Music and Sexuality
in Britten

Music and Sexuality in Britten

Selected Essays

Philip Brett

Edited by George E. Haggerty
With an Introduction by Susan McClary
and an Afterword by Jenny Doctor

UNIVERSITY OF CALIFORNIA PRESS

Berkeley   Los Angeles   London

University of California Press
Berkeley and Los Angeles, California

University of California Press, Ltd.
London, England

© 2006 by The Regents of the University of California

Library of Congress Cataloging-in-Publication Data

Brett, Philip.
    Music and sexuality in Britten : selected essays / Philip Brett ; edited by
George E. Haggerty ; with an introduction by Susan McClary and an afterword
by Jenny Doctor.
        p.   cm.
    Includes bibliographical references (p.   ) and index.
    ISBN-13: 978-0-520-24609-6 (cloth : alk. paper),
    ISBN-10: 0-520-24609-8 (cloth : alk. paper).
    ISBN-13: 978-0-520-24610-2 (pbk. : alk. paper),
    ISBN-10: 0-520-24610-1 (pbk. : alk. paper).
    1. Britten, Benjamin, 1913–1976. Operas.   2. Composers—Great Britain—
Biography.   3. Sex in music.   4. Gender identity in music.   I. Haggerty,
George E.   II. Title.

ML410.B853B64   2006
782.1092—dc22   2006003045

Manufactured in the United States of America

15   14   13   12   11   10   09   08   07   06
10   9   8   7   6   5   4   3   2   1

This book is dedicated
to the memory of
Philip Brett
1937–2002

CONTENTS

PREFACE

George E. Haggerty

Philip Brett tells the story of seeing Sir Geraint Evans's "moving production of *Peter Grimes* at the San Francisco Opera in 1973," at a time when he was for other reasons reading Dennis Altman's *Homosexual Oppression and Liberation* (see chapter 1). In private conversation Philip often talked about that experience as an epiphany, a moment of transition in his scholarly priorities as well as one of the sites at which "the new lesbian and gay musicology" was launched. All the work collected here was written after that thirty-five-year-old music professor was inspired to use his own personal experience as a tool for interpreting the music of Benjamin Britten. Again and again in these essays, Philip returns to the idea of oppression and the ways in which a culture marginalizes those who threaten it. He builds a more complex understanding of oppression and of the ways in which culture accommodates difference as he proceeds. But he never abandons that central theme. If oppression and marginalization stand out as the central tropes throughout this book, I know the continuity would have delighted Philip.

From just after the 1973 production I was Philip's partner, eventually his "domestic partner," and he recounted that experience for me several times. As he wrote more and more about Britten throughout his career, he often considered the notion of a "Britten book" that would bring his ideas together and take its place among other studies of that composer. At the very end of his life, after having written in addition to the essays collected here the magisterial "Benjamin Britten" entry for *The New Grove Dictionary of Music and Musicians*, 2nd edition (2001), that project was at the very top of his list. In fact, he was awarded a Guggenheim Fellowship for 2002–03 that he hoped to use for completing this project. He did not live to take up the Guggenheim, and he was never able to do all he hoped to do with his Britten work. This is a great loss for Britten scholarship. It is unlikely that Philip would ever have published these essays in their present form, nor would he have planned to see them appear outside the rich context of Britten's life, in which he hoped to place them. Still, these essays represent a substantial body of deep thought and lively argument about the works, and it makes sense to gather them here and to allow Britten scholars and other interested readers to see them side by side and to learn from reading them in this way just how Philip's own ideas developed and where they were leading him.

The great virtue of this collection is that it shows Philip coming at similar material over nearly thirty years and producing increasingly subtle and nuanced readings that suggest as much about critical practice as they do about their subject. Between "Britten and Grimes" (1977), the result of that first epiphanic moment, and "The Britten Era" (2000) or "Auden's Britten" (2001), written in the last years of his life, there is a world of learning and of personal experience. Even as Philip's earliest concerns remain inevitable and powerful, he chose to address larger and larger issues. From my perspective, as companion, proofreader, and scholarly sounding board, I can say that Philip's enthusiasm for this composer and his music, this larger scholarly project, never waned. Nothing thrilled him more than to attend a Britten performance, especially an opera, unless it was to perform a Britten piece himself, which he did throughout his career (an entire Britten program in 1977; the Spring Symphony in the 1980s; and other works at summer festivals and music camps. He also wrote informally for opera programs and CD-liners, and was delighted to give preperformance lectures, which he did in the last year of his life for *Billy Budd* (Los Angeles Opera) and the *War Requiem* (Los Angeles Philharmonic).

Benjamin Britten represented Philip's second field. He was also a scholar of English Renaissance music and the general editor of the complete works of William Byrd (*The Byrd Edition*). A companion volume to this one, edited by Joseph Kerman and Davitt Moroney, gives readers a chance to assess the complementary nature of this work. It was from Philip's perspective of course all part of the same project. His scholarship mattered to him only when it meant something personally powerful, and in the case of Britten that personal meaning is vividly expressed and deeply compelling.

The essays gathered here entail an inevitable degree of repetition of basic ideas and ways of developing an argument. If Philip had edited this collection himself, he would surely have found a way to eliminate these repeated bits. But to my mind, what matters is that they work well each time they surface, and the volume would suffer if they were removed. That leads me to suggest that readers approach the essays individually. The handful of favorite quotations and references will help readers to see "where I was coming from," as Philip would say. I did not include essays that seemed to me too repetitious, at times sacrificing new insights and different topics. What is more, only a few of these essays had primarily musicological audiences; some appeared as reviews rather than independent essays; and others were unpublished talks. I think the ones I have gathered offer the broadest perspective and the widest range of Philip Brett's writing on music and sexuality in the work of Benjamin Britten.

The following publishers and organizations have kindly allowed me to reprint articles that appeared in their publications: Cambridge University Press (chapters 1 and 3), Princeton University Press (chapter 2), Faber and Faber Ltd. (chapter 4), Musical Times Publications Ltd. (chapters 5 and 9), *repercussions* (chapter 6), The Regents of the University of California (chapter 7), Routledge/Taylor & Francis Books (chapter 8), and Indiana University Press (chapter 12).

I would like to thank Susan McClary and Jenny Doctor for their willingness to contribute essays to this volume and for their assistance in gathering materials; I also want to thank Joseph Kerman and Davitt Moroney for compiling their own Brett volume. Davitt has been a virtual coeditor of this collection as well, and I have been very lucky to have had him for bouncing off questions and concerns. Ruth Smith has been an enormous help, practical as well as emotional, and I am grateful for her involvement. Friends like Albert Johns, Robert Glavin, Sue-Ellen Case, and Susan Foster have kept me going through some tough times; and colleagues at UC Riverside have encouraged me in this project from the beginning. Byron Adams has made useful suggestions throughout; Katherine Kinney and Geoff Cohen have given me all sorts of moral support; and Nancy Rettig helped me to transform printed texts into computer files. I would also like to thank Chris Deviny and Kevin McCarthy, who enabled me to gather university information that made the collection stronger, and Louis Niebur, who assembled music examples. The greatest help of all, however, has been that of Mary Francis, my wonderful editor at UC Press. She has been an inspiration and encouragement from the very beginning, and as a Britten scholar herself, she has been an invaluable resource throughout this editing project.

Finally I would like to say a word about Philip Brett, who was my model of a scholar and a man, and who taught me how to make my own scholarship mean something to me. I will always cherish the twenty-eight years we spent together, and I will never outlive Philip's profound influence on who I am and how I think. Therefore it is appropriate that I dedicate this book to his memory. It is his book, after all.

Los Angeles, 2006

INTRODUCTION

Remembering Philip Brett

Susan McClary

I met Philip Brett one evening in 1986 at the annual meeting of the American Musicological Society in Cleveland. After several years of avoiding the meetings, I had come to this one largely because of my then-graduate student Lydia Hamessley, who wanted an introduction to the profession. As I remember it, the Cleveland meeting was exceptionally enervating, and I cringed at presenting a bright, young scholar to such dreary fare. But while trolling the lobby, Lydia and I spotted on the bulletin board a small note announcing a cocktail party for anyone interested in gay and lesbian issues. As it happens, I had a composition student, Steven Houtz, who had asked me about the possibility of gay music criticism, and I decided to drop in to see if anyone at the party had any information.

At the designated time, I entered a dark, empty ballroom about the size of an airplane hangar. Homosexual musicologists (of which there are legion) were assiduously avoiding not only the party but even the corridors adjoining it, for fear someone might otherwise draw some hasty conclusion about them. The individual who rushed forward to greet me identified himself as Philip Brett. A devastatingly handsome Englishman with killer dimples, Philip quickly engaged me in conversation. I felt, as did so many hundreds of other people who encountered him over the years, that our conversation mattered more to him than anything else in the universe. Recalling the mission that had brought me there, I asked him if there was any such thing as gay music criticism. He replied with his dazzling smile: "No . . . but don't you think there should be?"

Of course, Philip was being far too modest, for he had already published his first essays broaching these issues, beginning in 1977. But he quite rightly denied the existence of anything like a recognizable movement in that direction. As he and Liz Wood point out in their section on sexuality within the "Musicology" entry in *The New Grove Dictionary of Music and Musicians*, the discipline had not yet even ventured into feminist criticism. To be sure, several pathbreaking books and articles on women in music had appeared by this time, but they did not address the ways in which gender (let alone sexuality!) might inflect composition. I had considered the possibility of bringing over to music studies the exciting critical and theoretical feminist methods then transforming the rest of the humanities, but I still had done little more than dabble with ideas, occasionally throwing out a provisional reading during a seminar.

As Philip and I chatted that evening in Cleveland, however, we agreed to lend each other support as we moved forward into uncharted intellectual and political terrains; we joined hands and began to skip down the Yellow Brick Road together, our mutual pact rendering each of us slightly less vulnerable to the personal attacks we knew in advance we would endure ("Lions and tigers and bears—oh my!"). I would read and critique his experimental work if he would do the same for me. It is safe to say that without Philip I never would have had the courage to write the essays published in 1991 as *Feminine Endings*. That was my end of the bargain; Philip's brilliant series of articles and his founding of the Gay and Lesbian Study Group within the AMS represented his.

My allegiance with Philip and his agenda went far beyond mere collegiality and common cause. From the outset, he hailed me as (let's call it) a sister traveler, inviting me to participate in early panel discussions concerning gay issues and even encouraging me to write about Tchaikovsky or Schubert from a quasi-gay male subject position—something I could perhaps do with less personal risk at the beginning of this enterprise than gay men themselves, who might find not only their work but also their very persons assaulted as a result. Philip's endeavors and brave leadership quickly attracted a critical mass of gay and lesbian musicologists (among them the aforementioned Lydia Hamessley), who now properly carry out this crucial work in their own voices. But Philip always welcomed anyone who showed interest in contributing to gay and lesbian scholarship, regardless of the sexualities of the individuals involved.

Philip Brett was born in Edwinstowe, Nottinghamshire, on 17 October 1937. Most Americans took his English accent and supremely elegant demeanor as signs of an elite background, but his father was a collier, his mother a teacher. On two occasions I witnessed British scholars playing the class card on Philip, trying to put him back in his proper place. He chose to overlook the insults for the moment, though he later complained bitterly about the prejudices he had had to battle since his university days. I suspect that this experience fueled Philip's lifelong commitment to protesting injustices—whether in his accounts of William Byrd's struggles as a Catholic in Elizabethan England, in his insistence that musicologists claim the right to speak of matters related to sexualities, or in his unfailing support of oppressed younger scholars. When in 1990 he received advance word that his inaugural panel on gay issues at the AMS might be rejected by a squeamish program committee, he threatened to picket outside the meeting rooms—and he would have, too, if the committee had not backed down rather than face the prospect of this dignified gentleman standing in the hall voicing his grievances. When the editor of *The New Grove Dictionary* shamelessly mutilated his and Liz's entry on gay and lesbian music, he made available its unexpurgated version.[1] Without question, he acquired polish along with knowledge at school, but he remained very proudly a coal miner's son.

Like so many of the musicians in history, Philip attracted attention with his unusual talents as a choirboy. His beautiful voice and impeccable artistry made it possible for him to study at King's College, Cambridge, where received all his academic degrees (BA with Honors, 1958; MA, 1962; Ph.D., 1965). At Cambridge, he worked with notable figures such as the musicologist-performer Thurston Dart, Boris Ord, and Philip Radcliffe; he counted the novelist E. M. Forster among his friends. His dissertation focused on the songs of William Byrd, and over the course of his entire career he contributed many volumes to a critical edition of Byrd's music;[2] he was working on one of the final volumes of this series on the day he succumbed to his illness.

In all his work, Philip remained thoroughly grounded in the *practice* of music making—a grounding that always kept him from straying too far into abstraction, even when he was advancing innovative theoretical positions. He was a much-honored keyboardist and conductor: he received the Noah Greenberg Award in 1980 from the AMS for his dazzling performances of Jacopo Peri's *Euridice* and Claudio Monteverdi's *Orfeo*, and his recording of Handel's *Susanna* was nominated for a Grammy in 1991. Throughout his entire career, he was involved in major performances and recordings of early music, with occasional forays into contemporary repertories. He prepared, for example, the world premiere recordings of Lou Harrison's *Koro Sutro* and Morton Feldman's *Rothko Chapel*, both of which testify to his skill as a conductor and his eagerness to champion new works.

Philip is most widely remembered, however, for his pioneering efforts in introducing gay studies into musicology. At the peak of his career, he courageously—and over the indignant protests of colleagues—initiated the field of gay and lesbian musicology, now a thriving subdiscipline. In 1996, the Gay and Lesbian Study Group of the AMS instituted the Philip Brett Award "to honor each year exceptional musicological work in the field of gay, lesbian, bisexual, transgender/transsexual studies . . . in any country and in any language." In addition to scholarly editions of English Renaissance music and pathbreaking articles in a wide variety of fields,

Philip was coeditor of several pioneering collections concerning sexuality and humanistic study, including *Queering the Pitch: The New Gay and Lesbian Musicology* (1994), *Cruising the Performative: Interventions into the Representation of Ethnicity, Nationality, and Sexuality* (1995), and *Decomposition: Post-Disciplinary Performance* (2000).

Those opposed to gay-oriented scholarship in musicology often charge that it has no greater purpose than to expose the purported homosexuality of composers, to bring prurience to a field that otherwise transcends such matters. Philip's work stands as a powerful refutation of such caricatures. Not only does it meet the highest intellectual and ethical standards but it poses questions that have changed the focus of much subsequent work—queer and otherwise.

For instance, in his "Musicality, Essentialism, and the Closet," Philip examines the pervasive homophobic attitudes that underlie so many dimensions of musicking, especially in English-speaking cultures.[3] Like sexuality, musicality has been considered an essence—something inborn in certain persons. Moreover, the two categories often overlap in present day culture: to ask "is he *musical?*" (or "does he sing in the choir?") is frequently code for "is he gay?" This set of associations does not obtain even in most other European contexts, and there is no reason why talents in the sonic arts ought to be thus marked; yet they are and (as Richard Leppert has demonstrated)[4] have been in England since at least the eighteenth century. Taking such associations seriously instead of pushing them nervously aside allows for several important areas of investigation. It helps explain the cultural marginalization of music, the stigma attached to males who are drawn to music, the familiar overemphasis of masculinity in certain genres, as well as the place of music as a refuge—as a closet—for many who are in fact gay and who find in music a means of self-expression otherwise unavailable. It even allows us to make sense of the vehemence with which musicologists (far more than literary or art historians) have sought to forbid such inquiries: the personal and disciplinary stakes are unbearably high.

Philip's concerns also led him to interrogate the activities of performing and listening. Although we might assume that most people have some kind of erotic relationship to the music they perform or listen to, the anxieties related to sexuality and musicality have prohibited public admissions of such experiences—surely among the most important reasons we participate in music. Indeed, our almost exclusive use of the clinical language of music theory serves in part as a safeguard against reminders of the sensual delights music affords. As an openly gay musician who did not have to worry that his writing would inadvertently expose him, Philip (along with Liz Wood and Suzanne Cusick)[5] gave himself license to articulate at least his own pleasure in engaging with music.

His article on playing Schubert four-hand piano music,[6] for example, addresses the joys of having the body engaged in producing sound, of listening and responding on a moment-by-moment basis to the inflections of the other player, of simulating emotional and physical intimacy (though securely within the script presented in the score). Of course, nothing would prevent straight musicians from writing about music making in similar fashions—nothing except the fear that such confessions might threaten their need to maintain objective control. But such fears have constrained and stunted musicological discourse for too long. One of Philip's great legacies is his courageous example in writing about musical pleasure and the liberating invitation he extends to all of us to do likewise.

Finally, Philip wrote about music itself, thus invading the zealously guarded terrain too often restricted to formalist analysis. Significantly, his efforts in this direction centered on the dramatic works of Benjamin Britten—not because Britten's lifelong partnership with Peter Pears was an "open secret" (everyone knew but agreed not to discuss it) but because Britten's operas themselves seem to pose questions relating to sexuality. Philip fervently believed that these works acquired much deeper meaning when the interpretive process took these issues into account. He began moving in this direction in 1977 with the publication in the *Musical Times* of "Britten and Grimes," the first scholarly essay to broach the issue of Britten's sexual orientation and its possible relevance to the interpretation of the operas. Over the course of his career, he became the leading authority on this repertory: he produced the Cambridge Opera Handbook on Britten's *Peter Grimes* in 1983, published a brilliant series of articles and essays on Britten's life and works, and contributed the highly acclaimed entry on Britten in *The New Grove Dictionary.*

As with his pioneering essays on performing and reception, Philip's critical writing on these operas opened many more doors than those concerned specifically with sexuality or Britten. The occasional music theorist has thrown down the challenge of proving there was a gay chord or a gay form, thus revealing the absurd belief that chords and forms are the only proper units for analysis.[7] But Philip's readings pay attention variously to the explicitly homoerotic aspects of plots (in *Peter Grimes, Billy Budd, The Turn of the Screw, Death in Venice,* and others), to Britten's compositional choices in his affective settings of the libretti, to consistent associations by Britten of perverse sexualities with the Indonesian gamelan, and so on. He patiently and repeatedly explained that not all gay composers make use of these same elements and that these elements produce very different meanings in other contexts (needless to say, the gamelan has no such associations in its native lands). In his sophisticated interpretations, Philip demonstrated how to situate musical details within the larger universe of signification. His influence manifests itself not only in gay and lesbian criticism, but also in feminist, postcolonial, popular, and (increasingly) nearly all areas of musicology.

In the spring of 2002, Philip received a prestigious Guggenheim Fellowship to support him as he finished his long-awaited book on the operas of Benjamin Britten. This book was to bring together the many talents for which Philip was celebrated: his meticulous scholarship, his exceptional ability to analyze and write lucidly about music, his commitment to interpretation inflected by the composer's and critic's sexualities.

Despite a valiant struggle against cancer, Philip died only a few short months after the Guggenheim was announced and before he had had the opportunity to turn his undivided attention to this project. His passing deprives us not only of this gracious, humane individual but also of his *magnum opus* on Britten's operas. In lieu of that monograph, George Haggerty has assembled Philip's magnificent essays on Britten for the present volume. Reading all these pieces together reminds one of Philip's formidable contributions to musicology, even as it makes one mourn his untimely departure.

But Philip would not have wanted this introduction to his work on Britten to end on a low note; he would have had some hilarious quip, punctuated impishly with those killer dimples. The English editor of *The New Grove Dictionary* justified his cuts in the entry "Gay and Lesbian Music" by explaining that such issues were of concern only to North Americans. But Philip, a Californian by choice, frequently proclaimed himself "both British and homosexual . . . to the extent these can be distinguished in the American imagination."

Sexuality in music—an exclusively American phenomenon? I don't think so.

NOTES

I wish to thank Byron Adams for his thoughtful suggestions for this introduction. I only hope I have come close to what George Haggerty had in mind when he so generously invited me to write it.

1. See Brett and Wood, "Lesbian and Gay Music," ed. Carlos Palombini, *Electronic Musicological Review* 7 (December 2002), www.rem.ufpr.br/REMv7/Brett_Wood/Brett_and_Wood.html.

2. His coeditors were Joseph Kerman and O. W. Neighbour. A collection of selected essays by Philip on Byrd is being edited by Kerman and Davitt Moroney, to be published also by University of California Press.

3. Brett, "Musicality, Essentialism, and the Closet," in Brett, Wood, and Thomas, *Queering the Pitch: The New Gay and Lesbian Musicology* (1994), 9–26. This title contains several vintage Brettisms, including the pun on the British term for tuning ("queering") and the implication in the subtitle that there was an *old* gay and lesbian musicology—as, of course, there *was*, even if it dared not speak its name. See also Brett, "Are You Musical? Is It Queer to Be Queer?" *Musical Times* 135, no. 1816 (1994): 370–76.

4. Richard Leppert, *Music and Image: Domesticity, Ideology and Socio-cultural Formation in Eighteenth-Century England* (Cambridge: Cambridge University Press, 1988).

5. See Suzanne Cusick, "Gender and the Cultural Work of a Classical Music Performance," *repercussions* 3 (1994): 77–110; and Elizabeth Wood, "Sapphonics," in Brett, Wood, and Thomas, *Queering the Pitch*, 27–66.

6. "Piano Four-Hands: Schubert and the Performance of Gay Male Desire," *19th-Century Music* 21, no. 2 (Fall 1997): 149–76.

7. See, for instance, the special issue of *19th-Century Music* (ed. Lawrence Kramer) 17, no. 1 (Summer 1993), dedicated to questions of Schubert's sexuality.

CHAPTER ONE

Britten and Grimes

"I am firmly rooted in this glorious county. And I proved this to myself when I once tried to live somewhere else."[1] In this tribute to his native Suffolk, Benjamin Britten refers to his attempted emigration to America during the years 1939–42. He and his friend Peter Pears left England shortly before war was declared and hard on the heels of two friends and collaborators, W. H. Auden and Christopher Isherwood, whose departure stimulated a minor exodus of British writers and a considerable outcry in the national press. Britten, then a discouraged young composer, has described himself on arrival in the U.S.A. as "muddled, fed-up and looking for work, longing to be used."[2] Commissions quickly came his way, and in the next three years he wrote a number of considerable works, including the Violin Concerto in D minor, the String Quartet in D, the Michelangelo Sonnets, the operetta *Paul Bunyan* on a libretto by Auden, and the *Sinfonia da Requiem*. And it was a performance of this last piece in Boston that prompted Koussevitzky to offer him the grant that enabled him to write his first major opera. But the muddle did not clear up.

First published in *Musical Times* 117 (December 1977); reprinted with a new postscript in Brett, ed., *Benjamin Britten: Peter Grimes* (Cambridge: Cambridge University Press, 1983), 180–96.

If as Auden is reported as having said, "an artist must live where he has live roots or no roots at all,"[3] then it became clear that the anonymity and isolation beneficial to the poet did not suit the musician, and Britten gradually realized he must return to his native land, whatever the consequences to him as a pacifist.

The opera *Peter Grimes* has an intimate connection with the composer's decision to go back. It was in Southern California in summer 1941 that he picked up an issue of *The Listener* to which E. M. Forster had contributed an article on the Suffolk poet, George Crabbe. This seems to have been the turning point in Britten's decision not only about nationality but also locality. It was Crabbe's own Borough to which the composer repaired, no doubt with a sentence of Forster's ringing in his ears: "Yet he never escaped from Aldeburgh in the spirit, and it was the making of him as a poet." More important still, the article sent Britten to Crabbe's poems, which he had not previously read, and in *The Borough* he discovered not only a place to put down roots but also a series of characters and a plot for an opera.

Crabbe's Peter Grimes is one of the poor of the Borough, and though the poet grew up among the poor he did not like them. His portrait of the man whose cruelty leads to the death of three boy apprentices from the workhouse and whose guilty conscience drives him to madness and death is alleviated by few redeeming features: a bold and unusual choice for the central figure of a musical drama in the tradition of grand opera. True, there are other anti-heroes in twentieth-century opera, of whom the most famous is Wozzeck. But there is no assumption of basic decency in the Grimes of the poem, and he is not so obviously the downtrodden common man pushed into crime and insanity by the savage acts of those around him. It is true, of course, that Britten and his librettist, Montagu Slater, transformed him from Crabbe's ruffian into a far more complicated figure, one who can be recognized in certain lights, perhaps, as a distant foreign cousin of Wozzeck's. At the beginning of the opera Grimes has lost only one apprentice, clearly by accident, and the death of his replacement in Act II is also patently a mishap. The new, almost

Byronic, Grimes is rough, to be sure, but he is also a dreamer; and his music constantly invites compassion and concern. Yet there are still great difficulties with Grimes as the central figure, and the reaction of the critics ranges from Patricia Howard's prim little sentence, "His is not a character with whom we can admit to identifying ourselves" (*Operas*, 23), to Eric Walter White's more sophisticated but equally unhelpful remark that he is "what might be called a maladjusted aggressive psychopath" (115). In a comparatively recent review, Desmond Shawe-Taylor has gone so far along these lines as to find "a flaw in the conception of the central character." In his opinion, "the new Grimes is inconsistently presented. For all his visionary airs, the death of his second apprentice is directly caused by his roughness and callousness, so that the sympathetic Ellen Orford was in effect culpably wrong, and the 'Borough gossips' and the much-maligned Mrs. Sedley dead right."[4]

This statement raises a number of issues. It is of course usual and right for a society to protect the innocent and helpless from harm, but it is also generally recognized that it must observe due process of the law. The accident that befalls the second apprentice occurs when Peter, who is responsibly watching the boy, has his attention diverted and his paranoia understandably aroused by the arrival of the Borough procession, which observes neither due process nor common decency. That knock at the door just before the boy's scream reminds us in a very direct way that society precipitates what it should be guarding against, and therefore shares the responsibility with the individual. To put it in Forster's more trenchant words, there is "no crime on Peter's part except what is caused by the far greater crimes committed against him by society" ("Two Essays," 20). More important than what is indicated by the libretto, however, is what goes on in the score, because questions of right and wrong in opera are ultimately determined not by moral law but by music. We come away from the final duet of *Poppea* or the Liebestod of *Tristan und Isolde* believing if anything in the power of love, not the culpability of fornication, faithlessness, peremptory execution and banishment. Grimes is as undeniably sympathetic from the music he sings as Mrs. Sedley, on the other hand, is sinister. But what is finally disturbing here is not only that an experienced and respected member of the profession should wield a stick he would never use to beat earlier classics of the repertory, such as *Poppea* or *Tristan*, but also that he studiously avoids any truth that lies below the most obvious surface of the action. To discover why that should be is to take a further journey into the opera.

In the most sensitive account of *Peter Grimes* to date, Hans Keller, who draws usefully on psychoanalytic theory as well as a secure musical and dramatic instinct, points out that Peter "cannot show, let alone prove his tenderness as easily as his wrath—except through the music, which, alas, the people on stage don't hear. Thus he is destined to seem worse than he is, and not to be as good as he feels. *Peter Grimes* is the story of the man who couldn't fit in" (*Peter Grimes*, 105). It is this theme that Peter Pears explored in an article directed to the opera's first radio audience:

> Grimes is not a hero nor is he an operatic villain. He is not a sadist nor a demonic character, and the music quite clearly shows that. He is very much of an ordinary weak person who, being at odds with the society in which he finds himself, tries to overcome it and, in doing so, offends against the conventional code, is classed by society as a criminal, and destroyed as such. ("Neither a Hero nor a Villain," 152)

This is a clear explanation, so far as it goes, and rather more helpful than Britten's own statement that "in writing *Peter Grimes*, I wanted to express my awareness of the perpetual struggle of men and women whose livelihood depends on the sea" (introduction, 149). One of the greatest strengths of the opera is of course its vivid portrayal of the moods of the ocean—owing much, I suspect, to Britten's re-encounter with the Suffolk coastline. But, as in Crabbe, the natural detail is secondary to the human drama played out against it and which it sometimes reflects (e.g., in the Storm Interlude). In approaching this human drama, however, we need to go further than Keller's psychoanalytical abstractions, further too than Pears perhaps felt able, into the idea of the outsider, Grimes the unclubbable. His tragedy is of course relevant on a universal scale in our age of alienation, but I am interested in a particular interpretation that I believe solves some of the problems that have been raised.

It is clear from the music of the opening scene that Peter is not only telling the truth about the death of his first apprentice but also that he really is at odds with the Borough, and seeks in his own inner life a means of averting the harshness of his condition. All this can be heard in the orchestral motive played as he steps into the witness box, in his first words—sung on the same note as those of the bullying coroner but harmonized differently, and also in the way he cadences so frequently, not on the tonic, like Swallow, but on the seventh of the supporting chord (example 1.1). Peter cannot reply in the worldly manner of the coroner, then, just as later he cannot respond immediately to the approach of his schoolmistress supporter, Ellen Orford. She sets him off on a paranoid outburst that is literally out of tune with her E-major blandishments, and when she does bring him round to her key, what they sing together centers upon the minor ninth, the interval most associated with Peter's loneliness and his private fantasies, of which she is the unrealistic focus (example 1.2).

"I have my visions, fiery visions, they call me dreamer," sings Peter (in Act I, scene 1). And the tonal planning of the opera reflects the conflict between this fantasy life (generally expressed in D, E or A major) and the outside reality represented by, say, the E-flat of the storm and pub scene, or the B-flat of the courtroom and the final manhunt. It is easy enough to point to the self-destructive force of Peter's pride and of his fantasies, and to show how even his relationship with Ellen is doomed by his seeing marriage to her as the last step on the ladder of gaining respectability and "showing the Borough." But this still leaves him, in a sense, as an unexplained boy-beater, and it is only by looking more closely at his re-

Example 1.1. *Peter Grimes*, Prologue

Example 1.2. *Peter Grimes*, end of Prologue

lation with the chorus, representing the Borough, that a closer understanding of his nature can be reached. Eric Walter White has pointed out important distinctions between the handling of the chorus in *Grimes* and in Mussorgsky's *Boris Godunov*, with which it has often been compared (116). Britten was evidently concerned to characterize the minor figures who emerge now and then in order to emphasize that the crowd is after all a collection of individuals, each of whom, like Grimes in Crabbe's memorable phrase, "is at his exercise." Yet the most powerful moments are undeniably those—like the storm fugue, the round in the pub scene, the posse in Act II, the manhunt in Act III—when everyone on stage joins the chorus, only Peter himself standing out in contradistinction to the general will, which at one point, in the round, "Old Joe has gone fishing," he almost overcomes musically singlehanded. There is no other relationship so important in the opera: the boy doesn't utter a word; and Ellen—well, as we have seen, marriage with her is out of the question,

Example 1.3. *Peter Grimes*, climax of Act II, scene 1

and her parental response when she discovers a bruise on the boy's neck prompts her to a judgment which Peter can only interpret as desertion. The failure of their relationship leads to another and crucial step in Peter's decline. It is expressed musically in the second most important motive in the opera, a downward thrusting figure in which Peter, so to speak, accepts his fate (example 1.3).

But the break with Ellen is only symbolic of his final capitulation to the values and judgment of society at large, a point ironically underscored by the final "Amen" of the Borough at prayer. The congregation emerges, and starts a different chant: "Grimes is at his exercise"—set to the very notes of Peter's self-surrender. Is it quite clear at this point why the Borough people are so incensed? Clearly no one but Ellen combines moral fervor with sufficient human warmth to be unduly concerned about the misfortunes of a workhouse brat. It is Peter himself who rivets their hypocritical attention. He is an outsider not merely because of the unpleasant sides of his personality either, but because he is "different"— a difference accounted for on the surface level of the plot by his visionary side. His difference of nature—proud, aloof, rough and visionary— poses some sort of threat to the narrow ordered life of society struggling for existence against the sea, and therefore he is subjected to persecution, which is part of the ritual societies devise, whether subtly or in this case brutally, to maintain the bounds of what is socially acceptable.

The action of such a society upon an individual or minority in such a manner is simply stated as oppression. The word is overworked, but there is nothing better to describe the essence of a tragedy conceived long before the writings of the 1960s taught us the mechanics of the phenomenon outside purely political spheres. The dramatic treatment of this subject in earlier ages tended—as in, say, Milton or Handel's *Samson*—to dwell on the heroic aspects of the destructive but ennobling anger it can generate. But the anger of the nonheroic Peter is directed not toward some cataclysmic showdown with the crowd, but more dangerously against the defenseless boy, and still more dangerously, against himself. The moment when oppression becomes crippling and leads to tragedy is when it is accepted and internalized. And once we hear Peter falling under the spell of the Borough's values, we know that he embraces his own oppression and sets his soul on that slippery path toward self-hatred that causes the destruction of the individual.

First, it cuts off his means of escape: he is rooted, not only "by familiar fields, marsh and sand," as he admits to Balstrode in Act I, but also "by the shut faces of the Borough clans." Second, it leads him to think he can vindicate himself by making money, setting up as a respectable merchant, and even more unrealistically by marrying Ellen. Balstrode perceives clearly enough that a new start with a new apprentice will lead only to the old tragedy again, and Peter's acceptance of this unpalatable truth an act later is the pivotal moment of the drama (see example 1.3). And yet the most terrifying dramatic realization of his self-hatred is reserved for the last scene when, after recalling fragments from the opera in his delirium, he catches the sound of his persecutors calling his name through the fog. The Borough by this time has become a surrealistic caricature of itself as an oppressive society engaged in that ultimate fantasy of the oppressed— the manhunt. And Peter's response is to shout back at them, not abuse, but his own name—first in anger, but then as his energy subsides, in the self-loathing that longs for dissolution and death. On the appearance of

Ellen and Balstrode he curls up, as it were, into the womb-like state he associates with Ellen in his fantasy, and sings the melody first heard just before the Storm Interlude in Act I. This time the optimistic orchestral accompaniment is replaced by the fog-wreathed voices of his distant hunters, and he completes the descent from the rising ninth previously left unresolved.

Easily unnoticed, but highly significant, is the staccato figure (example 1.4) separating the lyrical arcs—modified in this last statement to emphasize the pathetic minor seconds more strongly. It is audibly an inversion of the angry crowd's motive in the courtroom Prologue. Bearing in mind that Britten combines an unconscious melodic gift with a highly conscious and responsible working-out of thematic connections, this can be taken not merely as a sign of Grimes's alienation but as a musical clue to his perverse relationship with the Borough through the inverting and turning inward of the outward forces of oppression. The true tragedy of Grimes, then, can be heard in his most eloquent moment of fantasy.

With this in mind, we can return to the question of why critics like Shawe-Taylor tend to be so uncomfortable about Grimes. Hans Keller provides one answer by observing that there is something of a Grimes in each one of us, though most have outgrown or outwitted him to the extent that they cannot or will not recognize him (105). Perhaps there is a more specific reason. The situation that gives rise to the oppression of Grimes—poverty and the nineteenth-century British apprentice system—is hardly relevant to opera-going audiences today, and it is consequently underplayed in the libretto. Instead, Peter's dreaming, visionary side is played up. We can safely take him as a symbol and the story as an allegory.

If Britten had been black, or had been a woman composer, he might well have addressed himself to the oppression of these groups. As a pacifist, he must have been engaged in the questions dealt with in *Owen Wingrave*, though 1945 would scarcely have been a good time to raise them, even in heavy camouflage. No, *Peter Grimes* is about a man who is persecuted because he is different. We may recall Peter Pears's explana-

Example 1.4. *Peter Grimes*, comparison of figures

a. Prologue

b. Act I, scene 1

c. Act III, scene 2

tion that Grimes "is very much of an ordinary weak person who . . . offends against the conventional code, is classed by society as a criminal and destroyed as such." To which he adds as a final line, "There are plenty of Grimeses around still, I think!" There is every reason to suppose that the unspoken matter is what in 1945 was still the crime that hardly dare speak its name, and that it is to the homosexual condition that *Peter Grimes* is addressed. At any rate, if we look at the opera in this allegorical way, the problems (both moral and dramatic) about Grimes's character fall away, the viciousness of the Borough's persecution becomes more explicable, and Peter's own tragedy, that of guilt and self-hatred, all the more poignant and relevant to people today.[5]

A number of Britten's other operas deal with male relationships, some of them—*The Turn of the Screw, Billy Budd* and *Death in Venice*—in a more specifically homosexual context than *Grimes*. Yet none of them is so vivid or urgent in quality. This can be understood in a variety of ways, not least in terms of the composer's youthfulness, but I should like to explore its connection with the circumstances of his removal to America in the wake of Auden and Isherwood. The reasons for their emigration have been explained in a number of ways, usually in broad terms embracing the decline of European civilization, the threat of Nazism, the stifling, censorious moral and artistic atmosphere of Britain in the 1930s, and so on.[6] All these reasons are plausible, but another fundamental impulse must also have been at work: namely that desire, so common in young gay men, to seek anonymity and freedom by going to the big city, the far-off country—any place, that is, away from the home where they feel at best half-accepted. But mere removal generally solves nothing. Every homosexual man, and in particular the artist, needs to come to terms with himself as well as society, and settle the linked questions of "roots" and sexuality in order to live, to grow, and to work fruitfully.

Let us consider the cases of two analogous British artists, both friends and collaborators of Britten's, who represent alternative possibilities at each extreme of the scale. Christopher Isherwood, who settled in the Los Angeles area, did not become any the less a British novelist for the remove. His perception of America was brilliant, but it was the view of an outsider, like the hero of his novel, *A Single Man*, who is a British homosexual man teaching at a Southern Californian State College. Yet as an exile Isherwood was able to write freely on sexual matters. He was the only writer of his time to explore the English phenomenon of male homosexuality, as a recent critic has pointed out (Heilbrun, 11), and it was not until Michael Holroyd's biography of Lytton Strachey that the subject so central to English intellectual life was treated in a manner, like Isherwood's, neither maudlin nor flamboyant. In his later years, moreover, Isherwood wrote and talked openly of his own experience of homosexuality, most notably in the two autobiographical books *Kathleen and Frank* (1971) and *Christopher and His Kind* (1976). Maintaining a reputation as one of the most distinguished writers of English prose of the twentieth century, he took a prominent part in the activities of the gay movement in the U.S.A.

The case of E. M. Forster is very different, though the two writers have many values in common, particularly those of honesty, gentleness and decency. Forster's most important experience abroad comprised the two visits to India (chronicled in *The Hill of Devi*) that provided the material for his masterpiece, *A Passage to India*, published in 1924. Ten years earlier, after a lean period following the success of *Howards End* in 1910, he had written *Maurice*, a homosexual love story. His reasons for not publishing it are often misunderstood: to quote the author's Terminal Note: "Happiness is its keynote. . . . If it ended unhappily, with a lad dangling from a noose or with a suicide pact, all would be well, for there is no pornography or seduction of minors. But the lovers get away unpunished and consequently recommend crime" (236). Forster did not want to face the possibility of being prosecuted; but the book, and some of what he called his "sexy stories," circulated among friends. The tension between society's conventions and demands on the one hand and his own wishes as a creative artist on the other finally led to the painful and difficult decision to abandon the writing of fiction for publication, as several entries in his personal diary indicate.[7] And if there should be any doubt about the price this sensitive and private man would have had to pay for what is now called "coming out," even in his later years, then one has only to contemplate the treatment of the posthumously published *Maurice* by the British critics, whose condescension on every other aspect of the novel barely concealed either a embarrassment at, or hostility to, the subject itself.[8]

Given Forster's love of England, then, his acceptance of himself as a homosexual had an effect amounting almost to suicide as a novelist. Britten, no less rooted in his native country, arrived at a less drastic accommodation allowing him to act upon his belief in music as a social activity. He wrote for particular people and places—a principle that began at home, so to speak, in the huge amount of music composed for his friend, the tenor Peter Pears, whose artistry and discrimination contributed enormously to Britten's own development. In addition to their work as singer and accompanist, these two men literally re-created English opera. They founded a national opera company, they initiated and successfully maintained a provincial music festival of international standing at Aldeburgh, and in their work with children and amateurs they played a large part in the dramatic transformation of English musical education since World War II. This great achievement above and beyond Britten's music would scarcely have been possible, in a country where homosexuality is tolerated as an eccentricity but not accepted as a way of life, if Britten had been as overt as, say, Angus Wilson or David Hockney.

Peter Grimes was conceived at the very moment when Britten decided to exchange uncongenial freedom abroad for unknown peril at home, when he forswore the advantage of Isherwood for a life that might entail the Forsterian sacrifice. The work therefore occupies a special place in his accommodation to society. After his return Britten always showed an affable face to his countrymen, and the artistic aristocracy lent him support and showered him with honors. I believe the other side of the coin, the dark side of his feelings as a potential victim of persecution and as an outsider in an established society, come out with tremendous force in *Grimes*. They were once again to emerge in 1953, the coronation year, when he scandalized conventional opinion by his treatment of the first Queen Elizabeth in *Gloriana;* but by the time of the *War Requiem* nine years later the voice of protest had become institutionalized in the oratorio form, and consequently muted.

In 1945, however, Britten had just returned to face unknown penalties from a repressive and embattled society on account of both his lifestyle and his pacifism. And I believe it was *Peter Grimes*, representing the ultimate fantasy of persecution and suicide, that played a crucial role in his coming to terms with himself and the society which he both distrusted and yet wished to serve as a musician. Unlike Isherwood, Britten needed to live and work where he had roots; unlike Forster he was not prepared to damp down the creative fires. Having made his choice, *Grimes* served as a catharsis, purging its agony and terror.

POSTSCRIPT

Two statements about the opera by its composer escaped my attention when I wrote "Britten and Grimes"; they provide different but connected ways of re-examining the concerns of the composer and his work. One of them, now frequently quoted, comes from an interview in which Britten recounts how he and Peter Pears came across Crabbe's poem and started working together on the outline of the plot:

> A central feeling for us was that of the individual against the crowd, with ironic overtones for our own situation. As conscientious objectors we were out of it. We couldn't say we suffered physically, but naturally we experienced tremendous tension. I think it was partly this feeling which led us to make Grimes a character of vision and conflict, the tortured idealist he is, rather than the villain he was in Crabbe. (Schafer, 116–17)

It was reassuring to find the composer confirming a symbolic view of the opera, stressing Peter Pears's involvement in its conception, and relating it to their personal situation. On the face of it, Britten's words contradict my view that "1945 would scarcely have been a good time to raise . . . the questions dealt with in *Owen Wingrave*" (see p. 19, above); but, to quote Michael Kennedy, "is it to be seriously doubted that 'and homosexuals' were unspoken but implied words in that statement? [after 'conscientious objectors']" (123–24). Though the opera owes a good deal to the composer's experience not only as a pacifist in wartime but also as an artist in a society he considered "basically philistine" (an expression he used twice in that same interview), its intensity must ultimately derive from the much earlier and more fundamental experience of the stigma of his sexuality, a stigma so strong that it could not be mentioned.

Peter Pears has said, "Ben had a marvellous childhood," and all one can discover of family life at 21 Kirkley Cliff Road in Lowestoft confirms this. A strict but gentle father who read Dickens to his children and took them on walks, a mother who pampered the boy and encouraged his musical talents, sisters who jumped up indulgently from the piano bench whenever he had a musical idea he wanted to try out—these were some of its happy ingredients. There was also a certain puritanism, which Britten regarded as an advantage to him as a composer because it inculcated disciplined working habits. Indeed, he remained nostalgic all his life for this ordered boyhood idyll (though when reconstructed it could prove a little stifling, as Auden pointed out to him in 1941 in a remarkable letter about "the demands of disorder").[9]

"His personality was outgoing, as a young child," writes Christopher Headington. "A later shyness came with adolescence" (17). Such a manifestation of the awkward age is familiar to many of us who had to confront our homosexuality while growing up in comparable circumstances. The dawning realization of sexual feeling can rarely be a simple matter; when it is homosexual feeling and when the family tie is strong, the resulting conflict can be devastating—for it is the special characteristic of the homosexual stigma (unlike that attached to being black or Jewish) that it is almost always reinforced at home and is thus the more readily "internalized," that is, accepted as valid and to a greater or lesser extent incorporated into the values and sense of identity of the person in question.[10] Attempting to imagine the special degree of guilt and shame he accumulated during this outwardly happy and unremarkable youth is, I think, the key to understanding Britten's sense of being an outsider, his insecurity and the resulting contradictions in his character. If imagination fails, some estimation of the damage his self-image sustained can be gained from his later attitude to his sexuality and from his hostility to the gay movement and to homosexual life-styles other than his own. According to Duncan "he remained a reluctant homosexual" (28), and Pears has said, "the word 'gay' was not in his vocabulary . . . 'the gay life,' he resented that."[11]

More important, the effect on Britten's work can be seen in the themes which crop up in it with some frequency: the difficulties surrounding male relationships; the loss of innocence; and the plight of the outsider. Perhaps even the more profound issues, the doubts about life and art that surfaced with such intensity in *Death in Venice*, derived at least in part from that early and crucial self-doubt. Not that Britten was totally obsessed by these things to the exclusion of all else in his dramatic music—far from it—but the importance in his creative output of an experience of human society resulting from his sexual preference can perhaps be gauged by comparing him with other leading composers of this century who happen to have shared the same orientation. In no other case does it seem so important an issue.

There is, however, no reason to see all his work as autobiographical. It is surely wrong, and perhaps crass, to identify Britten with any of his characters to the degree that both Davis and Vickers identify him with Peter Grimes in the literature accompanying the Philips recording. Equally suspect is the tendency to criticize the composer for failing to measure up to the implications of his plots and characters, as Peter Conrad does in his essay about *Grimes* and *A Midsummer Night's Dream.* The furthest we might go is to see Grimes as symbolic of something the composer recognized in himself. For if, as I suggested at the end of "Britten and Grimes," he came to terms with his worst fears about the darker side of society in this opera, he may also have explored there the darker and more violent sides of his own nature.

But at this point a distinction needs to be made. My ultimate concern is the social experience of oppression and its effects in the writing of *Peter Grimes,* not Britten's sexual preference. With appropriate changes to fit the conditions, I might write similarly about the social accommodation of another of England's greatest composers, William Byrd, who experienced another kind of oppression that affected his music. But the essence of Britten's sexuality or Byrd's religion is as inaccessible to criticism as the inner mystery of a work of art, "this stuff from the bucket, this subconscious stuff," as Forster calls it (*Two Cheers,* 123). Moreover, once we realize that, as several recent studies have emphasized, the very concept of "homosexuality" as a social and psychological category distinct from the "normal" or "heterosexual" is of comparatively recent origin (the word itself was not coined until 1869), the phenomenon of "homosexuality" becomes less relevant than the psychological effects of the labeling and its social consequences.[12] And Britten's preoccupation with a predominantly negative "homosexual vision" shows how crucial for him was the effect of this labeling and the concomitant oppression. Viewed as representatives or adumbrations of the "homosexual condition," Aschenbach, Oberon, Quint, Claggart, Vere and Grimes make a horrifying sextet; one almost forgets that the same composer wrote *Albert Herring*, that profound comedy of liberation. Furthermore, it is (to say the least) ironic that Britten, who enjoyed one of the most remarkable personal and professional partnerships in musical history, should choose for his final operatic "testament" the story of *Death in Venice;* for though one might join Tippet in saying "I think all the love which he had for his singer flowed into this work" (Blyth, 71), the fact that it centers on Thomas Mann's sad and lonely character seems to suggest that the oppression Britten sensed and internalized was much more powerfully present in his imagination than the well-regulated, shared and accepted life he led throughout adulthood.

Ultimately it is not the causes that are of greatest concern when one tries to come to grips with works of art, but the effects. While those who earlier this century sought completely to dissociate the work of art from its creator's life now appear mistaken, they did achieve what is surely the best focus for criticism. Our findings about the creator, the conception and the context of a work are put to best use only if they are projected in such a way as to sharpen our perception of its nature. The discoveries of Alfred Dürr and others redefining Bach's attitude to his work at Leipzig and Joseph Kerman's exploration of the significance of Byrd's Roman Catholicism are two examples of how radically a new interpretation of a composer's life can enhance our comprehension of his work. The taboo on all mention of composers' sexuality was of course partly a manifestation of wider repressive forces from which all of us, straight or gay, need liberating. In the case of Britten it was also an affront to critical intelligence, for it tended to force those who wrote about Britten's music into evasive tactics verging on intellectual dishonesty or, even worse, into euphemisms ("emotional immaturity" headed the list) that were themselves oppressive and insulting. On the other hand we should avoid making the simplistic claim that here lies the single key to Britten's creative personality: no inner mystery in the music is revealed by the simple acknowledgment of his homosexuality and its consequences, but the way is at least cleared for us to approach the works a little closer and with more understanding.

Britten's other statement may indeed help us in that quest. It comes from the article printed in *Time* magazine (16 February 1948) when *Peter Grimes* first opened at the Metropolitan Opera House in New York: "Britten regards this opera as 'a subject very close to my heart—the struggle of the individual against the masses. The more vicious the society, the more vicious the individual.'" This raises the moral question, familiar to social thinkers of liberal persuasion in this century, about the balance of responsibility between the criminal or delinquent and society, and relates it to the character of Grimes in a graphic way. When, at the climax of his quarrel with Ellen, Grimes accepts society's judgment, he also implicitly accepts the role forced on him by the prejudice and inhumanity of his fellow beings. He becomes the criminal he is thought to be. The question of whether or not he is technically guilty of the second boy's death—one I now see I was overanxious to answer—is (as Edmund Wilson saw clearly enough) beside the point. The intrusion of the posse in Act II, scene 2 was not merely a strategy to exculpate Peter, but more importantly a way of further dramatizing the moral question at the heart of the work.[13]

The connection between this question and the mechanics of oppression is a close one, for it is characteristic of stigmatized people to internalize society's judgment of them. This is the point Britten saw so clearly and (inasmuch as it did not gain general currency for another twenty years) so prophetically; it is also the one that critics of the opera like Shawe-Taylor, Garbutt and Conrad, who do not discern the source of Peter's apparent self-contradictions, have consistently failed to grasp. A common result of this internalization is that in the attempt to conform the person represses anger and eventually comes to distrust all feeling to such an extent that on top of the burden of insecurity and self-hatred is heaped the paralysis of depression.[14] Sometimes, however, the dam holding back the anger and guilt bursts with a resulting deluge of senseless violence. As I write, the newspapers carry two stories in which the "Grimes syndrome" reaches horrendous proportions. William Bonin, the so-called Freeway Killer of Southern California, and Wayne B. Williams of Atlanta have been convicted in murder cases concerning the deaths of large numbers of young men and boys. Both men are reportedly homosexual; Williams, whose victims were young blacks, is himself black. "Homophobia is the true murderer," wrote a correspondent to the *Los Angeles Times* (6 February 1982) in the wake of Benin's trial, pointing the same moral: that society's fear of homosexuality had sentenced Bonin to death just as it had destroyed his victims.

One reason why critics of the opera tend to evade this moral question is suggested by a passage in Adrienne Rich's *Of Woman Born* where she discusses a case of infanticide by an apparently devoted mother with a history of "depression" (256–80). The experts of modern society, she points out, instead of examining the institution of motherhood to discover root causes for such appalling tragedies, prefer to label those women who erupt in violence as psychopathological. Indeed, when Eric Walter White labels Grimes a "maladjusted aggressive psychopath" (116) or Arnold Whittall finds him immature in the sense that he cannot "conform" ("Benjamin Britten," 315), what we hear louder than their words are echoes of the conformist postwar era, when "unsocial attitudes," whether criminal or not, were equated with mental sickness or "immaturity," and when the tendency of psychiatrists was to put pressure on women and gays, for instance, to adjust to the expectations of society, thus increasing their guilt, suffering and sense of isolation. No wonder Grimes seemed as prime a candidate as Wozzeck for treatment," because far from being the romantic, Byronic figure Slater wanted—a character with the self-possession and self-will that, as we have seen, Peter notably lacks—he is in fact, as Pears puts it, "very much of an ordinary weak person." The successful realization of so modern a dramatic character is one of the main reasons for the opera's wide general popularity.

A common thread in all the murders mentioned above is that the violence was directed against those who were loved or who would have been the natural objects of affection but for the reversal of feeling caused by the long process of the internalization of society's values and the ensuing self-hatred and repression. "It has often been suggested (though seldom in print) that Grimes's inner struggle (like Claggart's, and perhaps Captain Vere's) is against a homosexuality that neither he nor, for that matter, his creator is consciously aware of," wrote Andrew Porter as long ago as 1971.[15] Grimes's outright demand for love from the boy in Pears's Amityville draft shows on the contrary that Britten must have been very well aware of this element, which adds its own touch of psychological realism to the story. The question of why all homoerotic overtones, as well as other aspects of Peter's background, were slowly but surely expunged as the opera grew has already been explored [ed.: see chapter 2, "Grimes Is at His Exercise"]. But one of the reasons not mentioned there, and perhaps ultimately of greatest practical importance, was that whereas universal meaning could have been extrapolated from the predicament of many other kinds of "minority" hero or anti-hero, an obvious homosexual—even an obviously repressed homosexual—in the title role would have either spelt outright failure for the opera or caused it to be dismissed as a matter of "special interest." As recently as 1979 Jon Vickers could claim on the one hand that Grimes is "totally symbolic" and that he could "play him as a Jew" or "paint his face black and put him in a white society," and on the other hand declare that "I will not play Peter Grimes as a homosexual" because this "reduces him to a man in a situation with a problem and I'm not interested in that kind of operatic portrayal."[16]

The opera was a long time in gestation. When Britten and Pears conceived the idea in 1941 they were adrift; they had recently escaped from Auden's dominating presence, and were without immediate responsibilities to society. It took exactly four years for the finished work to reach the stage, and those years were ones of tremendous development in their lives: first and foremost there was the return to England; then Pears, from having little or no operatic experience, quickly became a leading performer in the Sadler's Wells company; Britten meanwhile in 1943 worked out the theme of alienation in a different context in *Rejoice in the Lamb*; and both men gained a tremendous success with the *Serenade* in the same year. Moreover, with Eric Crozier excused his duties with the Sadler's Wells company in order to attend meetings with Britten and Slater in 1943, there must already have been some sense that the work might be chosen to celebrate the return to its true home of what was in effect, if not then in name, England's national opera. No wonder, then, that the homoerotic elements in the early drafts were censored.

More remarkable is the way in which Britten, in opposition to the ideas of his librettist, saw how to be true to his own feelings when turning the work into "a presentation of a general human plight—that of the outsider at odds (for whatever reason) with those around him" (Porter, "What Harbour"). For in order to make Peter so powerfully symbolic and to render the action of the opera so successfully allegorical, Britten could not allow the story to have homoerotic implications, much less an identifiably homosexual title figure. He had to desexualize Grimes, and furthermore rid him of his father-figure with all its attendant Freudian implications, in order that the work should not be misinterpreted as a "pathological" study. In doing this he made it abundantly clear that the opera's concern, implicit in its musical structure and thematic process, is the purely social issue of "the individual against the crowd": the one reflects the judgment and behavior of the many even while striving desperately to remain distinct. To watch Britten arriving at that conclusion and finding a solution, bit by bit, consciously or unconsciously, is to see how mature a dramatic composer he had by this stage already become; it is also to discover anew how from private pain the great artist can fashion something that transcends his own individual experience and touches all humanity.

NOTES

1. From a speech on being presented with the freedom of Lowestoft in 1951; quoted by White, 92.

2. *On Receiving the First Aspen Award*, 21.

3. Letter from Louis MacNeice in *Horizon* (July 1940), quoted in White, 30.

4. In the *Sunday Times*, 20 July 1975, echoing his views of thirty years earlier.

5. A reading of the first two chapters of Altman's work will show the connection clearly enough. I am happy to acknowledge that it was while reading this intelligent book and seeing Sir Geraint Evans's moving production of *Peter Grimes* at the San Francisco Opera in 1973 that this essay was first conceived. My use of the catchword "oppression," here and below, follows the sense developed by feminists and formulated by Altman (30–33): "Strictly speaking, oppression results from the fact that societies are divided along class, racial and caste lines and that some groups occupy positions from which they are able to dominate others. . . . But even when one concedes that, in these terms, oppression exists, it may seem difficult to conceive of groups being oppressed for their sexuality. This is, I think, largely because our concept of oppression has tended to be based upon a crude Marxist model that envisages oppression as a class or economic phenomenon, and there are those who still seek to incorporate all oppressed groups into such a uni-dimensional economic model. It is precisely the discovery that oppression is multi-dimensional, that one may be simultaneously both oppressed and oppressor that underlies the analysis of the sexual liberation movements. . . . The oppression faced by homosexuals takes on a number of forms, and at its most pernicious may be internalized to the point that an individual no longer recognizes it as oppression." Altman's book was enormously influential because it provided an intellectual basis for the gay movement, enabling it to reach many who had earlier remained aloof; his analysis of the various types of oppression is still retained implicitly in such important accounts as Weeks's *Coming Out* (190), but his concept of "liberation," while still basically valid, benefits from comparison with more recent directions of thought as outlined in Weeks, "Discourse, Desire, and Sexual Deviance."

6. A good summary appears in Spender, 252–54.

7. See Stallybrass's introduction to Forster's short stories, xiv.

8. The reviews of the first volume of Furbank's biography of the novelist show that concealment diminishes in proportion to the increase of embarrassment and hostility. In *The New Statesman* (22 July 1976) Paul Johnson, for instance, fills almost all the considerable space at his disposal fitting the young Forster into what might be called the "withered-sissy" stereotype, a stupid exer-

cise that concludes with the cruel and facetious remark, "perhaps it would have been better for the novels if he had never found out about sex at all."

9. Published in Mitchell, *Britten and Auden*, 161–62.

10. At that stage homosexual feeling need not, of course, be consciously identified as such for social and family judgment to be sensed and for feelings of isolation, exclusion and unhappiness to result; see Altman, 25–26: "In my case I had the sense of not belonging, of being excluded through some perception by my peers that I was apart from them. Like many others I had no idea why exactly that was (if it was); I put it down, as do others in similar situations, to excessive intellectualism or timidity or artistic bent, anything other than the real cause." This common experience is still little affected by the liberalization of social attitudes to sexual preference.

11. "The Good Companions." The use of "gay" as a term of self-determination (replacing derogatory epithets such as "queer" and "faggot" in the same way that "black" replaced "nigger") began in the early 1970s toward the end of Britten's life, and was initially threatening to most homosexuals (including much younger people) who had already arranged their lives in one way or another. For Britten, "the gay life" probably signified something of the type of existence he and Pears had encountered while living under the same roof as Auden; the influence of his upbringing was, I think, decisive in his rejection of this and also, perhaps, as Auden thought, in his idealization of "thin-as-a-board juveniles, i.e. . . . the sexless and innocent" and in his "aloofness" (see Auden's letter referred to above, note 3).

12. The "anti-essentialist" view briefly outlined here is elaborated from various vantage points in Plummer. The view of sexuality in general as a social and historical construction, rather than an inherent "drive," has been reinforced by Foucault's thesis; for a good exposition in the context of modern British history see Weeks, *Sex, Politics, and Society*, esp. 1–16. It is a paradox of the gay movement that while offering a new sense of identity for homosexuals it also looks forward to the eventual disintegration of categories based arbitrarily on sexual behavior or preference (see Weeks, 286–88).

13. J. W. Garbutt, who seems obsessed with the question of Grimes's guilt, conspicuously ignores the significance of the Borough's intrusion into Grimes's hut.

14. A straightforward guide to such typical reactions to oppression is Clark; see 22–28, 52–60, 146–49.

15. In a note for the New York Opera production of *Albert Herring*, the substance of which is also found in "What Harbour."

16. In an interview included in the literature accompanying the Philips recording. Vickers makes a more considered statement, but with little change of basic attitude, in a later interview with Michael Oliver, 364–65.

CHAPTER TWO

"Grimes Is at His Exercise"

Sex, Politics, and Violence in the Librettos of *Peter Grimes*

Grimes . . . is very much of an ordinary weak person who, being at odds with the society in which he finds himself, tries to overcome it and, in doing so, offends against the conventional code, is classed by society as a criminal, and destroyed as such. There are plenty of Grimeses around still, I think!

Peter Pears, "Neither a Hero nor a Villain"

INTRODUCTION

The modernist critical axiom that, in Joseph Kerman's classic formulation, "opera is a type of drama whose integral existence is determined from point to point and in the whole by musical articulation,"[1] was often used, we now realize, as a way of vesting sole authority in the composer, a male. Much work has now been done on recuperating the singer (usu-

---

The last and most succinct of several discussions on the development of the libretto of *Peter Grimes*, this essay appeared in Mary Ann Smart, ed., *Siren Songs: Representations of Gender and Sexuality in Opera* (Princeton: Princeton University Press, 2000), 237–49. Earlier versions include " 'Fiery Visions' (and Revisions): *Peter Grimes* in Progress," in Brett, *Peter Grimes*, 47–87; and "*Peter Grimes*: The Growth of the Libretto," in Banks, *The Making of "Peter Grimes*," 53–78.

ally female). It is a particular irony of the fifty-year-old repertory opera, *Peter Grimes*, that the singer who premiered the role of the protagonist— and still the only one apparently capable of singing the notes as written— was also the person who drafted the scenario, and even wrote bits of the libretto. He happened to be the composer's lover, whose auditions for that role were evidently as protracted and demanding as those for the role of Peter Grimes, which was originally conceived for a baritone, and given to him well into the course of the project.

There could be no better parable, in the twentieth century, of the social process by which operas come into existence, or, alternatively, of the bankruptcy of the modernist model of criticism based solely on the composer and the score. It is true, as Philip Reed has written, that "when Britten sat down at his desk in the Old Mill, Snape, in January 1944 . . . he was on his own" ("Finding the Right Notes," 79). Britten himself cultivated an image that encouraged the modernist view. The reclusive magician of Aldeburgh, drawing to him those he needed to realize his ambitious operatic dreams (and tending to drop many who were spent) could be made to fit an almost Wagnerian image of operatic creation. But there was always a great deal to consider before the notes—the libretto and its ideas, most obviously, and in Britten's case a physical sense of the stage and its design—without which they could not have taken shape or would not have taken the shape they did. In the case of *Peter Grimes*, for example, a whole two and a half years, much of it spent in conversation with others about the project, led up to that lonely moment in the Old Mill.[2] Many presences hover above and around this score, furthermore: some, like Pears and the Communist librettist Montagu Slater, with a direct bearing on it, others, like the poet W. H. Auden and the novelist Christopher Isherwood, played the roles of intellectual godparents. More shadowy but equally powerful forces, I shall argue, are the uneasiness in the relations of individual and state during a period when Europe was emerging from one of its most agonizing wars, an uneasiness which in Britain naturally focused on the class system but which in Britten's case, as for many of his circle, also included the unresolved questions sur-

rounding sexuality. Even at the personal level, Britten's single most powerful statement about the intent of the opera included Peter Pears: "[a]
central feeling for us was that of the individual against the crowd, with
ironic overtones for our own situation. As conscientious objectors"
(Schafer, 116–17). The remark was addressed to the social situation in
which the two found themselves—pacifism, in this instance as on other
occasions in Britten's life, doing double duty as a controversial but men-
tionable position for still unspeakable homosexuality.[3]

The opera was conceived in Escondido, California, where the two
lovers came across a copy of *The Listener* with the reprint of a BBC radio
talk on George Crabbe by the celebrated English novelist E. M. Forster.
The story of this exotic and epiphanic happening is familiar enough.[4]
Less familiar is the notion of how many people and connections were involved even at that initial moment—two musician-lovers inspired by the
words of another English homosexual male of the same leisured intellectual and artistic class about a poet who evoked "the sea, the estuary,
the flat Suffolk coast, and local meanness, and an odour of brine and
dirt—tempered occasionally with the scent of flowers."[5] Predictably
enough, the vivid drabness of the East Anglian coast where Britten had
grown up and which Forster brilliantly evokes survived in the score.
More remarkable are the intimations of those two Englishmen in California about the unpromising story of Peter Grimes as a subject for an
opera.

Unpromising? It is difficult to say this in hindsight, but Christopher
Isherwood thought so when Britten approached him to write the libretto,
and so he pleaded the claims of other work and the geographical distance
between them as an excuse to get out of it. Replying to this refusal, Britten let Isherwood know that "incidentally a lot of your hints . . . have
proved useful—thank you!" a remark that allows us to count Isherwood
as another contributor to the process and raises the distinct possibility
that his influence had some effect in pushing the story in a more socially
progressive direction.[6] Isherwood's various autobiographical books show
how clear he always was about the efficacy of anger in response to soci-

ety's attempts to dismiss him because of his being "queer" (the term he preferred to use as a reminder of the need for that anger). Was it Isherwood, possibly, who first nudged the two young Englishmen toward a view of Grimes that ultimately led to a classic modern reinterpretation of the subject of oppression?

In George Crabbe's poem, Grimes is an unmitigated ruffian. He spurns his father, gambles and drinks, becomes a poacher and trespasser but cannot finally be satisfied until he has "a feeling creature subject to his power." The three workhouse boys who serve this function as his apprentices "bear the blow of his outrageous hand" to such an extent that they forfeit their lives. Forbidden to hire more apprentices, Grimes sinks into melancholy, is tormented by visions of his father and dead boys, goes mad, and dies a pauper in a parish bed. As E. M. Forster later wrote, "Grimes is tough, hard and dull, and the poet must be tough with him, tougher than Shakespeare had to be with Macbeth, who possessed imagination. He must smash him up physically . . . and then place indubitable spectres in his path" ("George Crabbe and Peter Grimes," 16).

Crabbe was a realist, and a social critic rather then a reformer. His Grimes merely takes advantage of what the law allows. Unlike the villain of a Gothic novel, he does not have to resort to kidnapping to place another person under his control: he has only to apply to the nearest workhouse. The townspeople are implicated in the situation:

> But none inquir'd how *Peter* us'd the Rope,
> Or what the Bruise, that made the Stripling stoop;
> None could the Ridges on his Back behold,
> None sought him shiv'ring in the Winter's Cold;
> None put the question—"*Peter,* dost thou give
> The Boy his Food?—What, Man! the Lad must live:
> Consider, *Peter,* let the Child have Bread,
> He'll serve thee better if he's strok'd and fed."
> None reason'd thus—and some, on hearing Cries,
> Said calmly, "*Grimes* is at his Exercise."
>
> (*The Borough,* Letter XXII, lines 69–78)

When they do inevitably turn on Peter, the Borough folk are not interested in examining their own consciences; they want to find a scapegoat. We are reminded that Crabbe, though drawn back to Aldeburgh again and again, did not like the place or its people. As Ronald B. Hatch points out, "Grimes does not think he is doing anything out of the ordinary: nor do his fellow citizens. And in fact he is not. He is taking advantage of an accepted system. His individual savagery reflects the savagery of the society" (108).

That last sentence comes very close to something Britten told *Time* magazine in February 1948 just before the first New York performance of the opera: "The more vicious the society, the more vicious the individual" (16 February 1948). But he prefaced this by saying that Grimes was "a subject very close to my heart—the struggle of the individual against the masses." Unlike Crabbe, who saw Grimes as the embodiment of an evil society, Britten and his partner identified their character as the victim of that society, treated him with compassion, and cast him as Everyman.

In this makeover, Grimes becomes an artist, a dreamer, who can enter a pub during a heavy storm and sing about the stars, to the astonishment of the Borough regulars, who think him mad or drunk (I, 2). He is ambitious, though, to win their respect through the means he perceives them as admiring most, commercial success, and won't listen to the wise advice of the retired sea captain Balstrode, one of the few to resist the communal pressure to ostracize Grimes. Ultimately, his drive to succeed leads him to break his pact and friendship with the retired schoolmistress, Ellen Orford, and drag his new apprentice, whom she is minding, off to fish on a Sunday morning. This precipitates a crisis in the Borough, whose hypocritical citizens have been carefully introduced in the Prologue and first act: the pompous and lecherous coroner, Swallow; the ineffectual Anglican parson; the Methodist preacher, Bob Boles, who preaches temperance and drinks like a fish; the apothecary, Ned Keene, always ready to supply drugs under the table; and Mrs. Sedley, the "respectable lady" high on laudanum and low on charity, her nose in everyone else's business. A posse is organized (II, 1) and the men march off to Grimes's hut leaving the women (Auntie the publican, and her two loose-living nieces) to lament the foibles of men together with, and out of sympathy for, Ellen. As the posse reaches Grimes's hut (II, 2), distracting Peter, the apprentice misses his footing as he climbs out of the seaward door, and falls to his death down the precipitous cliff. The result is inevitable: the Borough condemns Peter (while continuing to display its own moral turpitude), and he is driven to madness and suicide.

I want here briefly to outline the process of the construction of the librettos of *Peter Grimes*—several versions reached publication—and to deal with some strands of criticism that connect with them. The development of the drama falls roughly into three main stages. To some simplified degree, these stages follow the categories of my subtitle, which may therefore provide subheadings.

SEX

The earliest scenarios, probably dating from that summer in Escondido, already display the main cast of characters—Grimes, the boy, Ellen and a Landlord of the pub (who later became Balstrode)—as well as some of the features of the plot; but there are some dead ends, such as a band of smugglers who disappeared from subsequent versions. Most striking is Pears's language about Grimes's relation to the boy: in the Pub scene, for instance, "Ellen acclaims boy as her child, Grimes (aside) as his apprentice (prey?)." An even more remarkable passage in the hut scene (II, 2) must be quoted in full:

> [Peter] admits his [the apprentice's] youth hurts him, his innocence galls him, his uselessness maddens him. He had no father to love him, why should he? His father only beat him, why should not he? "Prove yourself some use, not only pretty—work—not only be innocent—work do not stare; would you rather I loved you? you are sweet, young etc.—but you must love me, why do you not love me? Love me darn you."[7]

Pears must have recognized that this was going too far, for in another draft written on board the *Axel Johnson* the following spring as the young couple sailed to England, he changed the hut scene to emphasize Grimes's violence. Responding to his partner after he had heard part of the score, and perhaps acknowledging an earlier difference of opinion over the homoerotic question, Pears writes:

> The more I hear of it, the more I feel that the queerness is unimportant & doesn't really exist in the music (or at any rate obtrude) so it mustn't do so in words. P. G. is an introspective, an artist, a neurotic, his real problem is expression, self-expression. (Mitchell and Reed, 1189)

POLITICS

A second stage of the opera-making process is represented by the engagement of a librettist, Montagu Slater. Slater was not only a founder-editor of *Left Review* but also a Communist Party member, and the alliance between what one might call the 1930s homosexual/pacifist sensibility of Britten and Pears with the Marxist left had been foreshadowed by Auden and Isherwood and by other friends Britten had made while working in the film industry. In the musician's case it was an alliance that would not survive far beyond the completion of *Peter Grimes:* Slater was among many to be discarded as the couple moved toward the political center. Certain aspects of Slater's working habits, and his final act of aggression in publishing his own version of the libretto separately, may have accounted for this. At the time, however, the connection with Slater was an extremely important and effective one. It can probably be credited with giving Britten's first major opera a political twist that saved it from being "no more than a rather bloodthirsty melodrama"—Britten's own description of the first drafts in a letter to Isherwood—and possibly a rather gloomy homosexual bloodthirsty melodrama at that.

Slater's contribution was most important in the two episodes in which the tragedy moves beyond simply impinging on the community and actually spurs the community into action: the procession to the hut; what happens between protagonist and chorus there; and the manhunt in the last act. Commentaries on *Peter Grimes,* although frequently paying tribute to its status as a chorus opera, tend to ignore the first two of these crucial elements of the plot, which were not present in the earlier Britten-Pears drafts and are likely therefore to have been Slater's own invention.

The posse that sets out to inspect Grimes's hut for no better reason than "popular feeling's rising" (as the lawyer Swallow puts it) is formed in direct contravention of the due process on which the rule of law is founded, and of the convention of privacy that governs the individual's relation to the state in a democracy. The posse's approach throws the already overwrought Grimes into a paranoid panic, generating anger that is predictably directed at the boy ("Wait! You've been talking / You and that bitch were gossiping. / What lies have you been telling?"). But the effect of this on the audience is offset by what becomes the second turning point of the opera (the first being Grimes's rejection of Ellen and his symbolic acceptance of his role as outcast and failure in Act II, scene 1—"So be it, and God have mercy upon me!"—on a massive cadence in B-flat, the "Borough" key). Discerning the boy as "the cause of everything," Grimes decides to get out before the crowd arrives. The sequence of events makes it clear that even in his anger he has an eye toward the boy's welfare:

> PETER: Careful, or you'll break your neck
> Down the cliff-side to the deck.
>
> *Rope in hand he drives the* BOY *towards the cliff door.*
> CHORUS (*off*): Now the liars shiver, for
> Now if they've cheated we shall know:
> We shall strike and strike to kill
> At the slander or the sin.
> PETER: I'll pitch the stuff down. Come on!
>
> *He pitches ropes and nets.*
> Now
> Shut your eyes and down you go.

There is a knocking at the other door. PETER *turns towards it, then retreats. Meanwhile the* BOY *climbs out. When* PETER *is between the two doors the* BOY *screams and falls out of sight.* PETER *runs to the cliff door, feels for his grip and then swings quickly after him.*[8]

In other words, the community is directly implicated in the boy's death by means of the complicated symbol of "knocking at the other door," which momentarily distracts Peter from watching over him. Its significance must surely have been heightened by the sensitivity of many of its first audience to the devastating potential effect of this simple act, during the immediately preceding years, on the lives of those under the rule of the Nazis all over neighboring Europe. Separation from family or friends, confinement in concentration camp, or even death were among the possibilities of such an intrusion. This was perhaps the single most decisive change in the drama after the decision to reclaim the title figure, and the feature of the plot that has been least appreciated and examined. The manhunt of the last act is no doubt more musically remarkable. But the intensity of that moment can only work as well as it does by being part of a series of increasingly intrusive, aggressive, and finally inhuman, acts carried out by a narrow-minded, hypocritical community represented not only as in perpetual struggle with the sea but also as obsessed with conformity and enforcing "standards" to its own arbitrary liking. Without the preceding scenes this last and most powerful crowd event would have risked seeming merely surreal.

VIOLENCE (WITH SOME SEX)

Although Slater constructed the social aspect of the opera along lines that (so far as we can tell) Pears and Britten had not previously imagined, he did not feel the need for a complete change of direction in the characterization of Grimes. He appears rather to have relished the hints of loose-living and sadism in Pears's drafts, even those of homoeroticism. To Ellen's question "Peter, tell me one thing, where / Young stranger got his bruise and weals" Peter answers "Out of my true affection"; and in the hut scene at the point where Peter, suddenly losing his temper, "takes a short length of rope and whirls it around," a manuscript draft in Slater's hand presents a Grimes who would have severely hampered the opera's chances of success:

[PETER:]   By God I'll beat it out of you.
            Stand up. (*lash*) Straighter. (*lash*) I'll count two
            And then you'll jump to it. One.
            Well? Two.

            (The boy doesn't move. Then Peter *lashes hard, twice. He runs.* Peter *follows)*

            Your soul is mine.
            Your body is the cat o' nine
            Tail's mincemeat. O! a pretty dish
            Smooth-skinned & young as she could wish.
            Come cat! Up whiplash! Jump my son
            Jump (*lash*) jump (*lash*) jump, the dance is on.[9]

If this complicates Grimes in one way, then the apparition of his father during the hallucinatory episode later in the scene adds yet another dimension to his psychological profile. And Slater kept this sort of detail (but not the above passage) when he published his own version along with many of the other passages in which Grimes addresses the boy in charged emotional language.[10]

Britten, Pears and Eric Crozier, the stage director who at this stage became important in the process, may gradually have realized that Slater had only transformed the plot halfway. He had introduced community wrongdoing and injustice effectively while retaining the psychological profile that set up the audience either to pity the protagonist or to hold him in contempt, but not to identify with him. If the idea of the "individual against the crowd" was to work, and if the drama were to become an allegory of oppression (both external and internalized), then the process of Grimes's self-destruction had to be felt to be the direct result of his social situation, so that everyone in the audience could recognize a little of themselves in him. A set of psychological circumstances that would make his sadism explicit, or suggest a fundamental cause in an Oedipal conflict, would undermine this process. "Once we'd decided to make it a drama of the individual against the crowd," as Peter Pears once explained to me when I asked him why the father and dead apprentices had been excised, "then those things had to go."[11] And so it was at quite a late stage, from the beginning of composition right through to rehearsals and even beyond, that the third transformation occurred in which Peter Grimes lost the psychological or even pathological groundings which Britten and Pears had initially imagined and which Slater, having written them into the character, could not now be persuaded to relinquish.

The alterations to the mad scene in Act III are emblematic of the final process in the evolution of the drama of *Grimes*, in which the protagonist loses all those features of personality that might "explain" him outside the action of the drama and the aura of the music. Slater portrays a craven individual who rolls out his psychological credentials ("This breakwater with splinters torn / By winds, is where your father took / You by the hand to this same boat / Leaving your home for the same sea / Where he died and you're going to die."), defensively excuses himself for the death of his apprentice ("You're not to blame that he went down. / It was his weakness that let go."), and harps self-pityingly on his failings ("The drinking's over, wild oats sown") as he answers to Ellen, his mother figure, in person. The eventual version, concocted by Britten with the help of yet another collaborator, Ronald Duncan, soon to be the librettist of *The Rape of Lucretia*, tells the story of the opera in the music of the opera, recalling the inquest, the evil message of the posse ("Bring the branding iron and knife"), the soliloquy ("The Great Bear and Pleiades' setting") and the round in the Pub, and the friendship and betrayal of Ellen, culminating in the symbolic moment of capitulation to society, "And God have mercy upon me," brilliantly recalled sotto voce in E-flat, a step further into Borough tonal territory, and addressed now ("upon you") to Ellen and his persecutors, suggesting absolution as well as capitulation. This leads Grimes in turn to the desperately repeated enunciation of his own name as a prelude to its and his own erasure, and a brief recall of the storm soliloquy, sign of his inner life, literally dragged down to the Borough's E-flat as it concludes. Here, powerfully, music ends. Grimes is a nonexistent entity, finally, apart from the community and its actions, and this is what makes him an allegorical figure rather than a "character."

THE CRITICAL RESPONSE

Nothing better illustrates the centrality of Grimes's character in the plot than the speed with which ambivalence about him emerged, especially around issues of guilt and sadism. Even before the opera had been performed, Edward Sackville-West, a critic close to Britten, had written for the official introductory booklet an account of the music that includes, in the course of a rather specific programmatic interpretation of the Passacaglia, this rather surprising statement: "it would not do to shirk the fact that Grimes is guilty of manslaughter" (44). What the Borough court shrank from doing in the Prologue, then, and what Slater had so carefully circumvented in the hut scene, could readily be contemplated by one of the most intelligent and well-connected critics of the period. More extreme is Desmond Shawe-Taylor who, in his articulate review of the original production in *The New Statesman* (9–16 June 1945), declared that "what neither composer nor librettist seems to realize is that, after all, the sympathetic schoolmarm was wrong (and therefore, in effect, an accessory in the second boy's death), whereas poor Mrs. Sedley was dead right." Drawing a moral, he found "something shocking in the attempt to win our sympathies for a character *simply because* he is an outlaw and an enemy of society" and called it "an adolescent conception of man and society" ("Peter Grimes," 155). This conclusion alerts us to a specific phenomenon in Britten reception. "Adolescent" (like the more hostile labels "immature" and "clever" also often leveled at the composer) is a code word referring to a particular view of homosexuality during the period as a matter of arrested development leading to a failure to "adjust." Possibly what lies at the root of these and many similar rejections of the surface of the plot is the trace of something deliberately expunged from the plot that nevertheless made critics extremely uncomfortable, but that could not be articulated at the time. Tippett put his finger on it while talking much later to Humphrey Carpenter: "I don't think [Britten] seemed to understand that a problem would come over the question of Peter Grimes's relation to the boys" (Carpenter, *Britten*, 200).

Of course this could only have been true among the many who knew the "open secret" of Britten's homosexuality. Edmund Wilson, who caught one of the early performances on a visit to London, contextualized the problem of sadism in terms of the European war, which he considered to have degraded the victors as much as the vanquished. He saw Grimes as a symbol for "the whole of bombing, machine-gunning, mining, torpedoing, ambushing humanity, which talks about a guaranteed standard of living but does nothing but wreck its own works, degrade or pervert its own moral life and reduce itself to starvation" and observed that "the indignant shouting trampling mob which comes to punish Peter Grimes is just as sadistic as he" (*Europe*, 162). Hans Keller, a straight insider, on the other hand, refused to endorse the sadism of Grimes, even in his (rejected but now posthumously published) "psychoanalytic notes." He describes instead the chorus (at the appearance of Peter in I, 2) as "projecting their own repressed anal sadism on to him," and notes for good measure that "in view of the fact that even competent listeners have shut their ears to 'what the music clearly shows,' a quite important sidelight is here thrown on how musical understanding can be prevented by such mechanisms as projection."[12] Putting Grimes on the couch and impaling him on the twin spikes of anal eroticism and unresolved Oedipal complex, Keller manages almost completely to undo the social work of the libretto. No doubt aware of this, he confined himself in print to two paragraphs on Grimes's character that specifically address the social dimension and rather strikingly take account of the difference the music makes.[13]

In spite of Keller, and the statements of Peter Pears that he endorses, the views of Grimes as sadist and of *Peter Grimes* as a "problem opera" on that account do not go away. They surfaced most recently in Humphrey Carpenter's biography, where the materials I have discussed are used, without regard for the larger picture they form, to construct meanings for the opera that play down its political import and implicitly contradict its dramatic portrayal of the mechanics of oppression. Carpenter brings up the father image of Slater's early drafts, and draws attention to the word "murder" in the original scenarios of the hut scene drafted by Britten and Pears. Quoting Slater's more sadistic drafts for the hut scene (including the one quoted above), Carpenter asserts that the librettist "tried to show the audience much more of *what was really happening*" (my emphasis), as though there were a secret "real" text behind the opera linked directly to its composer's psyche, a special penetration of that psyche on the part of the librettist, and no problem at all with the use, in interpreting a work, of material rejected by its authors.[14] To unearth morsels from the sketches and drafts helpful to one's argument while ignoring the general flow of the evidence, is, of course, a danger of their being available. But there is something homophobic, too, in the tendency to confine a reading of Britten's operas, as opposed to those of, say, Berg, Janáček or Stravinsky, to the expression of the particularity of the composer's own psychology and inner life. It is true that one of the things Britten's operas (as well as his other works) seem to achieve is an exploration of various issues surrounding sexuality that the composer could not discuss in any other public forum (except obliquely through the code of anti-philistinism or the discourse of pacifism). His perseverance in this endeavor is one of the truly remarkable and even noble features of his career. Yet it is particularly ironic that *Peter Grimes* should come to be seen as a drama about Britten's own struggle with sadism in a homosexual or pederastic context when it was the work of so many hands nearly all of whom (except the straight Marxist Slater) were trying, toward its completion, to purge it of the particular and present it in terms sufficiently open for it to have significance for a wide range of people.

FURTHER EXPLORATIONS

There is surely an advantage to be gained in looking past the composer himself, however, toward the extraordinary set of events, political and cultural, that took place between the summer holiday in California in 1941 and the premiere in London in 1945. For, at a deeper level, *Peter Grimes* would seem to have tapped critical issues about modern society for which Britten and his friends were a rather surprising conduit—issues for which the controversy over Grimes's character acts as a kind of symptom. One, as we have seen from Edmund Wilson's account, prompted by World War II, is the nature of aggression and its deleterious effect on "both sides." Another, looking forward anxiously to the aftermath, is the (always unresolved) question of responsibility in the relation of individual and state in modern capitalistic democracies. The "more liberal view" espoused by the authors sees deviance, even criminality, as a symptom of society's failure, and tends to want to deal with it accordingly, by trying either to understand and allow for it, or, in a more problematic strategy, to control it by "medicalizing" it. The opposing view, espoused by conservatives who oppose state interference only when their own interests are threatened, insists on maintaining individual conformity and responsibility, and uses institutionalization as a means of control. *Peter Grimes*, not coincidentally, emerged at the dawn of the welfare state, and it reflects many of the questions that occupied British society at the dawn of that great social experiment.

An even wider issue stems from the ambiguous nature of the plot as an allegory and of the protagonist as a symbol. One feat of the music, one that disturbed Shawe-Taylor, is to create in sensitive listeners a warm sympathy for and even identification with a character who in the unmusical light of day may seem a brutal child abuser. To make matters worse, the ploy that critics so readily embraced in dealing with *Death in Venice*— of turning the protagonist into a symbol (of the artist) in order to avoid the (to them) embarrassing materiality of Aschenbach's declaration of love to a boy at the end of Act II—was simply unavailable in *Grimes*. This

strategy was unavailable mainly owing to Britten and Pears's "open secret": as an "ordinary weak person . . . who offends against the conventional code, is classed by society as a criminal, and destroyed as such" (as
Pears puts it in the quotation at the head of this essay), Grimes would inescapably be read as a symbol for the "homosexual."[15]

Since the trial of Oscar Wilde exactly a half century earlier, the male homosexual, as a notionally uniform but actually incoherent identity, had been
foregrounded in a special way in Anglo-American society and ideology, in
a manner analogous to that of the Jew in Fascist countries, as "the embodiment of a certain blockage—of the impossibility which prevents the society from achieving its full identity as a closed, homogeneous totality." Slavoj
Žižek, who has written with particular eloquence on the subject of ideology,
reverses the equation to display the mechanism: "Society is not prevented
from achieving its full identity because of Jews: it is prevented by its own an-
tagonistic nature, by its own immanent blockage, and it 'projects' this internal negativity into the figure of the 'Jew'" (*Sublime Object*, 127). By anal-
ogy, one might say that the impossibility, the "immanent blockage," of the
institution of compulsory heterosexuality that binds all the institutions of
the well-ordered capitalistic democracy without regard to the ethnic or class
differences that operate at other levels, is revealed in the return of the homosexual through all levels of that society and in all guises. The immanent
failure of the patriarchy is demonstrated by, and projected on, those who exercise its privilege as men but undermine the principles of sexual relation
and patterns of domination on which it is founded in the modern world.

Grimes marks the opening of a new stage in the debate over homosexuality, one that was perhaps inevitable as the result of the social
changes wrought by the war. It was to emerge, out of hints and innuen-
dos (like "adolescent"), into something closer to a witch hunt than a debate as the result of the defection of Burgess and Maclean from Britain
to the U.S.S.R. early in the following decade. "Conformity" and "ad-
justment" began to have special connotations, when even (one might say
especially) the gentleman's agreement that had existed between the authorities and homosexuals of the leisured class was abrogated in a horri-

fying series of arrests and trials. The overplaying of the disciplinary hand stimulated the growth of a movement which, beginning with the ameliorating but in many ways reactionary Wolfenden Report, led eventually to a modest reform of the law.[16] The point is not that *Peter Grimes* initiated or even participated in this debate, but that it stands as a symptom of the conditions of that debate. For one thing, its juxtaposition of the outsider with stereotypical masculinity and working-class affiliations preserved resonances of the Wilde scandal (marked as much by the crossing of class boundaries and the revelation of an underworld of lower-class male homosexuals as by the "offense" itself). In the context of theater dominated by Coward and Rattigan plays (and the Lord Chamberlain's embargoes), in which subversion was limited to innuendo and the characters reflected their audience in leisure-class appearance and values, even Peter Pears's aristocrat-manqué fisherman must for many have been disturbing, for it crossed the aesthete/hearty, homosexual/heterosexual binaries that were powerfully present in all kinds of representations.[17]

Fifty years later the story of *Peter Grimes* is still relevant as the broader conditions out of which it grew, the repressive social atmosphere of the 1930s, threaten to return—some would say *have* returned—to Anglo–North American life. The situation has been altered, of course, by the success of the gay and other movements in exacting recognition and discovering the efficacy of community and alliance. The protagonist of Suri Krishnamma's film *A Man of No Importance* (British, 1977), a bus conductor in the Dublin of the early 1960s, is still surrounded by oppressive figures comparable to those in the opera, but he externalizes his interior life by reciting poetry to his passengers and getting them to collaborate in his project to stage Wilde's *Salome*. Supported by his loyal band—all misfits themselves, we are allowed to realize—he is able almost heroically to defy the mean-spirited bus inspector, his Bob Boles, and retain the friendship (nothing more, mind you) of his bus driver "Bosie." But behind this almost tragic comedy lies the old set of social assumptions that *Grimes* dramatizes in an almost archetypal manner for a modern society policed out of homosexuality and other irregularities by certain myths and fears: the deviant is an ordinary person, not a hero, nor a camp matinee idol; his offense is not what he does but what he represents; and he is "alone, alone, alone . . ."

NOTES

1. *Opera as Drama*, 13. Kerman preserves this credo word for word in a recent revised edition (1988), 10; but in a new epilogue he significantly modifies the verbal constructions, e.g., "there seem to be three principal means [defining character, generating action, and establishing atmosphere] by which music can *contribute to* drama" (215; my emphasis).

2. See Philip Reed's "'Peter Grimes' Chronology," 21 ff.; the idea of making an opera out of Crabbe's poetry existed by 29 July 1941; the first mention of the title is in a letter from Isherwood to Britten (18 February 1942) about the novelist's not seeing "any possibility of collaborating with you and Peter on the PETER GRIMES libretto."

3. See, for example, Kennedy, 123–24. For a general essay on the complicity of pacifism and homosexuality in Britten, see Holloway, 215–26.

4. For the most recent and detailed account, see Carpenter, *Britten*, 152–58.

5. Forster, "George Crabbe" (1941), repr. in Brett, *Peter Grimes*, 4. The copy of Crabbe's works which Peter Pears bought that summer, most likely on a trip to Los Angeles, and which he and Britten marked up, is preserved in the Britten-Pears Library.

6. See Mitchell, "Montagu Slater," 34–36, and Mitchell and Reed, 979–80. In his letter to Britten, Isherwood went so far as to say "and frankly, the subject doesn't excite me so much that I want to *make* time for it"; in a letter to Donald Mitchell in 1981 he wrote, "I was absolutely convinced it wouldn't work"; and in conversation with me at his home in Santa Monica in 1977 he admitted that he had found the story homophobic.

7. An early scenario in Pears's hand, designated "L5" in Banks, 173–75; also printed in Brett, *Peter Grimes*, 50.

8. This is the final version, only slightly revised (largely by the interpolation of that particular chorus stanza) from the original draft. Stage directors, who are often unaware of the social implications of the opera, frequently omit the crucial "knocking at the other door": for example, Elijah Moshinsky in the Covent Garden production available on laser disc (Montvale, NJ: Pioneer Artists, 1982), as well as John Copley in the 1998 revival of an old San Francisco Opera produc-

tion—otherwise very realistic—that prompted my ideas about the opera when I first saw it in 1973 while reading Altman's work.

9. See Banks, 65–66, for the source citations of these quotations.

10. Slater, *Peter Grimes and Other Poems*, 43. This publication, undertaken perhaps to reclaim something of what Slater felt he had lost in revision, acts as a control on what he sanctioned in that process. At the beginning of the hut scene (Act II, scene 2), however, he included a two-stanza aria with refrain, amounting to an extra twenty lines, that are not to be found in *any* of the documents at Aldeburgh. They must therefore have been written expressly for the publication, in contradiction of the prefatory remark that "the present text is to all intents and purposes the one to which the music was composed." In his "Story of the Opera" for the Sadler's Wells booklet on the work, Slater uses his own version in quoting Peter's entire existing aria, even though he must have agreed to many of the changes in the vocal score: see Crozier, *Peter Grimes*, 23–24. Crozier informs us that Slater's book was on sale side by side with the libretto at Sadler's Wells during the first run of performances (in *Opera Quarterly* 10 [1994]: 16).

11. This was in 1981, I believe, as I was completing my earlier study of the sources. I didn't fully understand the remark at the time, and could not bring myself to ask Pears to elaborate—his statement sounded so final and perfect and unassailable.

12. *Three Psychoanalytic Notes*, 13, 43; "what the music clearly shows" is derived from Pears's statement, which Keller quotes, that "[Grimes] is not a sadist nor a demonic character, and the music quite clearly shows that" (*Radio Times*, 8 March 1946). One of the most interesting aspects of Keller's document is its open letter to the (plural) "Authors of *Peter Grimes*" (34), and the care with which Keller acknowledge Pears's contribution here and in his published writings on the opera.

13. The "two paragraphs" occur at the beginning of his "Story, the Music not Excluded," 105.

14. *Britten*, 210. To be fair, Keller falls into a similar trap. His scholarly instincts alerted him to the fact that the quotations in Slater's essay in the Sadler's Wells booklet represented an earlier stage: "The best means of immediately showing now that when we associate, in Peter's mind, his apprentices (children substitutes) with his father we are not forcing our ideas upon the drama, is to inspect a passage which occurs in a former version" (*Three Psychoanalytic Notes*, 30). On the next page he even allows himself to say that a psychoanalytic observer would have guessed as much anyway, but "would have been reproached with giving free reign to his phantasies." The use of the child-as-father-of-the-man ploy to evade pederasty and pin aggression on the unresolved Oedipal complex is of course a breath-taking move.

15. The writer Colin MacInnes, who at the time had sex with men without

considering himself homosexual, confided to his private notebook in the late 1940s: "The theme and tragedy of P. Grimes is homosexuality and, as such, the treatment is quite moving, if a bit watery. Grimes is the homosexual hero. The melancholy of the opera is the melancholy of homosexuality." See Gould, 82.

16. For an account, see Montgomery-Hyde, *Love that Dared not Speak Its Name.*

17. See Sinfield, "Private Lives"; and also his *Literature, Politics,* especially chs. 5 and 13.

CHAPTER THREE

Grimes and *Lucretia*

One of the sure tests of a composer's stature is how he reacts to success. The furore over *Peter Grimes* both at home and abroad after its premiere in 1945 was possibly more remarkable than that accorded any other opera this century. In the first few years of its existence *Grimes* was produced almost everywhere, even at La Scala, Milan, and at the hidebound Metropolitan Opera in New York. In connection with the Met production (a severe test of the work by all accounts), Britten's face appeared against a background of fishing nets on the cover of *Time* magazine, which ran a lengthy and informative article on him in its inimitable house style (16 February 1948). Not all the attention was adulatory, of course. As the anonymous reporter of *Time* put it, "English critics, having adopted Benjy Britten as a national hero, now insist on talking like Dutch uncles to him." When you examine the London reviews of the first run of performances at Sadler's Wells you cannot help being appalled by their superficiality and patronizing tone. Dyneley Hussey in *The Spectator* may be taken as an example: "There is no limit to what such a talent may accomplish, if the composer will aim at bold and simple effects, avoid excess of

Originally published in Nigel Fortune, ed., *Music and Theatre: Essays in Honour of Winton Dean* (Cambridge: Cambridge University Press, 1987), 353–65.

clever devices and subtle points that fail to make their effect in the theater, and above all, concentrate on the broad vocal melody as the central feature of his music" (15 June 1945). Another striking thing about these reviews is their tendency to begin enthusiastically and gradually to exert control, as though it would somehow threaten the critic's masculinity if he—and they were all men—were to write in response to his spontaneous feelings. Nevertheless, what journalists actually write is never so important as the amount of attention they show: it was clear to everyone that *Grimes* was a success from the start, and the sort of success that might have tempted a lesser composer to continue in the same vein. *The Rape of Lucretia*, first performed a little more than a year after *Grimes*, represents a radical departure from the earlier work in more ways than one.

The chamber proportions and scoring of *Lucretia* can of course be explained by practical considerations, which were always a challenge to creativity for Britten. The path to further grand opera had been closed off for the moment as a result of a row between the Sadler's Wells company on the one hand and those associated with Britten (including Joan Cross, Eric Crozier and Peter Pears) on the other. Indeed, it led to the withdrawal of *Peter Grimes* from the repertory after a surprisingly small number of performances. Moreover, Covent Garden's new operatic venture, which was to include *Peter Grimes* in its very first year, did not get under way until 1947 (see Crozier, "Peter Grimes"; and Brett, *Peter Grimes*, 90–91).

The idea of chamber opera must long have been fomenting in Britten's mind, and with the encouragement of Crozier and Ronald Duncan, whom he chose as his librettist for the new work, he apparently went ahead before there was any question of commitment from John Christie at Glyndebourne, where *Lucretia* was first performed (see Duncan, *How to Make Enemies*, 54–55). The change in timbre that resulted from the new medium naturally enough involved a change in musical style. And with *Lucretia* Britten's distinctive *secco* recitative first comes into its own. *Grimes* is not without good recitative, of course, most notably in the Pub scene. But the sheer bulk of information in the *Lucretia* libretto was a challenge to Britten to develop a characterful approach. Take, for instance, the opening of the opera, where the treacherous climb to power of the elder Tarquinius, who never appears in the opera, is marvelously set out in a declamatory manner that can make vital music out of such leaden mouthfuls of syllables as

> and always he'd pay his way
> With the prodigious liberality
> Of self-coin'd obsequious flattery.

The chief accompanying instrument is the piano, used in almost exactly the same way as it was used during this postwar period to accompany recitative in works of the seventeenth and eighteenth centuries. The punctuating ritornello from the full chamber band of single woodwind, horn, harp, percussion, string quartet and double bass hints by means of its reiterated chords at some of the tonal areas that will be important in the development of the musical argument, most notably C minor and E minor. With the entry of the Female Chorus, the background to the ensuing scene of an army encampment and its mood of frustration is suggested by an accompaniment seemingly locked to a chord constructed over B-flat. The mention of Christ and redemption causes a shift to a unison G, the dominant of the whole work, over which the Choruses sing their expressive C-major arioso. This is all done deftly and with an economy of means that is all the more striking after the expansiveness of the earlier opera.

Another distinct development in *Lucretia* is the characterization of arias and scenes by means of particular instrumental combinations—the instrumentation of *Grimes* is by comparison fairly standard. Take, for example, the opening aria for the Male Chorus, in the which the seesawing soft string chords, double bass punctuations (glissandi and pizzicati) and short falling pianissimo scales on the harp create the atmosphere of an oppressive summer night, complete with crickets and bull frogs—tone painting every bit as fine as, and rather more subtle than, anything in the Sea Interludes. The lullaby that portrays the sleeping Lucretia at the beginning of Act II is also worthy of attention. This is an early example of Britten's favorite combination of alto flute and clarinet, here combined with the muted horn; the harp harmonics that articulate the notes of the Female Chorus are a special touch. The passage is cast in an "innocent" C major, which provides the maximum contrast to the troubled C-sharp minor with which the act begins and also serves as a foil to the E major in which Tarquinius begins his ensuing aria, "Within this frail crucible of light," a more Grimes-like moment.

Even more notable than the development of musical style in *Lucretia*, however, is the radical change of subject matter and dramatic attitude. It was a change that most critics at the time deplored. Joseph Kerman, writing after the New York performance of 1949, contrasted the two works in this way:

> *Grimes* is straight melodrama, set in the early nineteenth century, written in *verismo* style; for all its faults it tells a story and tries to tell it dramatically. *Lucretia*, on the other hand, is a moral discussion, based on a classical legend elevated to a myth, and operates by means of narrative and contemplative choruses to such an extent that the tenor and soprano singing these choruses have the largest roles in the opera. There is no plot, properly speaking; the story, pared to a bare minimum, simply serves as a series of logical examples with the help of which Chorus and characters conspire to project a turgid metaphysic. (*Grimes*, 281–82)

After examining the effect on Britten of turning to the then self-consciously modern verse drama for a libretto, and quoting Duncan's lines for Lucretia at the climax of the drama with disapproval, Kerman concludes that "if there were not the example of *Grimes*, Britten's willingness to set this book would seem to convict him of complete inadequacy for dramatic composition" (283).

Finely composed though the score is, as Kerman gruffly acknowledges, its odd dramaturgy puts *Lucretia* among the most problematical of Britten's stage works. But this oddness can, I believe, be illuminated if not entirely explained by further comparison with the earlier, more traditional and more successful work. *Grimes* dramatizes with extraordinary power the conflict between the individual and society. Britten regarded it as "a subject very close to my heart—the struggle of the individual against the masses. The more vicious the society, the more vicious the individual" (*Time*, 16 February 1948). The extended poem on which Britten and Pears based the scenario they drafted before returning to England was "The Borough" by the eighteenth-century poet George Crabbe. Crabbe's Grimes is an out-and-out villain, the grim representative of a morally enfeebled society who merely takes advantage of the license allowed him under the poor laws of the time to brutalize the boys whom he buys from the workhouse. Britten changed Grimes—not as has been claimed (even by the librettist Montagu Slater himself [15–16]) into a Byronic hero but—into a victim of that society, who at the same time reflects its values.

The crux of the dramatic thrust of the opera occurs at the climax in Act II, scene 1. The passage begins (7 bars after fig. 15) with Ellen's challenge to Peter's compulsive desire to work and to succeed in worldly terms: "What aim, what future, what peace will your hard profits buy?" The F-major chord on "peace," sounding forced as though Ellen is engineering the drift of conversation toward a showdown, becomes the F pedal over which Peter sings, to an earlier melody signifying his stubborn pride, "Buy us a home, buy us respect [etc.]." But his determined D major is constantly undermined by the relentless thrust of the bass from A-flat to the pedal F. On this note the chorus then begins to recite the Creed—a "symbolum" indeed, not of spirituality but of the mob instinct "sanctified" by ritual. Though they fade out, a persistent repeated F on the horns reminds us of their continuing recitation. Staccato G-flat triads, suggestive in their relationship to the F of the minor ninth and second that characterize Peter's isolation, punctuate the conversation as Ellen first presses with seemingly genuine questions, then asks—in what David Matthews aptly calls "her sweetest even-note manner"—"Were we mistaken when we planned to solve your life in lonely toil?" Peter answers in lunging minor ninths supported by an even weaker set of D-major fragments in the bass. But Ellen can hear nothing and, lost to him, she changes her rhetorical question into a statement: "We *were* mistaken," the word "mistaken" sung here as elsewhere to a B-flat triad that hints at the devastation to follow. The saccharin sound of a solo violin underlines her falseness. Then, as she sings "Peter, we've failed, we've failed" to a rising octave on F, Peter strikes her, and the orchestra breaks loose in a melee created from the ironic superposition of Ellen's and Peter's melodies only to be cut short by the chorus, who sing a loud "Amen" to their unholy creed. Peter literally and psychologically takes his note from them to sing, on a massive B-flat cadence and to a downward plunging Lydian motive that informs most of the rest of the opera, "So be it then, and God have mercy upon me," a motive that the orchestra takes up in a rough canon as Peter stumbles off with the boy.

The passage is a brilliant musical illustration of cruelty masquerading as concern, and it also demonstrates how society inculcates what it sometimes eases its conscience by labeling paranoia. Even more powerfully, however, Grimes at this moment not only succumbs to the Borough, but also in his own mind becomes the monster he perceives they think him to be. After the enormously long dominant pedal, the cataclysmic cadence on B-flat—the key used to characterize the Borough right from the beginning of the opera—signifies as clearly as any musical gesture could the process in Grimes of what sociologists call "internalization"—the acceptance of society's values and judgment by the victim.

The opera argues, moreover, that the psychological process of internalization (and that of the "paranoia" that contributes to it) is a simple one resulting directly from social pressure and not from some subtle Freudian operation of the subconscious. While writing the work, the composer gradually jettisoned any matter that might be seized upon to manufacture psychological or pathological explanations for the central character. All mention was expunged of the father whose ineffectual attempts to control Peter the boy, Crabbe obliquely suggests, may partly be responsible for the villainy of Grimes the man. Britten's Grimes does *not* see the ghostly father and dead apprentices rebuking him—as was originally intended in the hut scene. Nor did the librettist's insistent de-

velopment of emotional ties between Grimes and his apprentice survive
the composer's intelligent scrutiny: it is with some surprise that we learn
that Peter's soliloquy before the Storm Interlude, as well as the aria, "And
she will soon forget her school-house ways," in the hut scene were both
originally addressed to the boy. All this had to go. By eliminating what
might have been interpreted as pathological elements, the composer insisted on the social message of the drama. (The critics who nevertheless
discerned psychopathy were for the composer part of the problem the
opera addressed).

A crucial moment in the scheme is the posse's arrival at the hut toward
the end of Act II, scene 2, an episode that is not in Crabbe, of course. The
loud knock which distracts Peter at the moment the boy falls symbolizes
society's implication in the death. We hear the posse approaching, its rising pitch suggesting the increasing suspicion and panic arising in its victim's breast. The cadence that heralds the knock signifies a kind of resolution, with the ensuing string and celeste tremolo suggesting the
suspension of time in a moment that is to prove fateful. As I have argued
at length, *Grimes* is a powerful dramatization of the view that crime is the
result of the workings of society at large, and that the individual reflects
society however hard he tries to remain distinct (*Peter Grimes,* 193–96).

A dramatic argument that places all the blame on society, reducing individual responsibility to such a degree, proved too much for most music
critics at the time, and still causes problems now. Whether or not Grimes
is technically guilty of his boys' deaths, a certain moral ambiguity has always been discerned in his portrayal. And as a visionary with no real emotional ties (*his* Ellen is part of his fantasy, the real one deserts him at the
moment of truth) he is so dissociated from the realism of his surround-
ings that in his alienation he becomes a truly existential figure. Britten,
however, was not by nature an existentialist. He later related this powerful drama of the outsider to his own predicament as a pacifist, and it
hardly needs now to be argued that it involved his sexuality as well. Conceived at the very moment when he decided to return to Britain after an
abortive attempt to emigrate to the United States, the opera served as a

catharsis, purging the darker side of his feelings toward the repressive and embattled society he had fled. Hence its intensity. Yet it was born not so much out of alienation as from an intense desire to be accepted and to play a part in society.

Perhaps even deeper issues were at stake. It is notable that the composer replaced Montagu Slater's text for the great soliloquy in the storm (it recurs at the end of the opera) with a verse beginning "What harbour shelters peace, away from waves, away from storms? What harbour can embrace terrors and tragedies?" This passage is one of the most powerfully symbolic in the work, because it juxtaposes Grimes's grandest sweep of melody, signifying his visionary side, with an inversion of a motive associated with the Borough in the inquest scene at the beginning, hinting again at the process of "internalization" and the seeds of destruction that it inevitably sows. The longing for peace, for resolution, is a theme that returns often in Britten's works. In *Grimes* it is not available. The protagonist goes silently to his death, a death, moreover, with no resonance, since society ignores the suicide of its victim as the daily round is resumed at the end of the opera.

Lucretia also involves death, a death that has political consequences in the myth, for it triggers the downfall of Tarquinius and the Etruscan rule at the hands of Brutus Junius, who thus becomes the focus in some accounts. It is not surprising that Britten showed no interest in this aspect of the story. The source of the opera is a play, *Le Viol de Lucrèce*, written by André Obey in the early 1930s for the Compagnie de Quinze, an idealistic group founded by Jacques Copeau to purify and revivify the French theater. Crozier mentions this company as an inspiration for the idea of the English Opera Group, and, much impressed by the play and its performance, he suggested it to Britten as a possible subject ("Staging First Productions," 27). Obey takes over from Shakespeare the element of what Ian Donaldson calls "magical thinking" about Lucretia's death. "Like a religious sacrifice, the suicide seems to cleanse the effects of pollution, and to restore innocence and purity" (25). To the notion of sacrifice in the play, the opera adds the theology of redemption. Critics were happy to assign this interpretation to the almost universally reviled librettist. Ronald Duncan later (in *Working with Britten*, 85) claimed that it was the composer's idea, and in view of the preoccupation with redemption in Britten's later works, this rings true.

In *Lucretia* the heroine is of course also, like Grimes, a victim. The society in which she exists is also portrayed as corrupt and oppressive, and she is raped by an Etruscan prince who embodies its worst features. But there is nothing the least alienated about her. In place of the broad cross-section against which Grimes is thrown in relief, *Lucretia* presents a tightly knit and balanced group of which the heroine is a fully integrated member. The allegory here is not that of the *out*cast oppressed, clearly. Duncan saw it, in typically high-flown terms, as "fertility or life devoured by death" and "spirit defiled by fate," with Lucretia symbolizing the former and Tarquinius the latter ("The Libretto," 62). But the musical opposition of motives built on adjacent notes symbolizing men and on thirds symbolizing women, outlined in some detail by White (148–54), suggests rather that Britten was making a point about the male and female principles in conflict. Furthermore, whereas Britten allowed Grimes's tragedy to speak for itself, he decided to present Lucretia's demise within a frame to enhance its personal meaning with a universal message. Obey's play already contained the two choruses that weave in and out of the action, taking on some of the functions carried over from the Shakespearian soliloquy, and also commenting on the tragedy from a contemporary point of view. It was Britten and his librettist, however, who made them specifically Christian.

Historically, Christianity has had some difficulty with the Lucretia myth, as Donaldson demonstrates (25–28). Though to most of the early fathers she seemed a natural proto-martyr, her example was eventually rejected because of the sin of suicide, which is clearly a stumbling block to any orthodox Christian interpretation. For Augustine, Lucretia's was not a heroic but a murderous act: failing to appreciate the Roman code of honor he asks, reasonably enough, "If she is

adulterous, why is she praised? If chaste, why was she put to death?"
Shakespeare, allowing his Lucrece to debate the Christian point of
view for three stanzas (1156–76), copes with the paradox by invoking
the body/soul distinction:

> Ay me! the bark pilled from the lofty pine,
>> His leaves will wither and his sap decay:
>> So must my soul, her bark being pilled away.
>
> Her house is sacked, her quiet interrupted,
> Her mansion battered by the enemy;
> Her sacred temple spotted, spoiled, corrupted,
> Grossly engirt with daring infamy:
> Then let it not be called impiety,
>> If in this blemished fort I make some hole
>> Through which I may convey this troubled soul.
>
> (1167–76)

But the metaphor and conclusion sound archaic and forced, as though
rehearsed from some midcentury anthology of sententious verse, and
Lucrece is immediately diverted by the contemplation of revenge in the
following stanzas.

Despite these difficulties, however, and quite apart from the question
of the composer's personal belief, there is a strong case for the introduction of Christianity in connection with this tale. A religion which celebrates the victim and therefore the very concept of victimization,
Christianity offers a universally understood context for the Lucretia
story as well as a personal and spiritual way of interpreting it. In *Grimes*,
Britten had of course represented religion only in its guise as a social institution, offering the basis in its hollow observance for hypocritical
judgment and ruthless persecution. In *Lucretia* we are asked to divorce
the moral and spiritual values of Christianity from their institutional
connotations as a means not only of seeing the universal significance of
the tragedy but also of finding a path out of the dilemma with which the
opera ends:

How is it possible that she
Being so pure should die!
How is it possible that we
Grieving for her should live?

Not quite articulated, but clearly underlying the work, is also the question of the ambiguous nature of beauty, one that exercised Britten a good deal, and came to occupy a central position in his last opera, *Death in Venice*. The pessimism of the later work had no place in *Lucretia*, however. In *How to Make Enemies* (134–36), the librettist reports that on reaching what was to have been the end—"So brief is beauty. / Is this it all? It is all! It is all!"—the composer begged for more words. That is, he demanded from Duncan a different poetic resolution because he did not or could not allow the musical argument to end: "from your point of view the opera is dramatically complete with Lucretia's death and the finale of epitaphs sung over her body, but I've just discovered that musically it's not finished. I want to write a final piece beyond the curtain as it were to frame the entire work."

Tonally, the piece revolves around and builds tension from an opposition of keys centered around C and E-flat, and keys centered around C-sharp and E. Peter Evans (138) goes so far as to see C-sharp minor as a symbol of sin and shame in Act II, and C as one of innocence and purity, and his reasoning is fairly convincing. C is very definitely heard as the key of untroubled innocent beauty when we find Lucretia sleeping in the passage already referred to above, and after that the E major in which Tarquinius sings seems another world of experience. As a result of this, the E that is a melodic pole of attraction for her is reharmonized when she awakes, and her C becomes C-sharp minor, the minor third of the melodic figure here being symbolically pierced by the horns brassy D-sharp (fig. 27) (a gesture that is repeated more violently in E-flat minor at fig. 41).

When Lucretia appears next morning her first arioso consists of chromatic confused utterances over a G pedal (fig. 71). The reference is to Tarquinius's music when he first wakes her (fig. 28), but in this context the pedal remains stationary so that Lucretia's C can be reinterpreted as C

Example 3.1. *The Rape of Lucretia:* the musical rhythm at the moment of Lucretia's death

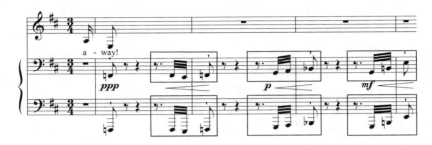

minor at the moment she sings her own name. At the appearance of Collatinus and Junius the insecure C slips to an unambiguous B minor for the denouement. As the heroine dies to a series of falling womanly thirds, the rhythm shown in the boxes of example 3.1 is heard and tried out on a number of pitches before the ground of the ensuing passacaglia emerges in E as unambiguously as Tarquinius's aria to her beauty earlier on. First Collatinus, then Junius, then the two maidservants, echoing Lucretia's falling thirds, sing over it. When the Female Chorus enters with a particularly far-fetched Duncanian metaphor, the ground migrates to the treble and the tonal complication grows. At the entry of the Male Chorus, the C-sharp-minor interpretation of the ground, latent in Junius's first statement, grows in strength, and it returns after the whole cast has tried to force a unison melody based on C against the ground to the crucial words quoted above, "How is it possible that she being so good should die [etc.]."

A stalemate has been reached at this point. Lucretia's tragedy is being viewed through eyes, the music seems to suggest, as human and sinful as Tarquinius's, and the burden of guilt cannot be lifted so easily. The music "is swept back into limp reiterations of its final thirds, 'It is all'" (Evans, 140). In an ensuing transformation and reconciliation as remarkable in its own way as the great B-flat chord in the epilogue of *Billy Budd* we are presented with a gradual resolution of the key conflict into a pure C major underpinning the correspondingly pure glimpse of the theology of

Christian redemption. First of all the Female Chorus asks questions each of which seeks to escape from, but is brought firmly back to, what is now a burdensome C-sharp-minor chord. When she finally reiterates the "Is this it all?" after mentioning the Crucifixion, a G-major dominant chord placed high on the strings, which have been silent since the end of the passacaglia, heralds the appearance of the Male Chorus, who gently takes up her note. Singing a melody in contrary motion to a bass that actually contains statements of the Tarquin motive, he resolves everything on to a B major which, as it were, purifies the B of Lucretia's shame in the simplest and largest arpeggio of the opera (beginning three bars before fig. 106). But even this is not all, for suddenly the fragmentary "it is all" rhythm appears all over the score like a galaxy of twinkling stars, and before we have time to assimilate it aurally, the bass gives way to G, a C pedal creeps in on a weak beat, and the Chorus sings its great melody, even-handed in its distribution of "male" tones and "female" thirds, for the last time.

This conclusion is irresistible and sure from a musical point of view. And as in so many cases in the history of opera, the music transforms the words. Here, as in the extraordinary prayer after the rape itself (reminiscent of the chorale in the trial scene of *The Magic Flute*, perhaps) we are helped over the perfumed High Church diction of a libretto written under the shadow of Eliot toward a vision of forgiveness and compassion that for Britten was evidently simple and real. Nonetheless, the Christian frame has raised serious problems for the opera, even among those most sympathetic to the composer. As Evans (most recently) has pointed out, "the tragedy could have been played out entirely in its own terms and the universal resonances would have been sensed" (141). More important still, once Christianity is invoked, it is no longer merely a question of "Great Love . . . defiled by Fate or Man": the sacrificial element of the religion comes into play ("But here / Other wounds are made, yet still His blood is shed") and the question of sin supersedes that of Fate.

The problem with sacrifice and sin in this context is that they are both made to devolve upon Lucretia. A careful reading of the libretto scarcely disturbs the notion that Tarquinius remains simply an agent of Fate—the cruel, degenerate, but inevitably attractive male whose phallic aspects Duncan is at pains to emphasize. Since the act of rape (after which he does not appear) is his chief purpose in the action, we cannot share his subsequent feelings. His one great moment, the exquisite aria "Within this frail crucible of light," possibly written in response to the phrase "the pity is that sin has so much grace" that precedes it, indeed gives some musical validity to the odd transference that occurs.

For Lucretia shoulders both. She is sacrificial lamb and at the same time the sinner begging forgiveness. Evans claims that the only view of her that makes any sense in the dramatic context is one in which she is both "revolted by Tarquinius' assault and horrifyingly attracted towards the realisation of a nightmare. . . . Her mental torture after the event suggests a recognition that revulsion and attraction can co-exist, that some part of her has shared the guilt" (141); and he quotes several aspects of both music and words that support this notion.

It is difficult to overcome revulsion at the view of rape which shifts the onus of responsibility onto the victim in this fashion. At first sight it may seem all too characteristic of that identifiable male approach which typically minimizes female rape either by denying its enormity or by throwing the responsibility for it back on to the woman. In his book on Richardson's novel, Terry Eagleton quotes V. S. Pritchett's extraordinary statement (in *The Living Novel*) that "Clarissa represents the extreme of puritanism which desires to be raped," and shows Ian Watt turning the ambiguous nature of Clarissa's feelings about Lovelace into her "unconscious love" for him (65, 68). Similarly, Ernest Newman in his first review of Britten's opera undercuts the work by referring to its central action as "the rather conventional mishap of Lucretia," and by finding the climactic point "too commonplace for stage representation" (*Sunday Times*, 28 July 1946). It would be disturbing indeed to find Britten in this company.

In fact, an examination of *Grimes* in the terms I have suggested clarifies the matter and shows why Britten countenanced this approach to Lucretia. As I argued earlier, what lies behind the exploration of the outsider's condition in the earlier opera—and what has been so misunderstood about it—is Britten's realization, no doubt gained from a cool assessment of his own predicament and perhaps some prompting from Auden and Isherwood, that those who are oppressed in one way or another tend to internalize their oppression. Grimes is a classic case, an unclubbable who can think of nothing better than joining the club while doing everything to ensure that he could never be accepted. Similarly, Lucretia in the second scene of Act II dramatizes the shame and guilt involuntarily experienced by rape victims even though they are totally innocent and have been wronged in a particularly horrible manner. Not sharing the attitudes of male heterosexual orthodoxy, Britten may well have been specially alive to this aspect of the tragedy.

And so, if we accept at face value the speech Duncan gives Lucretia at her moment of decision in Act II (just before fig. 94)—"Even great love's too frail to bear the weight of shadow"—then she stands convicted of lack of faith, and her suicide is a gesture of despair. If, however, the insistent B minor of her guilt is seen as symbolic of an involuntary, conditioned response—of internalization—and her words, her doubt, her guilt, even the whole panoply of Tarquinius's attractiveness, seen as the projection of an internalized role, then first her hysteria, and later her self-destruction, like Grimes's, begins to make sense. Her story becomes an equally modern tragedy.

But Britten is not even-handed with his victims. The fisherman whom we suspect to be at least partly guilty of the deaths of his apprentices is musically represented as a slightly tarnished yet still innocent victim of society. Lucretia, who on the other hand is the truly innocent victim of a ludicrous patriarchal order, is represented as at least partly guilty. Grimes's dreams give him an almost heroic stature and set him apart from society and the world of the audience, whereas Lucretia's dreams only betray her by turning natural desire into the material out of which her guilt is fabricated ("In the forest of my dreams / You have always been the Tiger"). By raping her, in other words, Tarquinius manages to make his desire her crime. And musically, the transference is accomplished quite literally by the recall of his "Yet the linnet in your eyes / Lifts with desire" (II, at fig. 32) during Lucretia's "confession" (fig. 88); also, on a symbolic plane his E major rubs off on her in the form of its dominant B, which also represents the fall from grace from her own limpid C major. In classical terms this tragic paradox must result in her death, but it becomes here in addition the very basis of the opera's Christian vision and the larger paradox that implies: "Though our nature's still as frail / And we still fall / . . . yet now / He bears our sin and does not fall / And He, carrying all / turns round / Stoned with our doubt and then forgives us all."

In musical terms, as we have seen, there is every reason to make the leap of faith this assertion requires; but it is an odd sleight of hand from an emotional or dramatic point of view, and one that may cause doubt or disquiet as we leave the theater. To make sense of it I think it must be seen in relation to Britten's lifelong preoccupation with the senseless violence of man and the attendant guilt by implication that he seems to have felt so strongly. In turning to Christian doctrine for relief and resolution in this opera he was attempting to answer the question that he had posed and left unanswered in *Grimes:*

> What harbour shelters peace,
> Away from tidal waves, away from storms,
> What harbour can embrace
> Terrors and tragedies?

Britten could not end yet again in the terrifying decrescendo to non-musical speech which, as Kerman put it, "is a powerful evocation of the dead hopelessness, past tragedy, of Grimes's ultimate predicament" (279). It is perhaps no accident that in *Lucretia*, written after the crisis of career and roots had taken place, Britten began the search for a more consoling and positive solution.

CHAPTER FOUR

Salvation at Sea

Britten's *Billy Budd*

The association of Benjamin Britten and E. M. Forster is one of the more interesting in the annals of opera. Less startling than the contemporaneous collaboration of Stravinsky and W. H. Auden (over *The Rake's Progress*, also completed in 1951), which by comparison was like two stars from different galaxies passing in unusual orbit, it seems to have been an almost predictable match between a literary-minded composer and a musical novelist who shared country, class and, to a large extent, beliefs. It also contained, for Britten at least, an element of the fateful. The two had met in 1936 under the auspices of Auden (then a major influence on Britten) and Christopher Isherwood (a close friend of Forster) during the staging of a play of theirs for which Britten had written the incidental music. Forster, then nearing sixty, was the "anti-heroic hero" (to use Isherwood's phrase) of this group of young liberal artists. He had given up writing novels after *A Passage to India* had appeared in 1924, but his creative energy was undiminished, and the tough words on personal liberty and humanitarian principle that issued in disconcerting ways from his superficially mild, understated demeanor shone as a guiding light to many

This revised version of an essay that first appeared in *San Francisco Opera Magazine* in 1978 is from Christopher Palmer, ed., *The Britten Companion* (London: Faber and Faber, 1984), 133–43.

in those days of gathering darkness. "I hate the idea of causes, and if I had to choose between betraying my country and betraying my friend, I hope I should have the guts to betray my country" ("What I Believe," 78). This is the most famous sentence from Forster's essay on his personal philosophy which, whatever its limitations, successfully maintained the primacy of personal relationships at a time when most intellectuals were succumbing to the siren songs of one ideology or another.

The independence Forster so cleverly maintained sprang not only from his Victorian liberal heritage but also from a profound distrust of authority that is common among members of a minority, but rarely in so articulate a form. Forster's acceptance of his homosexual nature, although on the one hand it caused him to stop writing fiction, had on the other strengthened his resolve and ability to be true to himself and his feelings. When Auden and Isherwood emigrated to the United States in 1939, they discovered similarly that their support for the various left-wing causes they had espoused simply could not take precedence over their personal destinies as men and writers (see Isherwood, *Christopher and His Kind* [317 ff.]). Britten and Pears soon followed Auden and Isherwood to the United States, probably with similar ideas in their heads. But Britten could not settle down, and Forster played an important part in the next stage of his life. By chance the composer came across an article in *The Listener* (29 May 1941) by the novelist on the minor Suffolk poet George Crabbe beginning with the words "To talk about Crabbe is to talk about England." And this clinched Britten's decision not only to return to England, but to take up residence in his native county in Crabbe's own town, Aldeburgh. The article also sent him to Crabbe's major poem, *The Borough*, where in the character of Peter Grimes he found the subject of his first and still most widely known opera.

The association then proceeded with overtures and pleasantries. Britten's third opera, *Albert Herring*, was dedicated to Forster quite appropriately, for it contains whiffs of Forsterian social comedy and a good dose of the message of the early novels. The famous novelist was also invited to the first Aldeburgh Festival in 1948 to lecture on Crabbe, and in so doing he remarked, "It amuses me to think what an opera on Peter Grimes would have been like if I had written it" ("George Crabbe and Peter Grimes," 20). The hint was pondered, and when in the same year Britten was commissioned to write an opera for the projected Festival of Britain he suggested they should collaborate. Forster was excited but hesitant because he lacked stage experience. Eric Crozier, the librettist of *Albert Herring*, was called in to help, and at this point Forster accepted. A subject had still to be found, however, and it is reported that the composer and novelist almost simultaneously hit upon Herman Melville's *Billy Budd* as the perfect choice.[1] It was certainly an unusual one, but when Crozier raised objections—for instance to the idea of an all-male opera—they are said to have been too impatient to listen; and it is safe to conclude that the subject answered a need for both of them.

Forster had written sympathetically about Melville (and perceptively about *Billy Budd* in particular) in his *Aspects of the Novel*. But the story offered him more than purely critical delight. He often gave sex as his reason for retiring from fiction: "weariness of the only subject that I both can and may treat—the love of men for women & vice versa," he wrote in his diary of 1911 (Furbank, 1:199). But in *Billy Budd* there was the opportunity to write about profound relationships between men: symbolically to evoke the power of homosexual love without being in any way sexually explicit. His first task, as he wrote to William Plomer, was to "rescue Vere from Melville," that is to say to correct Melville's excessive respect for authority, education and aristocracy as embodied in the Captain. This explains why Vere refuses in the opera to launch into the tirade that Melville causes him to deliver to his junior officers at the drumhead court. "How odiously Vere comes out in the trial scene!" Forster exclaimed in a little-known explanatory document.[2] The resulting vacuum, both in plot and in Vere's character, is filled by the most daring of all the Forsterian salvations: for just as the crippled Rickie (in *The Longest Journey*) is saved by the boisterous Stephen Wonham, just as Maurice is saved by the love of that other gamekeeper of English fiction, Alec Scudder, so the intellectual Captain Vere is saved by the love of his handsome sailor

Billy—with less reason, perhaps, and certainly more poignancy, for Vere still orders his destruction.

If Vere is vocal in Melville, Claggart is not. And in an effort to breathe life into the depraved Master-at-arms, Forster engineered a great aria toward the end of Act I about which he subsequently wrote to Britten, "It is my most important piece of writing and I did not, at my first hearing, feel it sufficiently important musically. . . . I want *passion*—love constricted, perverted, poisoned, but never the less *flowing* down its agonizing channel; a sexual discharge gone evil. Not soggy depression or growling remorse" (Furbank, 2:285–86). Clearly for Forster the apprehension of Billy's beauty and goodness by both Claggart and Vere includes sexual passion among other feelings. Forster himself was wont to project his feelings this way, as we learn from a most honest and revealing personal memorandum: "I want to love a strong young man of the lower classes and be loved by him and even hurt by him. That is my ticket, and then I have wanted to write respectable novels."[3] Billy was for him the center of the story, and perhaps in his creation of the young sailor there was an element of the wish fulfillment that is evident in *Maurice* and some of the posthumously printed stories.

For Britten, *Billy Budd* must have seemed a logical and necessary further exploration of themes he had already broached—most notably in *Peter Grimes* and *Albert Herring*. The heroes of these two earlier operas are both outsiders, odd men out in ordered and repressive societies. Grimes is destroyed by that society, but not before destroying himself by internalizing the oppression he suffers. *Herring*, as Andrew Porter rightly claims in "What Harbour Shelters Peace," is the happy counterpart of *Grimes*, in which Albert, the repressed youth tied to his mother's apron strings, breaks out after being unexpectedly "saved." I have argued at length that *Grimes* is fundamentally an allegory of homosexual oppression, and that in writing it Britten was somehow coming to terms with—by artistically experiencing the dark side of his feelings toward—the embattled society to which he was returning when he left the United States (see "Britten and Grimes"). While it is dangerous to connect an artist's personal life with his work too closely, it might even be suggested that there is some connection between the happiness and warmth of *Albert Herring* and the success of that particular decision in terms of the acceptance Britten found among English society. This "acceptance" grew over the years, and as Britten became more established so his mistrust of—even his connection to—society seems to have diminished, and his own private and deeply spiritual preoccupations came closer and closer to the surface: the corruption of innocence, the poignancy of age and decay, the theme of human reconciliation, compassion for the weak, lonely and helpless, and the Christian notion of salvation.

In *Billy Budd* the setting is still a hostile, uncomfortable environment dominated by oppressive forces. The hero, like Grimes, is destroyed by these forces, but in this instance he is pure, he is not alone against the crowd, and he is untouched by self-hatred. Instead, as innocent as Parsifal if more obviously flawed, he conquers the real evil and then "saves" the morally ambiguous figure who orders his destruction. Compared with *Grimes*, then, tragedy here is purified and made transcendental. And by framing the action between reminiscences of the aging Vere (whom Melville kills off shortly after the hanging), the opera is given a further push in the direction of a parable of redemption.

First and foremost among the difficulties in setting the libretto was the sheer technical problem of making an opera work without female voices. The composer thrived on such challenges, and as in this case, made them work to his advantage. The musical language of *Budd* as a whole is less demonstrative and colorful, more subtle than that of *Grimes*. It suggests most convincingly a certain gray monotony of life at sea, as well as the inner grayness of a character like Claggart in whom dwells, as Melville puts it, "the mania of an evil nature, not engendered by vicious training or corrupting books or licentious living, but born within him and innate."[4] The scoring forgoes the great sonorous orchestral tutti in favor of a separation of the various sections, with emphasis rather on the brass and woodwind than on the strings; and the effect of Britten's experience with chamber orchestra is also evident in the orchestral writing. It is in some ways a very delicate score, with a wonderfully conceived sound world all its own.

Another challenge was how to give musical purpose and unity to the opera while suggesting the mist, fog and moral confusion (the Forsterian "muddle") that are so essential to the librettist's conception. The opera was originally cast in four acts, and had a symphonic character. Act I covered Billy's introduction to the *Indomitable*, ending with a captain's muster in which Vere addressed his men, whom Billy then led in singing his praises. Act II was a "slow movement," depicting the vessel at night. The chase of the French ship acted as a scherzo, and the last act began with the ballad "Billy in the Darbies," and concluded with the hanging and the Epilogue. Britten revised this scheme in 1960 by tightening up the sequence of events into two acts without cutting anything essential (though the loss of the captain's muster is regrettable dramatically since Billy now swears to die for a man he has never seen). The atmosphere of moral uncertainty is suggested as soon as the curtain rises on the reminiscing Vere: an eerie string passage embodies a characteristic opposition between B-flat major and B minor that haunts the whole score. So much of the melodic material of the opera is ultimately derived from the opening statement. This tonal ambiguity, however, is projected on to a solid tonal framework that gives the opera a sense of progression as well as allowing certain key areas to be associated with certain crucial events. In Act I, the key scheme moves upward from this early and ambiguous B-flat major with a few significant diversions—to E major for Billy's first aria, and to F minor for Claggart ("Was I born yesterday?") and the novice's touching scene. It reaches C major by the end of the first scene, stays there for Vere and his officers, then proceeds up to E-flat major for the third scene, at the beginning of which the happiness of the men singing their shanty "Blow her away to Hilo" seems literally to blow away the doubts and fears of the ambiguous tonalities of the previous interlude in a glorious gust of E-flat—one of the opera's great moments. There follows Claggart's monologue, ending in his characteristic F minor, which then turns to F major to depict Billy asleep (the same motive as when later he is lying in chains), and the act concludes in G major with the duet between Billy and Dansker accompanied by an ostinato derived from Claggart's motive, to which Dansker sings "Jemmy Legs is down on you."

The tonality of the opening of Act II is again ambiguous, but in a more forceful way than that of Act I. The opening melody is in B-flat, but the ostinato which animates the scene reiterates the G which closed Act I, and G major is adopted as soon as the ship is called to action. From here the key scheme gradually winds down again—sometimes reverting to the B-flat-major–B-minor opposition as in the interlude depicting the mist and Vere's confusion—finally reaching C minor for Vere's aria ("Scylla and Charybdis") after Billy has killed Claggart. The court scene reverts to F minor, which turns to a radiant F major as Vere goes to tell Billy the verdict, and remains there for Billy's final scene. The hanging takes place in the remote key of E, and this incipient mutiny against the fated scheme of things both on stage and in the music is firmly quelled by an insistent B-flat which rings out with the voices of the officers. In the Epilogue the B-flat-major–B-minor opposition is finally reconciled by Vere's singing Billy's final ballad-like tune, which is firmly in B-flat, to the words, "I was lost on the infinite sea, but I've sighted a sail in the storm. . . . There's a land where she'll anchor for ever."

Another problem for Britten was to suggest those aspects or passages of the story that had perforce to be left out of the libretto. In Melville, to take a down-to-earth instance, we learn of the love and harmony Billy spreads among his shipmates from a speech by Captain Graveling of the *Rights of Man* (*Billy Budd*, 7–8). In the opera this slightly aggressive side of Billy's goodness is expressed in a series of rising arpeggios on triads a tone apart, first heard when the boat containing him and the other impressed men nears the *Indomitable* in Act I, scene 1. This motive subsequently forms the accompaniment to Billy's first aria ("Billy Budd, king of the birds!"), and when in his last scene Billy lies in chains, it punctuates the phrases of his ballad, played on the piccolo, still chirpy but lonely and forlorn. At the opening of Act II, however, it is transformed into the melody the whole crew sings in pursuit of the French ship, thus suggesting psychologically that this moment of unity is a product as much of Billy's influence as of the excitement of the chase. The unrest of the crew at other times, indeed the whole atmosphere of incipient mutiny in the aftermath of Spithead and the Nore, is suggested by a musical motive first heard in the Prologue, where it is set to Vere's "O what have I done?" (thus effectively showing his complicity in the state of affairs), and subsequently developing into the shanty "O heave away, heave," that runs through the first scene. It is heard every time the subject of mutiny occurs, and a variant of it forms Claggart's official accusation. At the climax of the opera, after the hanging, it turns into the wordless fugue which brilliantly suggests the famous passage in Melville:

> Whoever has heard the freshet-wave of a torrent suddenly swelled by pouring showers in tropical mountains, showers not shared by the plain; whoever has heard the first muffled murmur of its sloping advance through precipitous woods, may form some conception of the sound now heard. The seeming remoteness of its source was because of its murmurous indistinctness since it came from close by, even from the men massed on the ship's open deck. Being inarticulate, it was dubious in significance further than it seems to indicate some capricious revulsion of their involuntary echoing of Billy's benediction. (*Billy Budd*, 128)

Being a suggestive force, rather than a specific symbol, a musical motive can reflect such subtle changes of mood and meaning, the "murmurous indistinctiveness" Melville describes, and Britten was able to achieve such nuance in his depiction of the other main characters. Claggart, for instance, is characterized by a motive that contains two falling fourths. It is first heard against the ambiguous B-flat–B-minor chord in the Prologue, but reaches its most powerful expression against a stark F-minor chord bereft of its fifth, in such moments as the climax of the Act I aria. It is sad that Forster's Victorian ears could not hear the brilliance of Britten's music here, for it suggests a quality he had attributed to Melville in his *Aspects of the Novel*: he "reaches straight back into the universal, to a blackness and sadness so transcending our own that they are indistinguishable from glory" (98).

The motive of a perfect fourth, without the downward plunge of Claggart's depravity, effectively expresses the emotional charge behind the abstractions that both the Master-at-arms and the Captain use when they contemplate Billy: "O beauty, handsomeness, goodness," they both sing to the same melody, sharing alone among the ship's crew a special sense of and connection to the natural wonder of the Handsome Sailor, whose single flaw, his stammer (musically expressed by a trilling trumpet, the woodblock, and abrupt woodwind arpeggios), is a sign of the flaw in creation, of Original Sin.

Possibly the strangest and most daring moment in the score is the interlude after the trial and Vere's aria ("I accept their verdict"). It evidently expresses the intent of the chapter in which Melville tells nothing definite about what takes place when Vere communicates the verdict to Billy, but gives some hints and speculations which Britten and Forster worked up into the theme of salvation. What we hear are thirty-four clear, triadic chords, each of them harmonizing a note of the F-major triad, and each scored differently. They are vaguely reminiscent of the chords that occurred earlier whenever Claggart addressed Billy: in the sailor's last aria they appear at the moment when he begins to feel his full strength, and finally and triumphantly they underpin the climax of the Epilogue when Vere, singing Billy's B-flat melody, utters the crucial Forsterian lines, "But I've sighted sail in the storm, the far-shining sail, and I'm content."[5]

These chords lie at the heart of the musical treatment of the metaphysical overtones of *Billy Budd*. They seem to suggest that in Platonic terms, the love of Ideal Beauty can lead to wisdom, knowledge and forgiveness; and that in Christian terms, goodness and love have the power to forgive. This moment of unalloyed optimism is perhaps the crux of the opera, and the richest result of the collaboration between these two remarkable men. Interestingly enough, such optimism was not characteristic of either of them, and they both retreated in the following years. When in 1957–58 Forster wrote his last and finest short story, "The Other Boat," the two central characters, a young English officer and a young black man, destroy each other. This, Forster told his biographer, "was more interesting than the theme of salvation, the rescuer from 'otherwhere,' the generic Alec [Scudder, in *Maurice*]. That was a fake. People could help one another, yes; but they were not decisive for each other like that" (Furbank, 2:303). For Britten, too, there was a retreat from the idealism *of Budd*. When he came to write another work in which an upright, repressed man meets a vision of beauty, the result is less idealized. In *Death in Venice*, the composer's last opera, beauty enchants and then destroys: it leads as far as self-knowledge but does not reach the full distance to salvation.

NOTES

1. This and much other information is taken from P. N. Furbank's excellent biography of the novelist, to which I am deeply indebted. See the account of Forster's work on the opera, 2:283–86. Britten's own account, possibly a little idealized, appears in "Some Notes on Forster and Music," 85–86.

2. A "Letter to America," written in September 1951 for the *Griffin*, the still-extant monthly organ of the Reader's Subscription Service in the United States. This letter, kindly brought to my attention by Mr. Furbank after my essay was written, appears in certain ways to contradict what comes through in the opera. Perhaps, with his lack of operatic experience, Forster did not clearly perceive how firmly Britten was steering the ship, and in what direction. Forster thought the librettists' main problem was "how to make Billy, rather than Vere, the hero." Forster stated, "Melville got muddled"; "his respect for authority and discipline deflected him," and "every now and then he doused Billy's light and felt that Vere, being well-educated and just, must shine like a star." That the opera ultimately came out almost the opposite of what Forster intended, at least for one perceptive observer, appears from Andrew Porter's article in *Music & Letters*: "The librettists have made this secondary relationship [between Billy and Vere] the principal theme of their opera, and Vere its chief figure. The roles of Billy, the natural hero, and Claggart are reduced to those of actors who bring about Vere's tragedy and, indeed, the action is conceived as 'having been called up by Vere'" (112).

3. Quoted as a personal memorandum of 1935 by Oliver Stallybrass in his introduction to *The Life to Come and Other Stories*, xiv.

4. *Billy Budd*, ed. Milton R. Stern (1975), 61. Neither this standard edition nor the one, ed. Harrison Hayford and Merton Sealts, Jr. (1962), was of course available to Britten, Forster and Crozier, who were more likely to have used an edition such as *The Shorter Novels of Herman Melville* (1928) or *Melville's Billy Budd*, ed. F. Barren Freeman (1948). The matter is of more than merely bibliographi-

cal interest because of major changes in the 1962 and 1975 editions. The chief ones are the relocating of what used to be the preface and several other sections; the reordering of the title from *Billy Budd, Foretopman* to *Billy Budd, Sailor (An Inside Narrative);* and the change of the ship's name from *Indomitable* to *Bellipotent.*

5. Cf. the "Letter to America": "Melville believed in Fate, but kept seeing out of the corner of his eye a white sail beating up against the storm. Doom was fixed, the trap clicked, the body splashed, the fish nibbled. But he kept seeing the obstinate white sail." To be fair to Forster, then, it seems he was trying to suggest something more like hope than salvation, as other passages in the "Letter" indicate. The closest he comes to the latter is in the following sentence, the last before his signing-off paragraph: "The hero hangs dead from the yard arm, dead irredeemably and not in any heaven, dead as a doornail, dead as Antigone, and he has given us life." But opera, even in Britten's sensitive hands, is no match for the fine distinctions of the Forsterian vision, which that final B-flat chord, welling out of the orchestra, all but obliterates.

CHAPTER FIVE

Character and Caricature in
Albert Herring

The three Britten operas of the mid-1940s, *Peter Grimes*, *The Rape of Lucretia* and *Albert Herring*, are all at one level or another concerned with oppression. The remarkable thing about Britten's relation to that overworked word is that he seems intuitively to have grasped the thought behind the rallying cry of minority movements twenty years later—that the dynamics of oppression are not bound by a one-dimensional Marxist model but work in multifarious ways. The "oppressor" in one situation is likely to become the "oppressed" in another. And he seems also to have understood, probably from personal experience and again intuitively, that the damage of oppression stems not only from the exercise of oppressive power, but more devastatingly from the internal assimilation (internalization) of the authority of that power on the part of the oppressed and from the destruction of self-validity that results. Oppression is most effective and pernicious when its victims fail to recognize it as such (see "Britten and Grimes").

In *Grimes* a society bound together by its common battle against the sea ostracizes one of its own members because he does not fit in. Tragedy results, however, only when the victim accepts society's image of himself,

This essay first appeared in *Musical Times* 127 (October 1986): 545–47.

in a moment that is musically dramatized at the climax of the opera in Act II, scene 1, and lapses into shame and self-hatred. Shame is also the downfall of Lucretia, who allows her imagination to create her own guilt out of Tarquinius's crime: her self-oppression results in a sacrifice of the innocent that prompts (but perhaps does not dramatically justify) the introduction of Christianity to universalize the meaning.

Albert Herring is closer to home than the other works in many respects (set in a Suffolk town at the turn of the century, the kind of society it portrays was still thriving in 1947 and can yet be recollected if not recognized in England). It therefore injects into the debate the very English ingredient of class consciousness. Ten years earlier, when Britten and almost every other British artist had been so ardently left-wing, the opera might have sought to emulate the aims of a Marxist tract, but after the war Britten seems to have shed his socialist fervor as easily as Auden and Isherwood, and possibly for similar reasons—homosexuals and pacifists, unwelcome in any party that aspires to power, learn to keep their own counsel. What did come out of the Maupassant story, *Le Rosier de Madame Husson*, which the librettist Eric Crozier and the composer transplanted to East Suffolk, was again more prophetic than they may consciously have imagined: *Albert Herring* is a parable of liberation.

"Britten's purpose in writing *Albert Herring* could have been no more than a wish to entertain by apt caricature of the familiar." On the surface the composer's own recorded performance seems to bear out that assertion of Peter Evans's (145).[1] Yet for an audience today the element of caricature, festooned with local color and tricked out with schoolboy jokes and language, is the thing likely to become most quickly tiresome. And in Britain especially, critics are uncomfortable with what they perceive in the libretto as condescension—"the many mannered colloquialisms that depend for their effect on a willingness to snigger at the lower orders," to put it in Edward Greenfield's words (908).

Caricature and condescension: these aspects of the opera have been put into historical perspective by Peter Hall. His production at Glyndebourne in 1985 employed a new and unusual kind of realism: all the characters who in real life might have spoken with a Suffolk accent, including Albert, sang that way. I have heard only one excerpt from the performance (conducted by Bernard Haitink), one that was craftily chosen by Eric Crozier and Nancy Evans (in their talk about *Herring* at the 1986 Aldeburgh Festival) to show how vocally diminishing and therefore musically damaging to Britten's conception this policy was. The Glyndebourne singer screeched out Albert's Act I aria with twisted vowels and faulty intonation that make the ringing bel canto tones of the fifty-four-year-old Peter Pears (who created the role and sings it on the record) sound the model of youthful passion by comparison. Even more passionate and exciting was the younger Pears in an excerpt of the same passage from a 1948 recording that Crozier had found in the BBC archives.

This distinctly dialect *Herring* makes one listen to the recording again with different ears. Pears has a clever way of making his speech sound informal ("tuh" for "to" is the sort of change involved), but he makes no radical attempt to disguise his normally cultivated accent. Only the very minor roles are allowed to essay some kind of locality of speech (Emmie's interruption of that very aria of Albert's is an example), and what one hears is not of course real East Anglia but a variety of one of the accents used to portray (pillory, celebrate—your political orientation will suggest a suitable verb) lowlife on the classic British stage where traditionally local accents of an institutionalized kind (bearing about as much relation to the real thing as stage scenery to countryside) have been used to capture, almost always with some condescension, certain character types. Visitors to a recent straightforward National Theatre production of Congreve's *Love for Love* will reveal two "West-country accents" of the same sort—from characters whose siblings and parents speak the clipped "stage" English that is itself a reflection of upper-class speech. In this respect then, the Britten-Crozier conception of the opera simply falls in with a historical stage convention.

Peter Hall's gambit neutralizes stage history, and makes one think freshly about libretto and characters, by saturating the piece with accent (the real thing, not a stagey version). An incidental effect, in the excerpt

I heard, was its vindication of Crozier's ear. The phrase "Golly, golly, it's about time; golly, it's about time," which occurs at the end of Albert's single Act I aria referred to above, and which always sounded so public-school (to me) on Sir Peter's lips, fits right in with the North Norfolk sounds with which I happen to be particularly familiar. What had always seemed a comic device—the anti-climactic undermining of the intense feeling produced in the distinctly Verdian lyricism of the second part of the aria ("It seems as clear as clear can be")—now becomes part and parcel of the form, a natural coda which preserves the intensity up to the moment when Florence enters to announce the approach of Lady Billows and the rest.

If Britten had not reached, consciously or unconsciously, for something beyond caricature and condescension and had merely produced a cozy little provincial romp in the spirit of the escapist Ealing film comedies of the period, the opera would not have survived so well (two productions of it could be seen in Britain this summer) nor have been imported so readily by opera houses of other countries. I do not believe, with Stanley Sadie, that it is the "slightest among Britten's operas" (548), and I suspect that critical discomfort with it, like that over *Grimes*, ultimately derives from other sources.

In France and the Mediterranean countries the phenomenon of a man living with his mother is not unusual: it is a matter of no consequence in Maupassant's story, which concentrates entirely on the hero's decline into a legendary drunkard, and does not even suggest that he is mother-dominated. In the Protestant north, however, where oedipal implications translate easily into guilt and where manhood is won rather than granted as a birthright, Albert's position is more disturbing. There, but for the grace of God and some hefty pushing from the rest of society, goes every man. To be unmarried, and worse still, to be living for Mum, these are taboos in English society, which has contained them (and justified its self-image of toleration) within the concept of "eccentricity." One reason why the opera disturbs, why in a good production and performance it can have the effect of Mozartian or Shakespearian tears-behind-laughter, is that it presents an intensified version of a complicated situation every mother and son in the audience had experienced at one level or another. The sinister, obsessive nature of Mrs. Herring's music (surely one of the best of Britten's several predatory women, again a caricature rather than a character on the recording) and the true musical pathos of Albert create a viable central comic situation which, like all effective comic situations, is close enough to the truth to hurt.

On another level the potential tragedy behind the comic denouement of *Herring* is that of the unrealized self. Albert is a slave to someone else's ideas (to his internalized notion of a son's duties, if you like). And his liberation follows classic lines. First he finds his anger in the incredible Act I aria; it starts out memorably with his increasingly agitated recitation of his duties over pizzicato string chords that feel like the contractions of the muscles where anger is locked. Then in the second act he defeats fear, if only by means of Dutch courage parodied in German chromatics (as in *Tristan*, after all, the music knows the hero better than he knows himself), and asserts himself truly. But notice he does not "become a man." Critics have predictably dwelt on the *lack* of experience indicated in his night of shame/liberation. And so it is quite correct to think of Albert's self-liberation, as Andrew Porter has suggested, in terms of "coming out" (*Music* 208). Albert becomes himself in his own way without having subscribed to society's pattern of initiation: he returns without a trophy of any kind. Nothing more need be said.

Those whom he confronts and confounds on his return have just sung one of the most powerful and moving of Britten's many vocal passacaglias, "In the midst of life is death." Earlier critics often felt this piece overbalanced the work (as Winton Dean notes in his review of the 1986 Glyndebourne revival: *Musical Times* 127 [August 1986]: 454). I doubt if anyone thinks that now, but it would be easy to see why they did from the tenor of productions that bounced along emphasizing the fun. If Britten's intention was merely to "entertain by apt caricature of the familiar," then his subconscious betrayed him royally here (and subtly elsewhere in the score). Albert's condition can only be fully dramatized if those ranged about (and against) him are convincing characters, imbued with feelings that are never so intense as when their dreams and hopes are shattered, when they mourn the loss of their own power as well as of another human being.

If Lady Billows remains simply a caricature, then the opera cannot hope to be fully effective as comedy, never mind to engage its audience in the issues with which it is clearly involved, whether its creator realized it or not. The forces of repression often appear ridiculously puritanical, after all, but they are most potent and most real. And in our own time there is no lack of public figures, some comic and some less so, eager to legislate for the private lives of others and to persuade governments to carry out their programs. How any production of *Herring* can continue to preserve the myth of remoteness, as the 1986 Aldeburgh Festival production did, in the world of Lord Longford, Mrs. Whitehouse, Norman Tebbit, Jerry Falwell, William F. Buckley and Lyndon LaRouche, I cannot imagine. A present-day Lady Billows would undoubtedly want to have Albert compulsorily tested for HIV antibodies on return and shipped off to the nearest AIDS detention center; and her minions would each find a plausible reason to go along with her. The power of this remarkable score stems ultimately from Britten's own ambivalence about a society which on the one hand he desperately wished to serve and on the other he profoundly mistrusted. Behind *Herring* lies all the tension of *Grimes*, but projected through comedy, and softened by one rather unexpected element—the genuine celebration of physicality and sensuousness in the music of Sid and Nancy. Again, the composer must have realized that liberation cannot be achieved without repossession of the body and of feeling; and, puritan though he was, he found a way of encapsulating that thought in music.

The ethos of faithfulness to the composer's intentions that prevails in intelligent musical circles today, and that forms the credo of the early music movement, needs careful examining when in comes to works like *Herring*. As a statement of intention, the composer's recording is useful in setting a general style, indicating the likely interpretation of ambiguous matters, and stating the bounds beyond which lie distortion of the music. Yet if it inhibits the search for meanings that are latent in the score, but understated in that particular performance (for whatever reason), then I think its seeming authority must be resisted, however gently. I do not myself favor the Davis-Vickers recording of *Grimes*, simply because its undeniably powerful effects are too often achieved at the expense of a musical error (the tempo distortions in the Prologue are a specific example). But its idea of searching for meaning not made explicit in the composer's recording cannot be condemned. If Britten was prophetic in his art, as I suggested at the outset, then it seems false to his vision to emasculate that art by tying it exclusively to the musical tradition and social expectations of his own time. The real question, as always, is to know how and where to draw the line.

NOTE

1. The recording, made in 1964, is Decca SET 274-6; the cast is headed by Sylvia Fisher as Lady Billows and Peter Pears as Albert, with the English Chamber Orchestra conducted by Britten.

CHAPTER SIX

Britten's Bad Boys

Male Relations in *The Turn of the Screw*

There is a moment in Henry James's famous ghost story that gives away one of its secrets. The Governess, having seen a strange male figure around the house at Bly for a second time, elicits from Mrs. Grose that its features are those of Peter Quint, the master's dead valet. In her certitude that the ghost "had come for someone else" (than her), she jumps to a notable conclusion in her conversations with the kindly housekeeper:

> "He was looking for little Miles." A portentous clearness now possessed me. "*That's* whom he was looking for."
>
> "But how do you know?"
>
> "I know, I know, I know!" My exaltation grew. "And *you* know, my dear!"

Mrs. Grose does not demur, and shortly after goes on to clarify:

> "Quint was much too free."
>
> This gave me, straight from my vision of his face—*such* a face!—a sudden sickness of disgust. "Too free with *my* boy?"
>
> "Too free with every one!" (49–50)

Originally published in *repercussions* 1, no. 2 (Fall 1992): 5–25.

The "sudden sickness of disgust" in this context taps directly into the nineteenth century's discourse surrounding sexuality, and makes us realize that the haunting has a sexual purpose. The subject of male sexual practices has already been raised, indirectly of course, in the letter dismissing Miles from school for "an injury to the others." As Michael Moon has argued, it is the anti-masturbation tracts beginning with *Solitary Vice Considered* (1831) and rising to ever increasing heights of hysteria through the century in inveighing against a whole range of male practices for which "onanism" served as a label, that are the background to this "mystery (or nonmystery)" (256).[1] Their resonance for James and his reader would also immediately suggest the nature of the haunting of the boy by his corrupter. But how do both these women know that Miles is its object? The hints are all there in the Governess's description of the apparition which tie into the terms of what Moon calls the "anti-onanist terrorist literature":

"He gives me a sort of sense of looking like an actor."

"An actor!" It was impossible to resemble one less, at least, than Mrs. Grose at that moment.

"I've never seen one, but so I suppose them. He's tall, active, erect," I continued, "but never—no, never!—a gentleman." (47)

When we subsequently learn that he wears stolen clothes ("they're smart, but they're not his own") and that he is handsome ("Remarkably!"), we too can pull the pieces together. Created in the 1890s, a period which saw also the writing of *Billy Budd* and *The Picture of Dorian Gray*, and the staging of the three trials of Oscar Wilde, "The Turn of the Screw" plays a part in the definition and treatment of an increasingly urgent social construction of the time, one which has shaped a good deal of Western culture in this century.

Michel Foucault has shown how modern Western culture has put what it calls sexuality in a special relation to identity, knowledge and power; and he has analyzed how the entire network of social relations, from the eighteenth century onward, came increasingly to be sexualized—and thus subject to control—in terms of four major categories: the hysterical woman, the precociously sexual child, the Malthusian couple, and the perverse adult (103–14). Interestingly enough, "The Turn of the Screw" is organized around three of these charged figures. The Governess is all too obviously the first, the children, especially Miles, the second. The missing third one, the Malthusian couple, is, as it were, the ground from which the others spring, for in America at least, as the work of Moon and Caroll Smith-Rosenberg reveals, it is the publication of the first birth control books in the early 1830s, with their separation of sexual pleasure/indulgence from its hitherto supposedly inevitable biological consequences, that sparks off the anti-onanist literature and not only intensifies the effort to control the female body, but also contributes to a whole range of nonerotic discourses surrounding social matters.

But it is around the last Foucauldian category, represented by Quint, that the others are increasingly focused. As Moon sees it, the anti-onanist discourse "crystallizes around the figure of the depraved individual—servant, older relative, or older child—who, by teaching the young to masturbate, introduces sexual difference and sexual desire into what American moral-purity writers represent as the previously innocent—which is to say asexual—homosocial environments to which the young are committed" (255). (It is no accident that the Governess, on reading the Headmaster's cryptic letter, lights on the word "contaminate"—producing "corrupt" as a synonym for the uncomprehending housekeeper—rather than assuming that the "injury" is theft, bullying or some other relatively straightforward schoolboy crime ["Turn," 30].) In the larger sphere, for whatever reason, the other categories, indeed the whole panoply of nineteenth-century sexual categorizations, not to mention the many kinds of genital activity, came at the turn of the century to be organized around the pair—anything but simple in their ramifications—determined by the gender of object choice. And, as Eve Sedgwick observes, "It was this new development that left no space in the culture exempt from the potent incoherencies of homo/heterosexual definition"

(2). This pair of terms—not symmetrical and equal, but subsisting in a tacit arrangement by which the one term subsumes and excludes the other—has been, and still is, highly productive for art and literature. For, as Sedgwick has argued, they stand at the head of a number of pairs—such as private/public, secrecy/disclosure, minority/majority, foreign/domestic, even knowledge/ignorance—in which (as feminist theory has established) a pejorative use of one sets off the normative or privileged character of the other (11).

Benjamin Britten occupies a special place in this cultural discourse. It is not so remarkable that he was a homosexual composer—a large number have been and still are—nor are the forms his homosexual impulses and engagements took of unusual interest—as biographical revelations appear thick and fast, these are likely to complicate his position but not to alter it.[2] For what is so interesting about him is how he dealt at a public level, in his music and especially in his operatic works, with the concatenation of musicality and homosexuality. His own life was a curious mixture of publicity and privacy, the nature of his relationship to Peter Pears ("a congenial companion," he once called him) well known, though never publicly acknowledged or discussed. It was an "open secret," to give D. A. Miller's name to a familiar mechanism by which the tensions around the closet are kept intact (206). His puritanical middle-class upbringing (he was the son of a dentist) predisposed him to reject the word "gay" and all it came to signify in his lifetime (we have it on the authority of Pears). And at some level, as a history of depressions and insecurities testifies, he was, as one of his librettists put it, "a reluctant homosexual, a man in flight from himself, who often punished others for the sin he felt he'd committed himself."[3]

Whatever his public reluctance, however, he perceived fairly early in his career (around his thirtieth year), that his ambivalence toward, as well as his sense of, a homosexual identity would serve his art well. The immediate result of that realization was *Peter Grimes*, the opera which firmly established his reputation. What is remarkable about that work as an allegory of homosexual oppression is not so much the terrifying paranoia of the two manhunts, powerful though they are, but the realization of a musical process to mirror the internalized oppression which, as later became clear, is the most destructive aspect of minority social experience (see "Britten and Grimes" and its postscript).

Having mined this particular field, in *Grimes*, *Albert Herring* and a few smaller works, Britten moved on in his collaboration with E. M. Forster over *Billy Budd* (1953) to dramatize not so much the effects of the minority social experience as the dynamics of desire itself in a same-sex, closed environment. Far in advance of *Grimes* in dramatic and musical technique, *Budd* perfectly captures the nuances and innuendoes by which Melville suggests that Claggart is homosexual, and moreover dramatizes to a fine point the place that "starry Vere" occupies in the homosexual constellation, and the moral consequences of his dealing with Billy.[4]

The Turn of the Screw (1954) moves into an even more private space to explore the very heartland of the modern construction of sexuality. Arnold Whittall has summed up one aspect of the work as follows: "for the first time in his operas there are no significant public resonances or social perspectives: the conflicts are not seen as conflicts within society, or of tensions between a single 'outsider' and the rest" (*The Music of Britten and Tippett*, 158–59). So it may at first appear. But, as we have seen, the tensions that occur in the private area delineated in James's story play a determining if covert role in the organization of modern society. Though at one level Britten is clearly enjoying being able through the subterfuge of a literary ghost story to introduce same-sex attraction into his operatic world, he is also, at another level, equally preoccupied with the social concerns which are nonetheless social for being presented in this oblique guise.

The opera is presented in a series of sixteen scenes which closely follow the chain of incidents in the book, and preserve its episodic structure. Some events are telescoped, some omitted, but there are three scenes that are entirely (or almost entirely) new. The first of these is "the Lesson" (I, 6) which ends with Miles's song, "Malo" (example 6.1) This concentrated, thematically obsessive tune, with its triadic harp accompani-

Example 6.1. *The Turn of the Screw*, Act I, scene 6

Example 6.2. *The Turn of the Screw*, Act I, first theme

ment and plaintive viola/English horn countermelody, suggests very powerfully the abjection of the boyish masturbator—as if Britten sensed from his vantage point of half a century later exactly the resonances of James's tale. Every rising melodic figure suggesting awakening knowledge is complemented by a downward turn epitomizing abjection. Each occasion Miles and his harp accompaniment coincide on a common note is matched by one when he sings a seventh or ninth to the harp's root; the string of descending sevenths at the end of the third phrase provides a balancing languor to the notably clearer, more positive sounds of the consonant, rising second phrase. The inverted pedal of the viola and the quizzical interjections of the English horn add to the obsessive as well as melancholy quality of the music. Finally, there is a notable melodic correspondence between the opening of the song, rising from B-flat to E-flat through D-flat, and the celesta flourish first heard in scene 3 (fig. 15) when the Governess opens the Headmaster's letter, a flourish later associated with manifestations of Quint's presence. Needless to say, the "Malo" melody casts a long shadow throughout the rest of the score.

The other two added scenes are both in Act II: the first scene of the act illuminates the psychological states of the three principal adult characters, Quint, Miss Jessel and the Governess; and the fifth scene portrays Quint tempting Miles to steal the letter the Governess has written to his guardian. Both scenes serve to make the ghosts musically palpable in a way that contravenes James's subtle suggestiveness, but makes sense on the stage where unseen presences do not easily engage the audience's feelings.

The musical organization is closely, even obsessively, worked out throughout the opera. No other Britten score is so tightly ordered, no

Example 6.3. *The Turn of the Screw*, Act I, second theme

scheme of his more imaginatively devised to produce a musically claustrophobic quality. The fifteen interludes which punctuate the scenes consist of a set of variations on a theme that is announced at the beginning,
immediately after the expressive Prologue (example 6.2). Consisting of
three phrases of four notes each, this theme can be reduced to a set of
falling fifths (rising fourths) followed by falling thirds (or rising sixths)
which cover all twelve notes of the chromatic scale.

The first six notes, if laid out stepwise (in the order 1–3–5–2–4–6) can
be heard as the first six notes of the A-major scale. The last six, if similarly arranged (7–9–11–8–10–12), suggest A-flat. These are indeed the two
polar keys of the opera, A major signifying, in the broadest terms, the
Governess's world, A-flat the influence of the ghosts (and in this connection we should note that the "Malo" theme is initially presented in an
A-flat/F-minor tonal context). The tonality of the variations and scenes
of Act I ascend from the one to the other; those of Act II descend by an
exactly inverted path. Almost every other thematic aspect of the work is
somehow derived from this main theme, often in a way that is deliberately ambiguous.

An special example of derivation of this kind is the theme immediately
succeeding the main twelve-note theme (example 6.3). It is equally part of
the section labeled "theme" in the score, but because it is heard in an inner
part of the music that so interestingly suggests the movement of the coach
in which the Governess travels to Bly, or perhaps because it is so obviously
noteworthy but less abstract in its musical and dramatic effects, commentators tend to treat it as separate and not equal, even though the twelve-
note theme functions in a larger view of the harmonic rhythm as an upbeat to the cadence from which this new music springs. This second

theme is derived from the symmetrical series that precedes it by filling in the inversion of the first five notes, as Peter Evans first pointed out (214).

Inversion is a technical process in music which Britten had used before, in *Peter Grimes*, to symbolize the protagonist's internalization of society's disapproval. It cannot be simple-mindedly equated with the use of the word to mean sexual deviance in the language of nineteenth-century sexologists, but certainly the present theme operates along suggestive lines, and Peter Evans in his magisterial account of the structure of the opera concludes that its "crucial significance . . . is . . . clearly enough then, the corruption of innocence" (215).[5] It attaches itself in slightly different forms to the Governess, to Quint, and to the ghosts as a pair, and it will continue to be a matter of critical debate because its meaning is deliberately ambiguous.

The theme charts the important moments that reveal the Governess's state of mind, from her fear of her task in scene 1 and her arrival in scene 2 (where it hangs in the air on the high violins like a nervous thread) through her increasing awareness of the need to shelter the children to her ultimate realization, in scene 7 of Act I, that she "neither shields nor saves them." In scene 5 (five measures after fig. 46) it occurs as the Governess enjoins Mrs. Gross to "See what I see, Know what I know, that they [the children] may see and know nothing." This is the closest equivalent in the opera to the "I know, I know, I know!" of the tale. In Act II, the theme accompanies the Governess's growing recognition of failure, and a sense of having become tarnished in her efforts: "I have failed, most miserably failed, and there is no more innocence in me." Finally it occurs, plainer and perhaps coarser without its ironic final twist, as she declares possessively at the opening of the passacaglia in the final scene, "O Miles, I cannot bear to lose you. You shall be mine and I shall save you" (example 6.4).

The other face of this motive is its refashioning in the melismatic, extravagant chant in which Quint calls to Miles. Musically, then, the Governess and Quint are not only linked but also revealed as the central characters of the drama long before their final battle over Miles. And yet

Example 6.4. *The Turn of the Screw*, Act II, scene 8

the most important appearance of this motive is in the first scene of Act II, where its original association with the theme is reproduced, this time as a climactic conclusion to that theme. It is sung by the ghosts in "their" key of A-flat to the words which the librettist, Myfanwy Piper, imported from Yeats's "Second Coming." The words of the entire passage are:

> Day by day the bars we break,
> Break the love that laps them round,
> Cheat the careful watching eyes,
> "The ceremony of innocence is drowned."

Repeated in a fairly elaborate manner, the "ceremony of innocence" passage is immediately followed by the aria, "Lost in my labyrinth," in which the Governess declares, "Innocence, you have corrupted me." As Myfanwy Piper wrote: "The Governess's good intentions were destroyed by her experiences, whether real or imagined, and her love of Miles was corrupted, in that it became possessiveness and she was aware of it. Hence the last words 'What have we done between us?'"[6]

In recent years there has been a solid attempt to reduce the ambiguity suggested by the free-flowing associations of this, and other, musical aspects of the score. In the wake of an influential essay by Vivien Jones, we have been asked to see Britten's operatic adaptation as leaning toward one or the other of the "two stories" she discerns in the critical reaction to James. As the result, moreover, of the opening of discussion about Britten's homosexuality and its effect on his music, there have been several attempts to characterize Quint's portrayal positively—as, for instance, alluring, or, in one extremely gay-affirmative account, to make him the hero of the opera, and representing the relationship between him and Miles as "positive and liberating."[7]

The multiplicity of these accounts, and their different emphases, are a testimony both to the success of James's technique and Britten's musical adaptation of its essence. For what James set out to do was to liberate the old Gothic horror story from its reliance on apparitions and descriptions of horror by forcing the reader into the hot spot: "Make him *think* the evil, make him think of it for himself, and you are released from weak specifications," James wrote in his preface to the story (176). In pushing for resolution we are lost, whether we subscribe to the "first story" in which the children are corrupted by the ghosts or the "second story" in which the Governess in her hysterical condition conducts a battle for the children with ghosts whom she has imagined. The reader who accepts the "first story" creates the subjective horror of deceitful evil in innocent-seeming children; the one who accepts the "second story" creates a monstrous predator in the guise of womanly protector. The one springs from and endorses homophobia, the other misogyny. Between these two positions, moreover, there is little room to move.

As for the composer and librettist, well, the latter states unequivocally that "neither Britten nor I ever intended to interpret the work, only to re-create it for a different medium"—and quotes a significant Jamesian statement in support: "There is for such a case no eligible absolute of the wrong; it remains relative to fifty other elements, a matter of appreciation, speculation, imagination—these things moreover exactly in the mind of the spectator's, the critic's, the reader's experience" (Piper, 11).[8] The decision to personify the ghosts weights the opera perilously in the direction of the "first story," Vivien Jones reasonably suggests (13). But the way in which the composer suggests the mounting hysteria of the

Governess shows that he has not neglected this other story. One might point, for example, to the passacaglia of the final scene, where Miles's balanced utterances in the same rhythm as that of the upper instruments are countered by increasingly extravagant vocal outbursts from the Governess. Or one might hear the "second theme" (see example 6.3), first heard in connection with her, as being a projection of her hystericized condition so powerful that it conjures up more than musical ghosts.

The new school of critics referred to above takes its starting point from Piper's admission that what Quint actually says to Miles in the opera (all of it of course absent in James) is "laughably lacking in evil" (12). Averring that there is nothing sinister in Quint's music either, they see the ghosts as signs of the children's sexual awakening, neither good nor bad in itself, but drawing out the repressive instincts of the conventional forces arrayed around and against them, and goading the Governess into her hysterical reaction. In this view the "ceremony of innocence" is drowned in the adults and in the uses to which they put sexuality. The ultra-gay-male-affirmative reading of Clifford Hindley goes further still to portray Quint as representing a blameless "warmth of love" and as sharing a "mutually responsive relationship" with Miles, who is led by the Governess—"the victim of a destructive and . . . demonic delusion"—"to deny his love," to repress his "true nature" and thus to choose spiritual death; in this account Miss Jessel represents the only "palpable evil" in the ghostly apparitions (12, 17, 4).[9]

The opera, then, prompts as many scenarios as the personalities of its critics: projection and identification is everything here. These varying interpretations show that, as Wilfrid Mellers has rightly claimed, the Governess's and Quint's roles as heroine and villain remain ambiguous, and that "Britten's musical, encompasses James's poetic, vision" ("Turning the Screw," 152). They are also witness to the continuing potency as well as incoherence of the issues surrounding homosexuality, the closet and the related questions of power and knowledge. Like the Governess, critics are always tempted to claim they "know" when knowledge is likely to consist of confused and uncertain categories sensed rather than known.

What, we might ask in conclusion, are the signs, if any, of Britten's own attitude to the story. A composer who preferred to let his music speak for itself, he was careful not to give away hints in writing or conversation. Quint's music to Miles might be taken as a point from which to proceed. It is only in recent years, since Western ears have begun to recognize the full extent of the influence of Asian musics on Britten, that the sounds associated with Quint—the celesta flourish that announces his presence, for instance—have been traced to their source in the Balinese gamelan. Variation 7, preceding Quint's first scene with Miles, sets up a panoply of sounds—harp tremolandos, celesta arpeggios, gong strokes, and horn—which, as Christopher Palmer puts it, referring to Britten's subsequent ballet, *Prince of the Pagodas*, "all presage the Journey to Pagoda-land" ("The Colour of the Music," 105). And the cantilena in which Quint calls to Miles (example 6.5) is quite as exotic: its inspiration appears to have been the twelfth-century organum of Pérotin rather than some specifically "oriental" effect, though it is heard by Wilfrid Mellers as "recalling flamenco music and Moorish cantillation" ("Turning the Screw," 149).

Orientalism in music is as heavily encumbered as it is in other aspects of Western culture.[10] In his discussion of "the cult of the exotic" in music, which he dates from Glinka, the critic Constant Lambert concluded that in discerning the decline of the classic tradition in music it was necessary "to lay more emphasis on the fatality of that *femme-fatale* exoticism, than on her feminine charms" (139). This bracketing of the exotic/oriental with the feminine throws into question its use in Britten's music. Mellers and Palmer see Quint's cantilenas as "open[ing] magic casements"; in addition, Mellers, who actually calls them "arabesques," writes of them ambivalently as "revealing realms wildly mysterious, remote from the pieties of the Victorian house, yet as inspirational as they are malevolent—if, in musical terms, they can be called malevolent at all."[11] Those magic casements, it seems fairly clear, look out for most critics onto a landscape of

Example 6.5. *The Turn of the Screw*, Act I, scene 8 cantilena

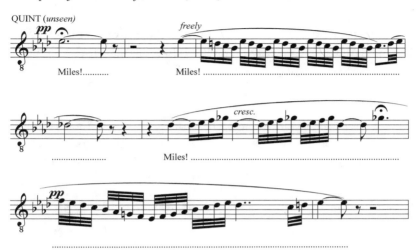

feminized ambiguity, of dread as well as allure. The "arabesque," moreover, also signifies a special status for those with whom it is associated.
Like the Governess's description of Quint in James's story, it sets him
completely apart as the Other, that which we, as audience, are (supposedly) not. There could be no clearer musical equivalent for the signs by
which Quint is marked as "the homosexual." After hearing this, we can
easily exclaim with James's Governess, "I know, I know, I know."

Britten's vision of innocence, of pre-nescience—an essentially nostalgic one—was tightly bound up with his discovery of the East. But
the displacement of the ideal from the familiar is only too clear an indication that it was not somewhere he would ever feel entirely at
home. And moreover, to propose the portrayal in this music of an ideal
Miles-Quint relation without hearing Quint's thirst for power and
dominance is also wishful thinking. If Aschenbach can give himself up
to the vision of a lovely boy in Britten's version of *Death in Venice*,
Quint's portrayal shows how predatory Britten feared such a "sacrifice"
can become.

A possible answer to the Quint/Governess dichotomy in this opera lies in a much-quoted letter to Britten from the poet W. H. Auden on the eve of Britten's departure from the States during World War II. In the following excerpt "Peter" refers of course to Peter Pears; "Elisabeth" is Elisabeth Mayer, the wife of the couple on Long Island with whom Britten and Pears went to stay for a weekend at the beginning of their sojourn in the U.S.A. and who ended up taking care of them for three years:

> Wherever you go you are and probably always will be surrounded by people who adore you, nurse you, and praise everything you do, eg Elisabeth, Peter. . . . Up to a certain point this is fine for you, but beware. You see, Bengy dear, you are always tempted to make things too easy for yourself in this way, ie to build yourself a warm nest of love (of course when you get it, you find it a little stifling) by playing the lovable talented little boy. (Mitchell and Reed, 1016)

Auden's words are born out in the unusual emphasis on the boyhood of Britten in all the biographical accounts, inviting comparison, of course, with Mozart, one of Britten's heroes. In a striking recreation of Auden's prophecy, Miles plays mock-Mozart/Czerny to win the attention of his indulgent female wardens in a scene (II, 6) which conjures up visions of the young Benjamin doted on by his mother and sisters. Stories related by Britten to his librettists, and told by them to the biographer Humphrey Carpenter, show that present in the composer's imagination, if not in reality, were two serious episodes of male sexual abuse affecting either him directly or his playmates in childhood. Fancifully casting the composer as Miles for a moment throws light on the ambiguity of the whole opera and on the way in which Britten, the "reluctant homosexual," might have been readily able to see life from the vantage point of a knowing innocent who is caught between a threatening lover and a stifling mother and for whom adult male power is as ominous and menacing as it is alluring.

Another possible identification worth exploring is the one that Britten may have perceived with Quint. The composer's own attraction for boys between the ages of about twelve and sixteen was strong: David Hemmings, the Miles in the original production of the opera (and on the London recording), apparently became the focus of one of the most powerful of his attachments, which, like many of their kind, were reportedly tender and fatherly, involving no physical activity beyond kissing and cuddling (Carpenter, *Britten*, 356–58).[12] With his own childhood experiences in mind, Britten may have felt keenly the knife-edge balance on which such behavior rested. In *Peter Grimes* he had originally set out to portray a child abuser, a figure slowly but surely eradicated as work on the opera proceeded and supplanted by a worst-case scenario of another and more general kind—the outsider whom society hounds to death on no legal or moral grounds, an outsider represented most viably in his case by "the homosexual" (see "Fiery Visions"). By means of James's tale he was able a decade later to return to the original theme, and also at the same time to exorcise—as he had in *Grimes*—a darker side of his own reality.

As I have tried to argue, James's tale is also a good place for us to start work on reconstructing the specific manifestations in Britten's music of the category that, as Eve Sedgwick has warned, we are only too liable to fall into the trap of naming, without regard for the varied present conditions of sexual identity and practice, "homosexuality as we conceive of it today" (44–48). The positiveness of a gay-affirmative reading is suspect not only because it sidesteps the social and personal context of these works, the tale and opera. In positing, as a conceivable alternative to the ending, a "liberated" Miles, who, overcoming the conventional forces of repression represented by the Governess and Mrs. Grose, accepts his "true nature" and goes on, say, to a cozy middle-class gay "lifestyle" (a softly lit portrait of Quint no doubt glowing on the apartment wall), it reduces the complexity of the tale and the opera in an essentialized reading. As we have begun to be aware, such readings ultimately put gay people of all sorts in collusion with the oppression we have suffered as a result of the dominant transhistorical notion of male homosexuality that has served so well the purpose of controlling our lives. It is rather, I would argue, in the specific nature of the homosexual images and personae—limited by class on the one hand and on the other by the discretion model that as a leisure-class homosexual male of his era Britten was almost bound to observe, but depicted so movingly in his music—that we may finally find our greatest source of inspiration. This is part of *our* history, and by pondering its meaning and coming to terms with it, by "telling the story in our own words" (and re-telling it) rather than accepting the framework in which it is presented by critics from the nongay majority, however sympathetic their intentions, we may be performing an even greater service for ourselves and others than that of affirmation.

NOTES

1. See also Smith-Rosenberg, who names other tracts: Sylvester Graham, *Lecture to Young Men of Chastity* (1834), which Moon calls "a founding document of the American male-purity movement" (254); S. B. Woodward, *Hints for the Young in Relation to the Health of Mind and Body* (1837); and R. T. Thrall, *Home-Treatment for Sexual Abuses: A Practical Treatise* (1856).

2. Mitchell and Reed contains plenty of hints; a biography by Humphrey Carpenter, due from Faber as I write, promises many more [ed.: Carpenter's biography was published in 1992].

3. Duncan, *Working with Britten*, 28; as one of those punished by Britten, Duncan was scarcely an impartial observer, it must be noted. "'The gay life,' he resented that," said Peter Pears in an interview with Gillian Widdicombe in *The Observer* (30 March 1980)—he also spoke the words in Tony Palmer's ITV documentary, *A Time There Was* (1980).

4. For a particularly fine recent account, see Whittall, "Twisted Relations."

5. Some indication of its varying intepretation can be gained from the different names used to characterize it by various critics cited in this article—e.g., "catalyst" theme (Howard), "tutelage" theme (Hindley). Evans, as might be expected, prefers the music-analytical label, "y" motive.

6. A letter to Patricia Howard quoted in her "Myfanwy Piper's *Turn*, 23.

7. Mellers, "Turning the Screw"; Palmer, "The Colour of the Music"; Stimpson; and Hindley.

8. The word "absolute" is italicized in the New York ed.'s preface in James's *Art of the Novel;* see 176.

9. This account is developed out of a similar, but more measured, view of the opera focusing on Miles's sexual awakening in Stimpson.

10. For a notable essay on this topic, see Locke.

11. Mellers, "Turning the Screw," 149; Palmer, "The Colour of the Music," 105.

12. On general patterns of behavior for pedophiles and "ephebophiles," a category into whose broad outline Britten fits, see West, 211–15.

CHAPTER SEVEN

Britten's *Dream*

For Sue-Ellen Case

"How can a minor third be gay?" This response from a prominent lesbian feminist on hearing that I was engaged in gay musicology encapsulates what is thought to be the main question. But we need not subscribe to its implied finality. Granted that music as many of us have studied it—my interlocutor was once herself a music major—has been presented most rationally to us both as a symbolic system with no connotations and as a series of works of transhistorical significance. As gay scholars we ought constantly to interrogate this training and its implications. One strategy would be to assert (and exert) the right to propose meanings that are grounded in an inside awareness of the cultural conditions under which homosexual composers in this century and before have functioned. Another is to insist on going beyond the text: what people perform or hear, what meaning they invest in it, and within what framework

From Ruth A. Solie, ed., *Musicology and Difference: Gender and Sexuality in Music Scholarship* (Berkeley and Los Angeles: University of California Press, 1993), 259–80. An earlier version appeared in *Performing Arts Magazine* on the occasion of a performance of Britten's *Midsummer Night's Dream* at the Los Angeles Music Center in 1988; the author explored the question further in a paper at the 1990 meeting of the American Musicological Society in Oakland, "Musicality: Innate Gift or Social Contract?"

they place it, will be a valid interest for gay inquiry; it will also put into question the fixation on the composer and his intentions which has dominated historical musicology for so long.

Another tactic is to question the unspoken assumptions behind the original question—that the minor third will have no part in a composite sign that includes words, that if it does the game is too easy, the results unfairly won. The superiority of "absolute" music is not merely an unhistorical notion but also an oppressive one: it must be contested all the time by being placed in its cultural and historical context. When we do overcome all the obstacles (including our own internalized reluctance to do so) we are liable to be the target of the latest and dirtiest word in academic polemics: essentialism. If so, let us be aware of the power relations involved: a graduate student throwing this word around may be plucky rather than homophobic; there is no reason to give an established male scholar the benefit of the doubt. It may be that the presentation of knowledge gleaned from a minority position ultimately enhances the authority of the dominant discourse: oppositional interpretations may "reinscribe" what they would erase. But before succumbing to this argument we should ask in whose interests it would be not to produce such knowledge. For what ought to be evident is that fear of certain kinds of meaning and knowledge are deeply ingrained in the musical community, and especially in its musicological component. It is hard to imagine, for example, that the spontaneous eruption of approval greeting an attack, at the 1991 Chicago meeting of the American Musicological Society, on Maynard Solomon's delineation of Schubert's homosexual circumstances sprang from genuine devotion to the detachment of scholarly method. At stake is the status of a major mainstream European master (rather than, say, a deviant Russian) and the energy that has gone into suppressing the notion that he might have been sexually as well as emotionally involved with others of his own sex is but one indicator of the fear and repression on which the notion of musicality and musical scholarship in the West is built.

Producing knowledge about homosexual artists of the past is not without its dangers, of course. One is a tendency to essentialize homosexual-

ity as a condition of creativity, a tendency which at its most grotesque reflects the elitism of certain kinds of privileged male homosexual subcul-
tures. For those of us who would abandon what Alan Sinfield, in a recent
article on Noel Coward, calls the "discretion model" for an explicit gay
identity, there is the almost opposite danger in decoding the work of closeted homosexual artists—not only of suggesting that all gay creativity
must be covert but of simply uncovering a depressing record of oppression and humiliation ("Private Lives").[1]

In this regard, the composer Benjamin Britten poses a problem comparable to, but different from, that of his contemporary the playwright.
Both were leisure-class individuals whose discreet homosexuality helped
to maintain the power of that troublesome mechanism the "open secret,"
which in D. A. Miller's formulation functions "not to conceal knowledge,
so much as to conceal the knowledge of the knowledge"; it reinforces the
dominant culture by confining homosexuality to the private sphere while
making it obscurely present in public discourse as an unthinkable alternative (206). Both wrote in forms that demanded a negotiation with the
dominant discourse in theater or music: until 1968 plays on the public
stage in England had to be licensed by a state official (the Lord Chamberlain), and until 1958 all mention of homosexuality was specifically forbidden; modern opera was almost a contradiction in terms, at least in England, until Britten almost single-handedly created a space for it.
Whatever subversive or oppositional encodings their works incorporate,
therefore, had to be contained, available only to a portion of their audiences. The very difference of their response to these conditions—the one
adopting a camp sensibility, the other rigorously rejecting it—under-
mines any fixed or stereotypical notion of a British homosexual subculture that might be used to dismiss them. It also supports Alan Sinfield's
conclusion that it is important to study such figures: "This is some of the
history that we have; it is foolish to imagine that we can be free of it, and
dangerous to leave its interpretation to others" ("Private Lives," 59).
After all, the conditions they worked under may all too easily return,
making the knowledge of how they dealt with them doubly valuable. And

yes, the power of Britten's music and its connection to the various stages of my own search for a means of self-determination are critically present in the following attempt to understand the broad outlines of his operatic development up to 1960.

When Benjamin Britten turned to Shakespeare for a libretto, he was a veteran composer of forty-six with six major operas and four other musico-dramatic works to his credit. The occasion for the opera was the remodeling of the tiny Jubilee Hall at Aldeburgh. Britten decided as late as August 1959 that a full-length stage work was needed to celebrate its reopening at the 1960 Festival: "There was no time to get a libretto written," he wrote, "so we took one that was ready to hand."[2] The statement can be taken with a grain of salt, for no composer's closet can have been littered with a greater number of unused libretti than Britten's. Nor had an apparent necessity ever prevented him from doing exactly as he pleased, at least in terms of artistic decisions. The drastically truncated version of *A Midsummer Night's Dream* that Britten concocted with the help of Peter Pears that fall finds a logical place in the composer's operatic output, representing a climactic end to a special line of development within it.

His three operas of the 1940s had all been concerned with a public world in which one individual is abused or victimized. They are fundamentally social, not psychological, dramas, and are all at one level or another parables of oppression. In *Peter Grimes* (1945) a society bound together by its common battle against the sea ostracizes one of its own members because he doesn't fit in. Tragedy results, however, only when the victim, internalizing society's condemnation at the climax in Act II, scene 1 ("So be it, and God have mercy upon me!"), succumbs to the shame and self-hatred that eventually lead to his suicide, which is utterly unremarked by those who have pushed him to it. Shame is also the downfall of the heroine in *The Rape of Lucretia* (1946): she allows her imagination to create her own guilt out of Tarquinius's crime and, like

Grimes, commits suicide as a result. *Albert Herring* (1947) mirrors *Grimes* more closely but reinterprets the predicament of the individual against the crowd through comedy: the young Albert turns the tables on his oppressors.[3]

In an unguarded moment, the normally reticent Britten related the story of *Grimes* to his and Pears's predicament as pacifists and conscientious objectors returning to England during the war (Schafer, 116–17). At a deeper level, however, the intensity of *Grimes,* and perhaps the composer's pacifism itself, had its roots in his personal experience as a homosexual—an experience which became central to his art but which he himself could never discuss or even mention in public.[4] Coming as he did from a cultured middle-class family, the security he undoubtedly felt was accompanied by those other middle-class characteristics, a compulsion to work and a puritan ethic from which he never really wanted to break free. His homosexual nature found expression in the lifelong relationship with Pears, which society could accept because its basis was ostensibly professional. But it also resulted in an equally lifelong sense of unworthiness and alienation.[5] The tension between these elements was apparently greater for Britten than it was for the many other twentieth-century composers who shared his homosexual orientation. It was a tension that could not be worked out in the usual ways, because of the puritanical streak that served him so well in other respects—we know that he was horrified by manifestations of gay subculture, and even by the word itself.[6] Prevented from any open discourse by the self-imposed silence on the matter of sexuality which he shared with most prominent homosexual men of his generation—a situation which has still not changed much in the world of classical music—covert treatment of the issues of sexuality in his music may have offered itself as a personally effective remedy. The result was an engagement in his work first with the social issues of his experience of homosexuality, later with the metaphysical ones, that trod various fine lines between disclosure and secrecy, allegory and realism, public and private—the binarisms that in our culture mark what Eve Sedgwick has aptly labeled the "epistemology of the closet."

Britten seems to have grasped certain truths intuitively: he recognized that oppression is not simply an economic matter along Marxist lines but a multidimensional phenomenon in which the oppressed in one situation is the oppressor in another; and he saw that its toll on the individual comes most devastatingly not by means of unjust acts (which tend to ennoble the sufferer) but through the ordinary individual's unthinking internalization of society's values and judgment. What makes *Grimes* so modern an opera is the very unheroic nature of its title figure. What makes it so brilliant from a political standpoint is that it forces the audience to identify with a figure they have been socially conditioned to spurn: the frightening alternative is to identify with the Borough (which of course several music critics have been willing to do). As an allegory that springs from his own experience, then, *Grimes* suggests that at some conscious level Britten realized that "the homosexual condition" is in essence a social construction brought about by labeling and its consequences. The works of the 1940s are in this sense prophetic, for such ideas were not current until the minority movements articulated them in the 1960s and beyond.[7]

Did anyone hear any echoes of all this in the music? The determination with which contemporary music critics avoided any mention of allegory in their responses to *Peter Grimes* suggests a collective subconscious effort to repel meanings that might lead down a dangerous path (such an effort is paralleled at the end of Britten's life by the opposite tendency to *invoke* allegory to get them out of a similarly tight spot with *Death in Venice*). Into this arena Edmund Wilson's intervention comes like a breath of fresh air; he attended *Grimes* and saw in it a message about the universally deleterious effect of war on the victors as well as the vanquished; his views on the brutalization of English society did nothing for his popularity at the time (*Europe*, 186–91). But there was at least one person who created a homosexual meaning for himself out of *Grimes*. The writer Colin MacInnes confided to his private notebook in the late 1940s:

> The theme and tragedy of P. Grimes is homosexuality and, as such, the treatment is quite moving, if a bit watery.

> Grimes is the homosexual hero. The melancholy of the opera is the
> melancholy of homosexuality. (Gould, 82)

MacInnes's odyssey—from someone who at the time of this note had had
sex with men without regarding himself as homosexual to someone who
at the end of his life wrote a column entitled "Captain Jockstrap's Diary"
for *Gay News*—was quite different from that of Britten (Gould 89–100;
227–28). (Especially attracted to men of color, MacInnes crossed the
boundaries of race; Britten did not.) Nevertheless, he pinned down here
an element that is always present in Britten's portrayal of the "homosexual condition," and he also hinted at its sentimental underpinnings.

Developments in Britten's own life and in British society made the
continuing exploration of the oppression/liberation theme an unlikely
way forward—the children's opera *The Little Sweep* (1949) was its last
manifestation. The repressive atmosphere of the 1930s, like so much else
in British life, was swept away in the aftermath of World War II. Yet, par-
adoxically, Britain under a socialist government seems to have been less
stimulating for left-wing idealism than those earlier days. Alan Sinfield
has shown how artists and writers responded negatively to the threat the
welfare state presented to the notion of individuality they prized so
highly as a condition of art (*Literature, Politics*, 43–58). In Britten's case,
his change of priorities may perhaps be further attributed to his detach-
ing himself from W. H. Auden, who had been a dominant (and dominating) influence in several spheres of his life. Furthermore, his increasing
acceptance by all levels of society began to alleviate his paranoia, at least
on the surface—already by 1947 the disgruntled Communist librettist of
Grimes, Montagu Slater, was complaining that Britten had become a
"court musician" (Mitchell, "Montagu Slater," 30).

The first opera of the 1950s occupies a special place in Britten's output, for it is one he himself preferred. The librettist was the novelist
E. M. Forster, who had endeavored to suggest elements of homosexual
experience in his fiction but who had given up writing novels altogether
while maintaining a position of great spiritual and intellectual authority

among the left-wing gay artists of the 1930s—Christopher Isherwood called him their unheroic hero. Forster and Britten lighted on Melville's *Billy Budd* with such enthusiasm that the co-librettist, Eric Crozier, could not even get them to consider the implications of their choice, that this would be the first all-male opera (Furbank, 2:283–86). The subject was still at one level that of injustice and oppression, but Billy's forgiving act of sacrifice for the inadequate Vere underpins the work with a universal quasi-Christian symbolism that did not (as in the less happy *Lucretia*) need to be spelled out. First and foremost, though, Britten's *Billy Budd* (1951) is a work of ambiguity, in which an apparent surface "libretto" truth is questioned at a deeper musical level: a remarkable example occurs in the Epilogue where the aging Vere's rapturous confidence in his salvation is undermined by the throbbing pulse of the militaristic music of the earlier sea chase. The almost embarrassingly epiphanic arrival of an otherwise unclouded B-flat chord in this epilogue, moreover, could be heard as almost literally anticipating Sedgwick's vision of Vere "retiring from his agonisitic public performance, only, once alone at last, to hug himself in delight under the covers, getting off on the immutable visual glory of the boy who 'ascending, took the full rose of the dawn'": the excitement of those drumbeats after all, the music obliquely suggests, is not entirely removed from the thrill of orgasm (Sedgwick, 118). If at some level Forster hints at a potential Ricky-Stephen or even Maurice-Alec alliance between the upper-class Vere and the Handsome Sailor, Britten seems to be admitting in this final moment that the captain is every bit as destructive as his less ambiguously homosexual (and evil) master-at-arms, John Claggart.[8]

While composing *Gloriana* (1953), his ambivalent act of homage to the new British queen, in his mind Britten was already working toward another chamber opera, commissioned for the 1954 Venice Biennale. It is with *The Turn of Screw*, an operatic version of Henry James's famous ghost story, that the composer entered the phase of development that was also to find powerful expression in *A Midsummer Night's Dream*. In *Billy Budd* he had already relegated his earlier concerns with oppression to second place in hinting at the metaphysical issues that lie beyond the dynamics of power within social relationships. A further way to explore relationships themselves, especially the irregular kind Britten was interested in and those dynamics in which they become entangled, was to cultivate dream, fantasy and the exotic.

There was another reason why, if Britten were to approach, through opera, matters of deepest concern to him, he would have to find stories that were in no sense "real." On his return to England from the United States in 1942, Britten was bidden farewell by his friend W. H. Auden in a letter that anatomized some of the composer's main problems as the poet viewed them. In opposing bourgeois complacency to bohemian lack of discipline, Auden was expressing the dichotomy (his own, as well as Britten's) that the composer was to explore so movingly in *Death in Venice*, his last opera. In characterizing Britten's bourgeois side, however, Auden drew attention to his attachment to "thin-as-a-board juveniles," and it is no secret now that Britten's homosexuality involved a fondness for, and an idealization of, young boys (Mitchell, *Britten and Auden*, 161–62).[9] It is of course misleading simply to throw the late nineteenth-century word *homosexual*, with its implications of pathology and "medicalization," into the ring with an older and more universal phenomenon of Western paternalistic society that has typically involved the teaching of younger men by older ones, sometimes with an erotic element (as in the case of that prototypical teacher, Socrates) and sometimes not. For modern society, however, pederasty is a dangerous area—the side of paternalism which when it manifests itself physically becomes "sexual abuse."

Just as Britten, who had never suffered real persecution for his homosexuality, came to terms in the terrifying manhunts of *Peter Grimes* with the paranoid fears common to most homosexuals, so in *The Turn of the Screw* the composer, who seems never to have forced himself on his young friends, explored (or exorcised) through the agency of Henry James the possibility of a dominant man-boy relationship implicitly sexualized. Bringing the ghosts alive and giving them words meant that the

Quint-Miles connection had an effect very different from the suggestive, ambiguous horror of the story (which depends for much of its effect on the reader's own vulnerability). Britten's Quint sings songs of allure and delight to which Miles fully responds. The ambiguity in the opera does not depend on whether or not the ghosts exist but springs from a musical question as to how different in kind are the relationships, and which is worse for the poor boy: that with the predatory ghost; or that with the smothering governess.

A deeper ambiguity surrounds the very nature of Quint's "threat" to Miles. The seductive theme in which he utters Miles's name in, for instance, scene 8 of both acts, and which is formalized in the Ceremony of Innocence episode (II, 1), is first vocalized by the Governess in scene 1, and is again heard on her lips in scene 5, after the disclosure by Mrs. Gross of the fact of Quint's death. "See what I see, know what I know, that they may see and know nothing," cries the Governess, singing this theme to the bewildered housekeeper. Are we to understand musically that Quint's relations with Miles are projections of her fears and desires? If it hints at that, the Ceremony of Innocence theme also suggests the crisis of secrecy, sight and knowledge constructed around the "love that dares not speak its name." And listeners' reactions confirm it. Disquieted by the implications of this theme analysts underplay the fact that it occurs first in the score under the heading "THEME" and is as much part of *the* theme as the 12-note motive that claims their attention.[10] In abstract serialism—however different from the Schoenbergian model—lies safety. The slippage here betrays the importance of the issue.[11]

It may seem a far cry from James to Shakespeare, but the progression from intense tragedy to more healing comedy had after all been traversed before, from *Grimes* to *Herring*. Britten, who was adept at covering his tracks, once said that *A Midsummer Night's Dream* appealed to him as the work of a very young man and as a story that involved three different and separate groups—the Lovers, the Rustics (as he called the mechanicals), and the Fairies—who nevertheless interact (White, 90). It seems more likely that after exploring the ambiguity of relationships in a realistic setting in *Billy Budd* and the fantasy of the unthinkable in the context of James's ghost story, the composer should have found in Shakespeare's subtle and adventurous play an ideal vehicle for pursuing his interests in the possibilities of relationships.

Until after World War II it was common to refer to plays like *A Midsummer Night's Dream* as Shakespeare's romantic or idyllic comedies. Productions emphasized the magical qualities of the play, its fairy enchantment and illusion, and its romance. Indeed, the first production of Britten's opera as designed by John Piper and Carl Toms, especially in its enlarged form at Covent Garden, had a share in that tradition (Herbert 275–78). Around the time the opera was written, however, C. L. Barber was arguing that Shakespeare's comedies were saturnalian rather than romantic and that they depended for their effect not on nineteenth-century notions of "character" but on ritual as embodied in holiday archetypes. In *A Midsummer Night's Dream* the lovers, like celebrants on the eve of May Day, run off to the wood at night and gain release from everyday restraint under the influence of Oberon. Both they and we gain clarification as a result. In accordance with this scheme, Shakespeare's play begins in town, in Theseus's palace, to which it returns, and into which Oberon and Tytania[12] enter, bringing the blessing of fertility to the bridal couples much as country gods brought their tribute when Elizabeth I was entertained (Barber; Montrose).

As the curtain rises on Britten's opera we cannot fail to notice a crucial difference from the play. Even without the scenery we know that we are already, in more senses than one, in the woods. It is almost impossible to resist the association with breathing and sleep, or at the least with the wood as a primeval force, that is so powerfully suggested by the eerie sound of the *portamenti* strings. We open at once into a world of dreams—clearly of the post-Jungian variety—the "real" world of the opera. In Britten's scheme it is the court of Duke Theseus that seems unreal and limiting, the final entry of the fairies marking a return to "normal." In other words, Britten has simply dispensed with the social context of Athens and with the background of reality as an initiating device.

He has moved here the furthest distance from the realistic borough of *Peter Grimes* into a completely private world, a world of possibilities rather than of limitations. The folk-festival or May-games aspect of Shakespeare's play, then, has been matched by a contemporary notion of misrule, the world of the libido.[13]

The very nature and conditions of opera, of course, appear to go against its expression of anything so radical. Opera is after all an anachronistic performance art, set in a museum context and patronized by a convention-loving public almost as exclusive as the aristocracy for which it was first created. But opera and masquerade have historical links, and today it is perhaps the carnivalesque, libido-enhancing as well as convention-bound characteristics of opera that give it a special place in gay culture.[14] Britten, moreover, had already shown ingenuity in injecting modern concerns into conventional formulas (most notably in *Peter Grimes*). In *A Midsummer Night's Dream*, operatic convention itself becomes part of the subject of the opera.

This concern is most immediately noticeable in the broad comedy of the mechanicals' play. Pyramus and Thisby's exploration of the crudest side of nineteenth-century opera exposes them to ridicule from the audience within the opera while giving a sense of superiority to the audience without. There is a feeling of wicked fun about the whole scene, from its more obvious effects to those little moments of malice, such as the Schoenbergian *sprechstimme* in which (as Peter Evans noted [253–54]) Snout wails out his song as Wall. The episode clearly appealed to Britten's schoolboy sense of humor, but it also constitutes his closest approach to camp, especially in the transvestite role of Thisby memorably performed by Peter Pears in the original production. Yet Britten's delight in parody here is tied up with a tendency of the work as a whole to parody convention in a more subtle way. As in other operas, the chorus opens *A Midsummer Night's Dream*, but it is a chorus of unbroken boys' voices, singing in unison—as different from the romantic notion of fairies (and opera choruses) as could be imagined. Shortly after comes the expected entry of the *prima donna* and the male lead, who in this case is far from the ardent tenor of the romantic era and as close as one can get nowadays to the *primo uomo* of eighteenth-century *opera seria*, the castrato. Along with the historical reference, however, goes the association of unmanliness, and thus of gender liminality, that haunts the modern image of the homosexual. Squeaking in a falsetto voice, the emasculated, misogynistic, boy-desiring Oberon is almost literally a figure of the closet (Castle, 35–36).[15]

The casting of Oberon as a countertenor (the part was written for Alfred Deller) sent Britten back for models to his beloved Purcell. In Oberon's first set piece, "I Know a Bank" (I, at fig. 47), we can hear echoes of the fantastically elaborate style of Purcell's "Sweeter than Roses," which Britten had once arranged for Pears. The formality of the slow march that announces the fairy king and queen and accompanies several of their moments together also harks back to the seventeenth century. We notice that the fairy denizens of the wood, whether in Oberon's florid aria, Tytania's ecstatic "Come Now, a Roundel" (I, at fig. 94) or the attendants' bouncy "You Spotted Snakes" (I, at fig. 97), are much more likely to sing in rounded set pieces than are the Rustics or Lovers who invade their territory. Theirs is a world of formality, of decorum, of a certain innocent perfection and ultimately, of course, of nostalgia as well.

Britten's treatment of the role of Puck also suggests a difference from—as well as a reference to—a historical convention. The role of hero's friend or servant in opera is traditionally assigned to the baritone (as in such diverse works as *Don Giovanni, Don Carlos, Tristan und Isolde* and even *Peter Grimes*); yet Britten's Puck is a boy tumbler who speaks (in an adolescent parody of baritone in the original production) rather than sings. We may remember that the rift between Oberon and Tytania is caused by Oberon's desire for "a little changeling boy / To be my henchman." But Oberon already has a henchman in Puck, a freer spirit than Miles, and one who snaps to his master's attention with even greater alacrity than Miles to Quint's. Theirs is the central relationship of the wood: it is certainly the one that holds the power in this labyrinth.

The appearance of a quartet of lovers who are constant in all but their affections (as Cecily puts it in *The Importance of Being Earnest*) prompts a modern audience to think almost automatically of *Così fan tutte*. Britten, however, is truer to his poet in suggesting through them the blind, irrational, compulsive—and painful—state of love. These four figures tend to avoid the voluptuous strings of thirds that characterize Mozart's score: they sing lines that are eternally syllabic, in even notes. This is a sure sign in Britten's musical language, as in the case of Grimes's Ellen Orford, that although they are conventionally "good," there is something wrong with them, or limited about them. It is only after very close hearing that we begin to notice the typically Brittenesque subtleties of characterization that distinguish them. Moreover, it is not until their awakening in Act III that their "unending melody" is exchanged for something like a set piece. This is the litany-like chorus that Britten builds out of a speech of Shakespeare's Helena, which she initiates at figure 19a: "And I have found Demetrius like a jewel, / Mine own, and not mine own." On the one hand this suggests that their experience in the ordered/disordered kingdom of the *Dream* has taught them something, and on the other it seems to consign them to a lifetime of little more promising than doubledating: what many modern critics and directors see as Shakespeare's own gloomy prognosis for love and marriage in patriarchal society finds a modern echo in Britten's own pessimism about it (Orgel, 10–13, 26–28).

One relationship in the play/opera is purposely grotesque. Interestingly enough, Britten puts it literally at the center of the opera, halfway through the second act, and lavishes on it some of his most luscious music. As Bottom, singing an out-of-tune song, wakes the sleeping Tytania, she bursts into a rapturous lyricism that suggests a truth beyond irony. "Certainly on the evidence of her music Tytania's love for Bottom misconceived seems deeper than whatever it is she feels for Oberon," as Wilfrid Mellers puts it ("Truth," 188). Her final statement before they fall asleep together, couched over the four chords that encompass the experience of the wood as well as the notes of the complete chromatic scale, sounds, in its range, its rhythm and phrasing, and the way its fall complements the orchestra's rising pitch, to embody perhaps the most complete and definitive statement in a drama whose indeterminacy is one of its chief characteristics (see Slights).

Tytania's forswearing of her love for Bottom in Act III, contending with and contingent on the earlier moment of musical truth, seems to me to suggest that the opera, like the play, places emphasis on the indeterminacy of meaning and on the disruption of patriarchal power, not its restitution. Women in Britten's operas tend to run to the extremes—they are either victims or predators (see McDonald). Tytania is a curious amalgam; she takes over Bottom and at the same time is utterly dominated by Puck and Oberon, whose cruel triumph (as Patricia Howard suggests) causes her eventually to forfeit not only her Indian boy but also the very stuff of her independent authority, her vocal brilliance—a fate worse than death for a diva (*Operas* 169–70). In Act III she sings comparatively restrained phrases in duets or ensembles initiated and controlled by Oberon: both her waking moment (eight bars after figure 9) and her final entry with Oberon (figure 98) are governed by the falling third, G-sharp F-sharp E, the motive that acts as an *ostinato* to their quarrel in Act I and becomes more clearly identified with Oberon's patriarchal power as the opera proceeds.

If we are led to wonder about the misogyny implied by the composer's treatment of Tytania in Act III, we are also reminded of the power and beauty of her extramarital encounter during Bottom's awakening. At the climactic moment of this scene, when the weaver names the ballad in which he intends to celebrate his experience, he recapitulates Tytania's crucial phrase. Britten provides only enough differences of detail to accommodate the new words and situation (the forceful dynamic marking *fppp* suggests the waking jolt with which a truly remarkable dream is recalled). Tytania's language of passion, we now realize, was in some way shared by Bottom, who even usurps Oberon's falsetto voice in recalling it. This moment, comic in the richest sense of the word, and open to a number of interpretations in performance, brings with it the realization that the Tytania-Bottom relationship is the only one that crosses the rigid class boundaries of the play's three estates, the only one in which possession and power are not fundamental issues, the only one in which each partner is a victim, the only one in which pure sensuous enjoyment is uncomplicated by societal rights and duties. It is the high point of the carnivalesque side of the opera, and Bottom's waking reverie gently nudges us to savor its transgressive quality.

Another episode of ambiguous meaning occurs at the end of the Act II as Puck arranges the lovers into correct pairs. In the play he speaks in short lines and country proverbs:

> Jack shall have Jill
> Nought shall go ill,
> The man shall have his mare again
> And all shall be well.

Britten gives this speech to the boy-fairies, who sing it to a shapely melody in thirds over rapturous repetitions in the orchestra of the four "motto chords" of the act. The irony of Shakespeare is thus replaced by a statement of faith, if not quite of resolution—the final note of the melody is not vouchsafed in the ending ritornello. Sung by "thin-as-a-board-juveniles," it is hard to interpret it as anything but the vision of innocence and purity that Britten seems to have tried to recapture all his life.

In Auden's terms, of course, this trait was a symptom of the composer's "denial and evasion of the demands of disorder." Certainly when the evening's magic has worn off the critical listener will wonder about this passage. But part of the attraction of Britten's art is the knife-edge it walks between the genuine and the sentimental, between honesty about life's difficulties and a longing for resolution and comfort. It was not until *Owen Wingrave* (1970) and *Death in Venice* (1973) that he went on, after the ritual purification of the Church Parables (1964–68), to deal directly as well as profoundly with the two major issues of his life, pacifism and homosexual love. *The Turn of the Screw* and *A Midsummer Night's Dream* represent a stage at which he searched for the clarity that eluded him, projected his doubts about the "innocence" he could never recapture and mulled over the nature of human relationships in a private world created out of the stuff of ghosts and dreams—the private world of the male homosexual and his closet. "He was," as Pears once said when explaining Britten's dislike of "the gay life," "more interested in the beauty, and therefore the danger, that existed in any relationship between human beings—man and woman, man and man; the sex didn't really matter" (Palmer, *A Time There Was*). That sex really did matter is shown, paradoxically, by the de-sexualizing of the creatures of the wood in *A Midsummer Night's Dream*.

Danger is the word that leaps out of Pears's statement, and it is one that bears thinking about. The closet is maintained by the threat, the "danger," of discovery and its reprisals, real or imagined. Even among openly gay people today the feeling lingers: there is after all enough potential menace from any number of our institutions (law, religion, the military, medicine, psychotherapy, business, etc.) to strike terror into the most sanguine person. The closet is a dynamic, not static, shaping presence and homosexuals with long experience of it can hardly be expected to imagine human relations without its corrosive effect.

But a specific historical situation ought to be in our minds when we consider Britten's music of the period from *Billy Budd* (1951) to *A Midsummer Night's Dream* (1960). In May 1951 the homosexual British diplomats Guy Burgess and Donald Maclean defected to the Soviet Union. The British authorities, urged on by the Central Intelligence Agency of the United States, where the McCarthy era was in full swing, increased surveillance. Use of police as agents provocateurs resulted in a dramatic increase in arrests (fivefold the number from 1938). And it was not simply the "man in the street" who was affected. In 1952 the mathematical genius and computer pioneer, Alan Turing, was sentenced to submit to estrogen therapy; he committed suicide two years later. A year afterward began the much more notorious and highly publicized series of prosecutions of Lord Montague of Beaulieu and his friends. One effect of the public hysteria generated by the popular press and the blatant dishonesty of the police was the move toward reform: the Wolfenden Report on prostitution and homosexuality (1957) led (after another ten years) to the "consenting-adults" law.[16]

Britten and Pears may not have been directly affected by any of this—puritans both, they were unlikely to have been picking up men in public places. But someone as sensitive to injustice as Britten cannot have remained indifferent. The climate both encouraged the kind of bravado that seems (in the circumstances) to mark Angus Wilson's *Hemlock and After* (1952), or Britten's *The Turn of the Screw* and at the same time prompted a certain instinct for self-preservation and reticence. It may be true, as Peter Conrad avers, that in his version of *A Midsummer Night's Dream* Britten leads his characters back from the "atonal dubiety" of nature to the shelter of courtly ceremony, that he "flinches from psychological exposure" and "hadn't the fortitude to remain in the wood," but such judgments (which seem not even to pause before projecting the composer directly into his work) reflect a later age in which "danger" is presumed to have been exorcised.

If danger stalks the score of *A Midsummer Night's Dream*, what musical form does it take? For an answer to that question we must go back to *The Turn of the Screw*, and specifically to the music in which Quint awakens desire in Miles. The celesta flourish which announces Quint's presence, the remarkable variation 7 with its panoply of sounds—harp tremolandos, celesta arpeggios, gong strokes, and horn—and the cantilena in which Quint calls to Miles: all these belong to a preoccupation of Britten's with the music of Asia that goes back at least to his association in the States with Colin McPhee and its effect on *Peter Grimes*. The Sunday Morning Interlude in Act II, which bears an obvious resemblance to the coronation scene from *Boris Godunov*, also derives from Balinese music transcribed by McPhee for piano duet and recorded by him and Britten (Matthews; Mitchell, "What Do We Know," 39–45). Britten's musical version of orientalism here surely answers to Edward Said's classic description of it as producing "one of [Europe's] deepest and most recurring images of the Other" and yet being in essence "a sort of surrogate and even underground self" for the West (1–2). Even more pertinently for the present case (in the words of Leo Treitler in relation to the interpretation of chant), "the Other is, in effect, a projection of the Self, or rather of an unacknowledged aspect of the Self that is supposed to be unacceptable to that identity that is the speaker for the Self" (290). Quint is the quintessence of that Other in Britten's presentation. And his music spills over into the *Dream:* "If it is an accident that E-flat is the key both of the immortals in *A Midsummer Night's Dream* and of Quint's evil in *The Turn of the Screw*, it is the kind of accident that happens only to genius," as Wilfrid Mellers noted ("Truth," 191). If Quint/Oberon is decidedly Britten's Erlkönig, in the *Dream* it is even more noticeably the process itself of erotic binding and power embodied in the juice of the flower that is invested with the "Oriental" sound of the celesta, accompanied in its most sinister appearance—the bewitching of Tytania at the end of Act I (at fig. 102)—by harp, tremolo strings, glockenspiel and the like.

There was clearly no way forward from here. Britten's visit to Asia in 1955–56 planted a seed of understanding in his mind about the actual music of Bali and Japan, which he then heard in context for the first time. In a letter to Imogen Holst about the Balinese gamelan he praised the music as "*fantastically* rich—melodically, rhythmically, texture (such *orchestration!*) and above all *formally*" and said, "At last I'm beginning to catch on to the technique" (Headington, 114). There occurred at this time no less than a crisis in his career (one that many commentators seem to see as the beginning of his decline). The first large work after the *Dream* was the *War Requiem*, completed in December 1961. Hans Werner Henze conveys something of its importance when he says that it is "a work whose urgency had banished all stylization"; that it represents "the other side of Ben's music: a world in which the lyrical is denied, and whose contours have been elaborated in a hard and indeed temperate and unornamented manner" (254–55). Even greater severity is characteristic of *Curlew River*, not completed until 1964. This church parable engages with the music of Asia on terms that are not at all patronizing, because they put so much of Western musical history at risk in an attempt at a genuine relationship that acknowledges and celebrates difference: Britten's grounding of his work musically in Western chant and dramatically in the English mystery play provides the basis for a clear-headed reinterpretation of and homage to Eastern conventions. Such a strategy seemed almost to acknowledge the appropriation and projection that had been involved in the earlier works, especially those of the 1950s. *Curlew River* and its successors *The Burning Fiery Furnace* (1966) and *The Prodigal Son* (1968) were the narrow strait that had to be navigated successfully before Britten could turn back to opera in a more recognizable mold.

One element shared by *Owen Wingrave* and *Death in Venice* is a personal "coming out" drama constructed in the one case around the young hero's rejection of family values in favor of personal integrity and in the other around the aging writer's abandoning himself to a vision of beauty embodied in the adolescent male whose attraction he has never allowed himself to recognize let alone enjoy. Pacifism and pederasty are distinct issues, and no doubt they occupied separate areas of Britten's conscious thoughts. Yet they are linked here musically in an orientalism more utopic than threatening—both peace and the beauty of boys are evoked by the gamelan—and dramatically in the powerful images of "the closet" and "coming out," which condense so many of our Western oppositions into one powerful figure (Sedgwick). But both operas downplay the public/private issues of Britten's *Grimes* period in favor of a search for inner peace on the part of the protagonists. Owen's battle with the slightly caricatured living representatives of the Wingrave family and their allies is far less than what he goes through as the result of the terrible hurt done to the boy with whom he identifies in the ancestral legend. When Aschenbach sings "I love you" at the powerful climax of Act I in his key of E major, there is no avoiding the sense of personal declaration, the importance of which rests entirely in the private sphere—both for the character Aschenbach and by implication for the composer Britten. Such a declaration, it may be thought, would even so have its public effect in robbing the open secret around Britten of its remaining power for his audience. But the way that critical debate grabbed at the straw of allegory offered by the libretto of *Death in Venice* (invoking a round of binarisms such as discipline/licentiousness, classic/romantic, and Apollonian/ Dionysian) affords a classic instance of the workings of the open secret and, consequently, of the double bind under which the discerning of sexuality in musical drama operates: "In a mechanism reminiscent of Freudian disavowal, we know perfectly well that the secret is known, but nonetheless we must persist, however ineptly, in guarding it" (Miller, 206).

NOTES

1. See also *Literature, Politics* (1989), 301.

2. "A New Britten Opera," *The Observer,* 5 June 1960; quoted in White, 90.

3. Britten's own recording and the productions with which he was associated emphasized the comic, even patronizing, elements in the opera, rather than its serious side. For the arguments concerning this latent side, see chapter 5 ("Character and Caricature in *Albert Herring*").

4. Robin Holloway made the connection in an interesting passage on *Owen Wingrave* and the *War Requiem* in an essay on the Church Parables: "The private, almost fetishistic quality of this word [peace] in Britten's output explains itself— warrants its full warmth—only if it is understood as the pass- or code-word for his sexuality" (224).

5. The biographies give the telltale signs—indications of black moods and utter depression, an avoidance of direct conflict, a lack of confidence and even sense of failure in the midst of tremendous success—which most gay readers will immediately recognize. The testimony of Ronald Duncan, who harbored a good deal of resentment as a rejected librettist, cannot be taken uncritically. There is surely some truth, however, in this description of Britten: "He remained a reluctant homosexual, a man in flight from himself, who often punished others for the sin he felt he'd committed himself. He was a man on a rack"; see *Working with Britten,* 27–28.

6. See, for instance, Headington, 34–35, and Peter Pears's statement that "the word 'gay' was not in his vocabulary . . . 'the gay life,' he resented that" in the ITV film *A Time There Was,* dir. Tony Palmer, quoted in Brett, *Peter Grimes,* 191.

7. Particularly important texts for the gay movement in this regard were McIntosh and Altman.

8. Ricky and Stephen are half brothers who end up living together (before Ricky's death) in Forster's novel *The Longest Journey;* Maurice is the chief character in the posthumously published *Maurice,* and Alec Scudder, the other gamekeeper of English fiction, is his lover.

9. Mitchell has stated that *"Death in Venice* embodies unequivocally the powerful sexual drive that was Britten's towards the young (and sometimes very young) male"; see *Death in Venice,* 21.

10. Peter Evans with his usual perspicacity notes its derivation from the inversion of the first five notes of that chromatic series (214).

11. Patricia Howard goes so far in not seeing/hearing as to claim that the theme "first occurs in Act I, scene 1 at a significant point in the governess's musings" quoting the passage 7 measures after figure 3 ("O why, why did I come?") to support her observation; see *Turn of the Screw,* 82.

12. I have adopted Britten's spelling "Tytania," derived from the quarto, rather than the more usual Titania. In Britten's performances the first syllable was pronounced as a long "i" (as in "tie") not a short one.

13. Ruth Solie has suggested to me the possible connection of this opposition between court and wood to that between "the two fundamental types of sociality: the Norm and the Festival" as proposed by Jacques Attali in his analysis of Breughel's painting *Carnival's Quarrel with Lent;* see Attali, 21–24. It may be useful to consider to what degree Britten's explorations of a transgressive order here and elsewhere have to do with his patent efforts to change the "political economy" of music-making in post–World War II Britain—by starting the English Opera Group, founding the Aldeburgh Festival, exploring alternative performance-spaces and methods (in such works as *Noyës Fludde, Saint Nicolas* and the Church Parables) and by the immense effort to encourage music in schools, an effort in which he played a leading role (and which the Thatcher government reportedly did its best to dismantle). My notion here, however, was derived from C. L. Barber and enriched by ideas of the carnivalesque associated with Mikhail Bakhtin and articulated in the English context in Castle.

14. Terry Castle indicates the historical association of masquerade and opera in London—the first public masquerades, like Handel's first productions, took place at the Haymarket—and points to the survival in "the conservative institution of the opera" of masquerade in such works as Verdi's *Ballo in Maschera* long after it had been exhausted as a topos in literature (339–40). Representing flamboyant feelings beyond those allowed in "real" circumstances, opera offers sol-

ace and promise of fulfillment to gay men (no strangers to repressed emotions); hence its potent role in the social control of homosexuality (see Morris).

15. In an extended and fascinating demonstration of the connection (in singing manuals and other documents) between the falsetto voice and unnaturalness and degeneracy, Koestenbaum shows how "the discourse of degenerate voice (one of several models of the unnaturally produced self) enfolds and foretells the modern discourse of the homosexual" (see 217–23).

16. Standard accounts are Montgomery-Hyde, *The Other Love;* and Wildeblood. Chapter 5 of Sinfield's *Literature, Politics* includes analyses of literature of the time. On Turing (and a for wonderfully thoughtful appraisal of the decade) see Hodges, ch. 8.

CHAPTER EIGHT

Eros and Orientalism in Britten's Operas

In what seemed a rather bold gesture during my student days at King's College, Cambridge, I persuaded a friend of mine with one of those classic Cambridge baritone voices to perform with me in a College Music Society concert the *Four Indian Love Lyrics* of Amy Woodforde-Finden. This was the closest I could have been said ever to have come, as a highly repressed and not-at-all gay boy, to camp. Any success it might have had as camp, however, was entirely owing to my straight baritone friend, who did incredibly unsuspected and virtually obscene things to the articulation of such phrases as "Pale hands, pink-tipped" in the song "Pale Hands I Loved beside the Shalimar."

Those who know the songs presumably know them for what they are usually taken, a brand of popular turn-of-the-century kitsch. In the erotic lyrics, written by a woman with the male nom-de-plume of Laurence Hope, the gendered female figure exists in a lightly masochistic relation to the dominant male ("Less than the dust beneath thy chariot wheel, / Less than the rust that never stained thy sword, / Less than the

From Philip Brett, Elizabeth Wood, and Gary C. Thomas, eds., *Queering the Pitch: The New Gay and Lesbian Musicology* (New York: Routledge, 235–56). It draws directly on material from "Britten's Bad Boys" (chapter 6), but because the case made here is ultimately a more general one, it seems correct to let these repetitions stand.

trust thou hast in me, my Lord: / Even less than these, even less than these!"). Woodforde-Finden complements their brand of sexual fantasy with a musical style that embodies the exotic in the simplest of ways—a modal inflection here and there, a vaguely "Eastern" ornament in the melodic line—but otherwise wavering somewhere between late-nineteenth-century Italian operatic rhetoric and the Sullivan of Gilbert and Sullivan. Their undying appeal has led Boosey and Hawkes to reissue them quite recently.

After the performance, a don whom I liked and who I knew had been in the Indian civil service came up to us with port on his breath and tears in his eyes. "I haven't heard those songs since India, where they were often sung at the club," he explained. It has dawned on me since that in that setting, men and women, servants of the British raj, would have been applauding and thereby sharing in the performance by one of their own kind of songs hinting at species of erotic acts that though they might have performed they could never admit to. These erotic fantasies, however, could be displaced onto an Indian persona. Of course, this persona bore no relation to any real Indian, either those standing silently as servants ready to do the sahib's bidding at the club, or those who, far vaster in number than the British masters, would in ordinary circumstances hardly be noticed by them: one thinks of the terrifying anonymity to which Harry Coomer finds himself consigned when he becomes Hari Kumar in his native country in Paul Scott's *Raj Quartet*. Nor had the songs necessarily to be linked to India itself, for anywhere south of the Pyrenees and east of East Grinstead would do: among Woodforde-Finden's other works are a cantata, *The Pagoda of Flowers* (1907), located in Burma, and a song cycle entitled *A Lover in Damascus* (1904). She and her reception belong to a phenomenon in which Far, Middle, and Near East coalesce into what Edward Said calls "one of [Europe's] deepest and most recurring images of the Other" (1). It is the phenomenon that he calls orientalism.

Orientalism, in Said's usage, is the negative term of one of those many "binarisms" whose deconstruction in recent years has helped us to understand more about the culture of Europe and North America. In the context in which I have raised the topic, that of the erotic, musical and colonial, we can see all at once the projection of a male fantasy of the feminine, and the identification of a subject race that, according to the imperialist fantasy, is begging to be subjected. Said sees orientalism as bound up with questions of power, that of rulers over subject races (207), of gender, because orientalism as an academic discipline "was an exclusively male province" (207); and of sexuality. In a sentence that indicates one of Said's few failures of nerve, he writes: "Why the Orient seems still to suggest not only fecundity but sexual promise (and threat), untiring sensuality, unlimited desire, deep generation energies, is something on which one could speculate" (188).

Nineteenth- and early twentieth-century music is, of course, deeply implicated in the general Eurocentric perception of the Orient, particularly in France and Britain, the countries Said points to as having the longest tradition of orientalism. A recent study by Ralph P. Locke of Saint-Saëns's *Samson et Dalila* indicates in extensive detail its musical consequences in French nineteenth-century opera, from Félicien David onward, and its reverberations in modern American culture up to and including Bernstein's *West Side Story* (1957). Susan McClary's work on *Carmen* raises the issue in a feminist context, prompted by the portrayal of the title figure in the typical alluring-but-forbidden model of the exotic female Other. British music remains to be studied in this respect: among composers there are obvious candidates like Delius and Granville Bantock, but the repertory will undoubtedly reveal a great deal more with careful combing—even the severe Holst wrote an "oriental suite" entitled *Beni Mora*.[1] In this essay I want to focus on rather specific examples of what I see as orientalism in the music of Benjamin Britten.

In the last decade, Donald Mitchell has revealed the extent of Britten's involvement in the musics of Asia; and Mervyn Cooke has charted the provenance of Britten's musical derivations quite precisely in even more recent work.[2] Britten's first exposure to this music, according to these scholars, was through the Canadian composer Colin McPhee, who had spent a good deal of the 1930s in Bali, and had become an authority on its music.[3] The two met early in Britten's American sojourn at the Long Island home of the Mayer family, where they were both welcomed like many other gay men in music and literature whom Elisabeth Mayer entertained and befriended.[4] The same age as Aaron Copland, another member of the Mayers' circle, and a generation older than Britten, McPhee was a prickly customer with a history of depression, drinking and sponging off his friends. Yet the two hit it off well enough for Britten to make a special farewell visit to McPhee in October 1941 when the latter had a residency at Yaddo, an artists' retreat at Saratoga in upstate New York;[5] and it transpires that the Canadian composer tried, along with Copland, to influence the younger Englishman to a greater degree than has previously been recognized. In a letter to Elisabeth Mayer, McPhee refers to an article he has been writing—and the reactions of its subject:

> Ben seems to have winced at quite a few passages; I am glad of it. We've talked this all out before, but if (even if it doesn't get published) my negative phrases can help him, it will have been worth while. No one but Aaron has ever picked certain things in Ben to pieces—that is not what I mean—we don't want to do that, but try to make him see the futility of certain things. I understand Ben so well, and his fear that he can't. If he is only wanting a career (and I know that is not it), and a career that I know would be very short, then he need not change. But if he wants to survive, to be played with love later on, even during the later years of his life, he must search deeper for a more personal, more *interesting* idiom. Alas, this is so; in the order of today good craftsmanship is not enough—that is why I can't, won't write.[6]

One aspect of the "more personal, more *interesting* idiom" that causes Britten's music "to be played with love" even to this day derives from the very music of Indonesia that McPhee championed so fiercely, and it is worth asking how the far less successful Canadian composer made such an impression, with immediate as well as long-range consequences, on the younger Englishman.

One area of mutual respect must have been established through piano playing, for McPhee had been a concert pianist and was probably a closer match for Britten in this respect than others of the circle. At any rate, Britten played with McPhee the latter's *Balinese Ceremonial Music*, a set of four pieces transcribed for two pianos, four hands; in 1941 they recorded them for the publisher Schirmer. McPhee inscribed a copy "To Ben—in the hope that he'll find something in the music, after all." Ben indeed found something in their heterophonic technique and exotic sound with which to characterize the "blue moon" episode of *Paul Bunyan* in the same year. And whatever ambivalence McPhee sensed must be weighed against Britten's playing the pieces again in a Wigmore Hall concert with Clifford Curzon in 1944 after his return to England: they had undoubtedly left their mark. Furthermore, as Bayan Northcott first discovered, chords from one of them turn up in the Sunday Morning Interlude of *Peter Grimes*, which otherwise looks toward another exotic model, the coronation scene of Mussorgsky's *Boris Godunov*, to produce its sonorous picture of an English Sabbath.[7] Similar traces of "Asian" sonorities can be found or sensed in subsequent pieces, but it is not until *The Turn of the Screw* (1954) that, as we shall see, they become attached to a dramatic trope.

As Britten became more involved with these sonorities, the passages containing them became less recognizably related to the "pure gamelan" of McPhee's transcriptions and more generally "exotic." On hearing the examples for this paper, some listeners have resisted the suggestion that they owe anything to gamelan music at all, possibly because of the nature of my interpretation. Yet I am not proposing any new musical identification at all. Every passage mentioned in this essay has been heard and marked as exotic, oriental, or quasi-oriental by other Britten critics, principally Cooke, Mitchell and Palmer. And it is Mitchell and Cooke who have invested the Britten-McPhee relationship with primary importance in the matter. Britten seems not to have been involved with other American composers of gamelan-inspired music, such as Cage, Cowell and Harrison, though gamelan is a gay marker in American music, as Stevan Key has pointed out to me.[8]

As it turns out, there is a European counterpart who may have helped significantly to reinforce the initial impact of gamelan on Britten—a homosexual composer much closer to camp in his aesthetic than the severe Englishman would ever have allowed himself to be, but one whom Britten nevertheless befriended, supported, and admired. Francis Poulenc's Concerto for two pianos in D minor, written the year after the 1931 Exposition Coloniale de Paris at which he heard a Balinese gamelan, contains a passage at the end of the first movement that is closer than McPhee's transcriptions to the sound of Britten's post-1956 gamelan music. The passage is heralded by the only eerie moment in this ebullient score, and subtle allusions to it occur at the end of each of the other two movements; the two composers were the soloists in a performance at the Albert Hall on 6 January 1945. The previous summer, Poulenc had finished his first opera, *Les Mamelles de Tirésias*, in which, just after the Theatre Director urges the audience to "make children—like you never have before" at the very end of the prologue, there occurs another "Balinese" moment that, like the two fleeting allusions at the close of the second and third movements of the concerto, is much closer to the kind of pseudogamelan effect I am principally concerned with here. I do not know whether Britten saw the score then, but he thought highly enough of the work to present its first English performance at the Aldeburgh Festival in 1958 and to play the piano part himself.[9]

In 1955–56, Britten, Pears and their friends the Hesses went on a world tour during which the composer heard not only Balinese gamelan music, whose technique—which he found "about as complicated as Schönberg"—he now became involved with, but also Japanese music drama (Cooke, "Britten and Bali," 320). The first of these exposures bore immediate fruit in the 1956 ballet, *The Prince of the Pagodas*, in which the pagodas themselves are depicted in gamelan music. Much later, in 1964, came *Curlew River*, the opera (comparatively long in gestation) that demonstrated the full extent of Britten's engagement with Japanese Noh drama. After this point, Asian music, particularly Balinese gamelan music, turned up with great frequency in Britten's works, making its most extensive appearance, possibly, in *Death in Venice*.

The revelation of the extent of Britten's engagement with Asian musics was important if only because it also revealed the parochialism of those critics who, in a curious evocation of an essentially imperialist vision of London as the center of a Eurocentric world, saw (and still see) Britten as having cut himself off in his later years, to the detriment of his musical development. This anxiety, revealed in a particularly virulent attack by Tom Sutcliffe, music critic of *The Guardian*, in the television documentary series *J'accuse* on Channel 4 during the spring of 1991, has strong links to concerns over his "going native"—for every British critic who accepts the gamelan and heterophony as part of Britten's language there is another who loathes what they represent.[10] But the revelation of Asian influences also opened up new ways to explore the dramaturgy of the operas. In an essay of 1985 in the Cambridge Opera Handbook on *The Turn of the Screw*, Christopher Palmer made the association, crucial for my purposes here, between the gamelan-like sonorities and pentatonic melodic shapes one the one hand, and the opera's treatment of erotic desire and sexuality on the other.[11]

The musical organization of *The Turn of the Screw* is closely, even obsessively, worked out. No other Britten score is so tightly ordered, no scheme of his more imaginatively devised to produce a musically claustrophobic quality. The composer may well have realized that the "technical skill [that] always comes from the bourgeois side of one's nature" could—and must for him—be made to produce something more powerful and dramatically compelling than the "large unfeeling corpses" Auden had warned Britten about in a famous letter.[12] The fifteen interludes that punctuate the scenes consist of a set of variations on a theme that is announced at the beginning, immediately after the expressive Prologue. Consisting of three phrases of four notes each, this theme can be reduced to a set of rising fourths (or falling fifths) followed by falling thirds (or rising sixths), which cover all twelve notes of the chromatic scale. The first

Example 8.1. *The Turn of the Screw,* variations on a theme

six notes, if laid out stepwise in the order 0–2–4–1–3–5, make the first six notes of the A-major scale; the last six, if similarly arranged (6–8–10–7–9–11), cover the hexachord E-flat–C, suggesting E-flat or A-flat. As it turns out, A major and A-flat major are the two polar keys of the opera, the first signifying, in the broadest terms, the Governess's world, the latter the influence of the ghosts. The tonality of the interlude/variations and of their subsequent scenes in Act I ascend from the one to the other; those of Act II descend by an exactly inverted path. Almost every other thematic aspect of the work is somehow derived from this main theme, often in a way that is deliberately ambiguous (example 8.1.)

Perhaps because of the organicist ideology underlying most music analysis, or because of a fairly simple-minded wonder that comes over most commentators on encountering a theme in Britten's music incorporating all twelve notes of the chromatic scale, no one pays attention to the actual musical effect generated here—and again when the theme is heard in a similar juxtaposition at the beginning of Act II. The dynamics, the phrasing, the prolongation of each pitch and the steady rise in pitch level associated with an exactly reiterated rhythm, all culminating in a $\frac{3}{2}$ measure prolonging the twelve-note dissonance almost unbearably, lead the ear to hear the passage as an introduction, a giant upbeat if you will, to what happens next, at fig. 1 (example 8.2). The portentous quality of the gesture is scarcely matched, of course, by what follows—a

Example 8.2. *The Turn of the Screw*, Prologue

theme played by flute, clarinet and the two violins over an internal pedal on A, and therefore not fully foregrounded.[13] Most notable perhaps is its disturbingly asymmetrical rhythm, which is taken over completely by the timpani and tenor drum as the main element of the first scene, "The Journey," suggesting all at once the uneven roll of the carriage wheels, the palpitations of the Governess's frightened heart and intimations of sensuality, the first delicate hint of exoticism in the score. *This* journey, evidently, is going to take us somewhere further than an English house in the country. The second theme, which Peter Evans ingeniously derives from the twelve-note series by filling in the inverted version of its first five notes, is equally important in the construction of the work and even more important dramatically than the twelve-note theme that precedes it. It migrates from character to character, subtly changing under the pressure of the dramatic situation.

It first attaches itself to the Governess, charting the significant moments that reveal her state of mind, from her fear of the task at hand in scene 1, and her arrival in scene 2 (where it hangs in the air on the high violins like a nervous thread), through her increasing "knowledge" of the situation, and the awareness of her need to shelter the children as Act I proceeds, to her ultimate realization, in scene 7 of Act I, that she "neither shields nor saves them." In Act II, it accompanies her growing recognition of failure, and of her sense of becoming tarnished in her efforts: "I have failed, most miserably failed, and there is no more innocence in me." Finally it occurs, plainer and perhaps coarser without its ironic final twist, as the Governess declares possessively at the opening of the passacaglia in the final scene, "O Miles, I cannot bear to lose you. You shall be mine and I shall save you."

The theme also attaches itself to the not-so-ghostly ghosts. Their most important enunciation of it occurs in the first scene of Act II, where its original association with the twelve-note theme is reproduced. Here, the introductory feeling of the twelve-note theme is intensified by a gradually increasing harmonic rhythm as well as by growing rhythmic activity in the bass toward its climax-provoking end. When the second theme arrives, it is in the ghosts' key of A-flat, and it is sung to the words that Myfanwy Piper, the librettist, imported from Yeats's *Second Coming:* "The ceremony of innocence is drowned." It is precisely at the arrival of the second theme and Yeats's memorable phrase that the pseudogamelan effect that Palmer identified occurs, provided here by flute, harp, and celesta over gurgling woodwind trills, with gong and cymbal strikes reinforced by string *pizzicati* on the downbeat of each $\frac{3}{2}$ bar (example 8.3).

The water imagery that Christopher Palmer writes about is likely to have arisen because Britten, who liked concrete images, responded to the word "drowned"; yet, as Palmer notes with respect to the last scene of Act I, in which a similar sound is projected, this imagery is directed, surely, toward the particular meaning of loss of innocence associated with erotic, or even purely sexual, practices ("The Colour of the Music," 106).

Since sex, once discerned, is so willful in its signification, and so easily gets out of hand (as it does, rather, in Palmer's account), it is wise to look first toward the historical context for a specific practice that might in particular apply to a tale such as this by Henry James and its transformation into an opera by Britten. In view of the "sexual awakening" theme here, and the involvement of children with supervisory adults in a nineteenth-century setting, masturbation is an inescapable choice. As Michael Moon has pointed out in his work on what he calls "the antionanist terrorist writing" of America in the nineteenth century, its target became increasingly "the *social* pursuit of this nominally solitary activity" (my emphasis). Its discourse, he continues, "crystallizes around the figure of the depraved individual—servant, older relative, or older child—who, by teaching the young to masturbate, introduces sexual difference and sexual desire into what American moral-purity writers represent as the previously innocent—which is to say asexual—homosocial environments to which the young are committed" (255).

The Turn of the Screw, written half a century after the inception of the anti-masturbation campaign, which comes to be an anti-homosexual campaign through the mechanism noted above, is for Moon a prime example of that mechanism:

Example 8.3. *The Turn of the Screw*, Act II, scene 1, second theme

One has only to recall how much in the tale turns on the mystery (or non-mystery) of little Miles's having been sent down from school for shocking misconduct toward some of his schoolmates—conduct into which he may have earlier been initiated by the literally haunting figure of Peter Quint—to perceive how resonant the figures of the boy and his corrupter, figures first disseminated on a mass scale in male-purity discourse, remained in the imaginations of James and many of his readers. (256)

It is surely not stretching the point to add the composer to those "readers," for if anti-masturbatory literature and the homophobic myths associated with it were still widely circulated during my own childhood in Britain, how much more present would they have been in the 1920s when Britten was reaching puberty? Indeed it appears that he told two of his librettists separate horror stories of childish corruption close to home, one about his being raped by a master at school, the other about his being implicated in some obscure way in the mechanics of his father's homosexual desire (Carpenter, *Britten*, 202–5).[14]

Whatever we make of these stories, whether true or strongly present in the composer's imagination as figured forth to his librettists, the music itself lends substance to the notion of Quint as corrupter, and we may remember that it was Britten himself who insisted to Piper that he "should sing—and sing words (no nice anonymous, supernatural humming or groaning)" (Piper, 11). What we hear Quint sing in his first vocal entry, however, is a perverse transformation of what we have been calling the second theme (largely by an elaboration around the flattened seventh, the "blue note" of the original) into something preliterate. If we listened for a word, which I doubt anyone does on encountering this passage in the theater, we would hear the possessive, self-involved, long-enunciated "my," closing only at its moment of dying pleasure into the name of the Other whom it calls "Miles." This is a voice from Lacan's imaginary, rather than symbolic, order, conjuring up an echo of the original cry that objectifies the voice into an instrument of pleasure, or the mother's voice, from which the child first feels the pangs of separation.[15]

According to Lord Harewood, the extraordinary cantilena in scene 8 (example 8.4) was suggested to Britten by the sound of Pears singing a Pérotin monody, but most auditors apprehend the exotic, something— in Wilfrid Mellers's account—"recalling flamenco music and Moorish cantillation."[16] We have only to remember the tendency to conflate various parts of the East to appreciate the orientalism of the gesture. Mellers and Palmer hear Quint's cantilena as "open[ing] magic casements" for Miles: in his ultra-gay-male-affirmative account Clifford Hindley hears it as, simply, "love" (11). But, given the orientalist context, the landscape onto which those magic casements open must be one of dread as well as allure; for orientalism is one of the means by which desire unacceptable to or feared by the (Western) Subject can be projected onto the Other. As if to confirm this diagnosis, this first vocal entry of Quint's, placed very carefully near the end of the first act, is heralded by and intertwined with echoes of variation 7, the first place in the score in which the pseudogamelan sounds fully assert their presence—sonorities derived from an encounter fifteen years earlier that Britten was now using to conjure up the distant world that the problematic McPhee had extolled and to delineate a character he himself had perhaps adumbrated.[17] In short, given the difference of the homoeroticism portrayed here, Britten's strategy belongs to the same cultural context as the lyrical effusions of Amy Woodforde-Finden, however distinct the musical effect.

Five years after *The Turn of the Screw*, in composing *A Midsummer Night's Dream*, Britten had recourse to a similar strategy in portraying Oberon. "If it is an accident that E-flat is the key both of the immortals in *A Midsummer Night's Dream* and of Quint's evil in *The Turn of the Screw*, it is the kind of accident that happens only to genius," writes Wilfrid Mellers in rhetoric characteristic of Britten criticism ("Truth," 191). If Quint is marked as homosexual and threateningly so by his "oriental" music, then Oberon is similarly designated by his countertenor voice; as Wayne Koestenbaum points out in a recent essay, the association of *falsetto* with unnaturalness and perversity in the singing manuals of the nineteenth century prefigures the discourse of homosexuality (217–23). Furthermore, Oberon at his most threatening and evil, as he evades the

Example 8.4. *The Turn of the Screw*, Act I, scene 8 cantilena

fairy sentinel to dispense the erotic binding power embodied in the juice of the flower, sets off another stylized pseudogamelan, with the ever-prominent celesta aided by harp and glockenspiel and with pianissimo tremolo strings set off by the pizzicato double basses playing a derivative of the melody in canon (example 8.5).

The device of the exotic attached to Oberon and Quint may have been simply aimed at capturing aspects of Shakespeare and James. The transgressive, carnivalesque atmosphere of the wood outside Athens could be apprehended by a post-Freudian composer in such a way as to suggest a positively Bakhtinian reading. Similarly, Britten would have pondered

Example 8.5. *A Midsummer Night's Dream*, Oberon's theme

long and hard over how to recreate James's effect—Piper's view, after all, stated unequivocally, is that "neither Britten nor I ever intended to interpret the work, only to re-create it for a different medium" (11). What James set out to do, of course, was to liberate the old Gothic horror story from its reliance on apparitions by forcing the reader into the hot spot: "make him *think* the evil, make him think of it for himself, and you are released from weak specifications," James wrote in a preface to the New York edition of the tale (*Art*, 176). In pushing for resolution in interpretation, then, we are lost, whether we subscribe to a "first story" in which the children are corrupted by the ghosts, or a "second story" in which the Governess in her hysterical condition conducts a battle for the children against an imagined foe. The reader who accepts the "first story" creates the subjective horror of deceitful evil in innocent-seeming children; the one who accepts the "second story" creates a monstrous predator in the guise of womanly protector. The one springs from and endorses homophobia, the other misogyny. Between these two positions, moreover, there is little room to move.[18]

The opera offers a focal character in the Governess. But she is distanced through James's framing device, which Britten, despite his liking for such frames, adopted at a comparatively late stage. Moreover, she is implicated in Quint's identity (in whatever way the listener likes to imagine) through the common basis of the theme they share, projected though it is in musically different ways. Britten himself could readily have found points of identification with both of them. But I should like to imagine him for a moment cast as Miles. The perceptively offensive Wystan Auden once wrote to the composer to say "You see, Bengy dear, you are always tempted . . . to build yourself a warm nest of love (of course when you get it, you find it a little stifling) by playing the lovable talented little boy" (Mitchell and Reed, 1016). Miles playing mock Mozart/Czerny to win the attention of his indulgent female wardens (II, 6) conjures up Auden's image rather evocatively. Seen from Miles's vantage point of abjection ("I am bad, aren't I?"), moreover, the ambiguities of the tale recede a little as we see the lovable boy caught between a dominating lover and a possessive mother in a struggle that no side wins and that ends inevitably in death—a catharsis even more intense than the capitulation of Peter Grimes to society's persecution and his own internalized oppression.

But there is also a good deal that Britten may have perceived of himself in Quint. The composer's own attraction for boys between the ages of about twelve and sixteen was strong: David Hemmings, the Miles in the original production of the opera (and on the recording conducted by Britten), apparently became the focus of one of the most powerful of his attachments, which, like many of their kind, were reportedly tender and fatherly, occasionally passionate, but involving no sexual exploitation (Carpenter, *Britten*, 341–55).[19] With his own childhood experiences in mind, Britten must have felt keenly the knife-edge balance on which such behavior rested. In *Peter Grimes* he had originally set out to portray a child abuser, a figure slowly but surely eradicated as work on the opera proceeded and supplanted by a worst-case scenario of another and more general kind—the outsider whom society hounds to death on no legal or moral grounds, an outsider represented most viably in that case by "the homosexual."[20] By means of James's tale he was able a decade later to return to the original theme, and also at the same time to exorcise—as he had in *Grimes*—a darker side of his own reality.

How then do we conceptualize an attitude toward the orientalism by means of which Britten casts such a web of ambiguity around Quint and Oberon, the powerful and predatory, but also alluring, figures who haunt the two last operas before an Eastern mode was adopted by Britten in earnest? Let me begin by making a distinction. Britten's is not comparable to the authorial anxiety exhibited in the *Alexandria Quartet*, in which, according to Joseph Boone's deconstructive reading, "the imaginary geography of Durrell's eroticized Egyptian landscape helps to throw the modernist and masculinist tenets of his text into disarray" and to "overwhelm the coherence of its representations of masculine heterosexual competence." In Durrell, as in the case of Flaubert, which Said discusses without revealing the threat of pederasty, "the exotic otherness of sexual 'perversion' [i.e., homoeroticism], is figured as the threat of erasure, the negation of artistic vitality or 'sap.'"[21] This is not true of Britten, who rather indicates a rich if dangerous enhancement of life and art beyond the world that imprisons him (and Miles). Nor is the composer's strategy that of feminizing the Other, so typical of orientalist responses. After his cantilena, Quint emerges in a series of quite specifically phallic, if veiled, personae—"the riderless horse, snorting, stamping"; the hero highwayman; King Midas—before relapsing back into less personified images—the hidden life; the unknown gesture; the soft persistent word.

One way of looking at Britten in this regard is to put him a little farther down the line from Durrell on a continuum of sexuality. What if the coherence here is represented by consenting homosexual love between two adults, as represented by his life with Peter Pears, the exotic otherness and threat of erasure by pedophilia, the love of "thin-as-a-board juveniles" with which Auden taunted Britten? (Mitchell, *Britten and Auden*, 161–62). Orientalism in its sexual mode in these two operas is, after all, attached exclusively to boy lovers, boy dominators, or boy seekers, that is to Quint and Oberon. This connects in turn to the pederasty that (as Boone notes) Said evades discussing in his account of Flaubert. The very dust-jacket picture of Said's book is Gérôme's "The Snake Charmer," depicting a naked boy entwined with a snake facing a crowd of men who (it is suggested to the implicated Western male gaze) are enjoying the spectacle of a titillation offered to the spectator only in the form of graceful buttocks.

On the other hand, Britten was himself identified, through a process that links the oriental to elements in Western society, such as delinquents, the insane, women, the poor and, of course, homosexuals, as "lamentably alien," to use Said's phrase. He was not the representative of a male heterosexist order, like Durrell, but of a group that, in the period of the operas under discussion, was particularly at risk of persecution as a result of the defection of Burgess and Maclean to the U.S.S.R. and the subsequent intervention of the CIA into British domestic policing. Britten began composing *The Turn of the Screw* on 30 March 1954, less than a week after the conclusion of the notorious trial that resulted in the imprisonment of Lord Montagu, Michael Pitt-Rivers and Peter Wilde-blood; Humphrey Carpenter has turned up evidence that some time in January of the same year (or slightly earlier), Britten was interviewed by Scotland Yard, whose gentlemen's agreement with the leisured classes was terrifyingly abrogated during this period, as part of their "definitely stepping up their activities against the homosexuals" (Carpenter, *Britten*, 335, quoting a letter from Percy Elland, editor of *The Evening Standard*, to his proprietor, Lord Beaverbrook). Do we understand, then, the de-monizing of the homosexual through the orientalism of these works as a means of expressing fear, shame and defiance all at once? Are we to in-voke a particularly complicated configuration of the dynamics of op-pression to explain away the case?

However one theorizes the Britten syndrome outlined here—or that of Amy Woodforde-Finden and Laurence Hope, which is promisingly complicated owing to their gender—a fresh view should probably be taken of Britten's subsequent operatic musical relations with the East. An important note by the librettist of *Curlew River*, William Plomer, shows how uncomfortable he was with the original idea for that opera of mak-ing it simply a translation of *Sumidagawa*, preserving the Japanese locale and character names. Britten also shows, in a letter of April 1958, how in-creasingly worried he became about the idea of creating a pastiche of a Noh play.[22] In insisting on the move into a comparable Western tradi-tion, that of the mystery play, Britten opened up conditions in which he was able to pay homage to an Eastern tradition by adapting and imitat-ing some of its musical and dramatic procedures without patronizing it, and without using it as a vehicle for the projection of Western fantasies. It is a project that tries hard to avoid the colonizing impulse, though of course it reflects the romantic utopianism also associated with the phe-nomenon of orientalism in the West.

When Britten returned to mainstream opera, he reverted to the de-ployment of gamelan music—this time notably closer to the original model—to denote moments of significance. In *Owen Wingrave* the game-lan makes a special appearance for Owen's biggest aria, his lyrical statement of belief about peace. In view of the earlier works the use is suggestive, so that when we hear the character exclaim, at the climax of the aria, before the emergence of the ghosts who are to seal his doom, that "peace is love," we may be pardoned for wondering what kind of love is involved. The use suggests the nonspecific erotic sensualism of the pagodas, those warm, slightly phallic but nonthreatening presences in the earlier ballet, *The Prince of the Pagodas* (1956). The suggestion of polymorphous perversity they entail points us in the direction of a world of prepubescent sensuousness, again preverbal, at a stage before entry into the symbolic order signified in the ballet by the phallic trumpet motive with which the prince emerges from the salamander. Owen is regressing into Britten's world of what has been called by the commentators "innocence," but which is beyond innocence and guilt, and rather "nescience," the presymbolic state hymned in "A Time There Was" of *Winter Words*, and indicated in Britten's music either by aggressively triadic tonality or by these echoes of the East.

The difference from the pseudogamelan of *The Turn of the Screw* and *A Midsummer Night's Dream* is striking, and it is further emphasized by a reversal in the assignment of the gamelan in Britten's last opera, *Death in Venice*. Here the orientalism is mapped not onto the adult male lover, but onto the distant, inarticulate figure of the boy who is beloved. Not only is this dramatically apt, since Aschenbach, through whom we as audience perceive Venice and Tadzio, would naturally project them in the image of orientalism, but it allows for a wider critique of the European dialogue of Self and Other. Like *A Passage to India* in Sara Suleri's brilliant reading, it could be said to be "both an engagement with and a denial of a colonial homoerotic imperative" (147). As the slowly circling figure of Tadzio leaves Aschenbach crumpled onstage at the end of the opera, we are reminded of the forces tearing Fielding and Aziz apart during their near-engagement at the end of the novel. For two generations of upper-middle-class Englishmen, trained in the humanist liberal tradition that promised so much and performed so little, the climax of their creativity coincided with a scene of denial and pessimism.

NOTES

1. *Beni Mora*, composed 1909–10, first performed 1912. I am indebted to my colleague Byron Adams for drawing my attention to this work, which has drawn a mixed reception from Holst critics.

2. Mitchell, "What Do We Know" and "Catching on to the Technique." Cooke, "Britten and the Gamelan" and "Britten and Bali."

3. McPhee recounted his experiences in his *House in Bali*; his treatise *Music in Bali* is still consulted.

4. A page from the Mayers' visitor's book shows Britten and Pears's names appearing for the first time on 21 August 1939, followed shortly by that of McPhee on 7 September; see Mitchell, *Pictures* (pl. 115), which also contains photographs of McPhee and Britten together in the garden at Amityville and of the score of *Balinese Ceremonial Music*, mentioned below, that McPhee gave to Britten. For two different accounts of life at the Mayers', see Mitchell and Reed, 679–83 (also 724 for Britten's own account); and Carpenter, *Britten*, 133–36. McPhee was treated for depression by Dr. Mayer, a psychiatrist; he also taught Elizabeth Mayer the piano; see Oja, 154–57, 179–80.

5. The visit is referred to in a letter to Britten of 1 October (1942) from McPhee (in the Britten-Pears Library at Aldeburgh). After opening with "just a brief note to say I love you and think of you often," McPhee writes that "by the time you get (if you do) this letter, it will be just a year since you so very sweetly came to Saratoga." Written from Woodstock, where Copland lived and where Britten and Pears rented accommodation when they first arrived in the States, the letter goes on to give news of Marc Blitzstein, Victor (Kraft, Copland's lover), Oliver (Daniel, who worked at CBS), David Diamond, and M(argaret) M(ead). These were McPhee's friends, of course—Copland and Daniel lent him money endlessly as well as promoting his work—but it is interesting to speculate that Britten may have met Margaret Mead through McPhee. McPhee gave his own birthdate as 1901, but Oja has verified the date 1900 from his birth certificate; see Oja, 1.

6. Postmarked 10 July 1941 and written from Yaddo (bold letters printed with the red ribbon of the typewriter). Britten had put McPhee in touch with an editor, David Ewen (see letter 309, Mitchell and Reed, 907–8). According to a further letter of McPhee's to Elizabeth Mayer, on 30 October: "Ewen's book has been given up, and I am glad, for though I hope to publish something about Ben, in the same tone, I would like to develope *[sic]* it more. The other thing was too hasty."

7. As indicated in Matthews, 122–24. Further on the pre-1954 music, see Cooke, "Britten and Bali" and *Britten and the Far East*.

8. Private communication.

9. For an account of Britten's relations with Poulenc, see Mitchell and Reed, 249–50. The two composers gave a further performance of Poulenc's two-piano concerto on 16 January 1955 at the Royal Festival Hall in London; see Buckland, 228 and 393. Peter Pears sang the part of the Husband in the Aldeburgh production of *Les Mamelles*.

10. Sutcliffe describes Aldeburgh, Britten's home and the place where he held his music festival, as "a haven isolated from the radical intellectual milieu Britten enjoyed in the thirties in London." Like many other observations in the program this has the ring of truth—Britten certainly became increasingly conservative as he aged; what is extraordinary is the anger expressed against the composer for not measuring up to the examples of Elgar and Vaughan Williams, for not being the national composer he was expected to be, and, ultimately, for exploiting an "emperor's clothes" situation. Thus the Church Parables, described as "a new brainwave recipe mixing plainchant and monks and Japanese Noh theatre and percussive Balinese timbres" are "proof enough that Britten was producing exactly the emotional corpses that Auden [in the letter cited in note 12] had predicted."

11. Palmer, "The Colour of the Music," 101–25, especially 110–13 and 124. It is worth noting that a connection between sensuality/sexuality and Bali had been made in a different but equally revealing way by Colin McPhee in a letter to William Mayer (postmarked 2 September 1942 and preserved in the Britten-Pears Library at Aldeburgh):

> I remember that at nineteen I was filled with the idea that I had something precious to say, and that at twenty-three I no longer believed it. I already felt lost, filled with despair, and took refuge in living completely for the moment. Many times there was a decision to be made between some important opportunity and a sexual (homosexual) relationship which was purely sensual. I never hesitated to choose the latter. This I did deliberately and would do again and again, for it seemed the only thing that was real. The Balinese period was simply a long extension of this.

12. Saturday (31 January 1942), printed in Mitchell and Reed, 1015–16.

13. Patricia Howard goes so far in not seeing/hearing it as to claim that the theme "first occurs in Act I, scene 1 at a significant point in the governess's musings"—in the passage seven measures after fig. 3 ("O why, why did I come?"); see "Structures," 82.

14. Carpenter is extremely judicious in handling these accounts given to him by Eric Crozier and Myfanwy Piper. The second story hinges on Piper's statement, "He did say that his father was homosexual and that he used to send him out to find boys" (23).

15. It was after I conceived this passage that I came across the extracts from Michel Poizat's *Opéra, ou le cri de l'ange;* Poizat usefully analyzes just such ef-

fects—the proleptic effects—of the "blue note" conceived in a wider sense than I originally intended here, as applying themselves in opera "towards a supreme mark of the failure of speech and the signifying order, namely, the cry" (201). In connection with the other presymbolic experience, not the first cry of the *enfant* but the voice of the mother, it is interesting that one of Britten's early playmates has observed that Peter Pears's voice sounded like that of Britten's own mother. See Mitchell's preface to Mitchell and Reed, 14.

I am indebted to Roger Parker for pointing out to me the similarity *as gesture* of this moment in Britten's score to the introduction to the famous Bell Song from Act II of Delibes's *Lakmé*, an orientalist opera if ever there was one. What Carolyn Abbate says about this piece in her opening discussion (4–9) applies equally to Quint's vocalizing: "Such moments enact in pure form familiar Western tropes on the suspicious power of music and its capacity to move us without rational speech." The differences between the two passages are revealing. If Lakmé's "overtly seductive performance . . . extracts one erotically fascinated listener [Gerald, the besotted British officer] from the crowd," Quint's song is even more powerfully focused on its one onstage auditor, Miles. If Lakmé, whose music dissolves into fragments "becomes *explicitly* a body emanating sonority," Quint is a disembodied vocal threat from the start.

16. Harewood's observation appears in Kobbé, 1494. It is confirmed by Rosamund Strode; see 89–90. Strode identifies the piece in question as *Beata viscera Mariæ virginis*, printed in the widely used Davison & Apel, no. 17c; and she points to Pears's performance of the monody to open the Purcell Singers Concert (conducted by Imogen Holst) on 16 June 1954 at the Aldeburgh Festival as the one that "suggested to Ben exactly what he wanted for Quint's unearthly and alluring calls to Miles" on the grounds that he was writing *The Turn of the Screw* that summer. But Myfanwy Piper "vividly remembers 'amazing crashes' accompanying Quint's calls to Miles" when Britten played through the work in progress during a mid-May visit, according to the account in Carpenter, *Britten*, 337, where it is also reported (a) that Britten wrote to Lennox Berkeley on 6 July saying that "rehearsals start in a month & I have 5 scenes still to write—O Law!" and (b) that the composition sketch was finished on 23 July (355). Mellers, "Turning the Screw," 149.

17. Oja is reticent with details of McPhee's sexual tastes and partners in Bali, but she notes that his marriage to Jane Belo, who financed the venture, foundered partly on his relationship with an indigenous male: "I was in love at the time with a Balinese, which she knew, and to have him continually around was too much for her vanity" (letter to Sidney Cowell, in Oja, 142). McPhee was also devoted to Balinese children, particularly the talented dancer Sampih, a boy of about

eight when they first met in 1932, who subsequently lived at the McPhee house and whom he loved intensely (88–89); McPhee founded a children's gamelan—*gamelan angklung*—as related in *A House in Bali*, 195–201, and in his children's book, *A Club of Small Men*, copies of which Britten possessed. Britten's feelings about McPhee must have soured when the latter described the *Seven Sonnets of Michelangelo* as "baroque and pompous show-pieces, pastiches that hold little interest" in "Scores and Records," 48–49; writing to Elisabeth Mayer on 13 May 1944, Britten comments "I know how fickle the musical public is, & how superficial their judgements (although I was a bit grieved by Colin's attack on the Michelangelo Sonnets);" see Mitchell and Reed, 1201–2. If the music associated with McPhee nevertheless remained in Britten's composing consciousness, as Mitchell, Cooke, and others argue convincingly, why are these same commentators so fastidious about the characteristics of the person behind the music, especially the homoeroticism that was so strongly intertwined with his love of Bali?

18. Nor when we turn to the opera is Clifford Hindley's "third story"—of a blameless Quint offering Miles the fulfillment of his "true nature," the Governess the victim of the delusion that such relationships are all evil, and such evil as there is being projected onto Miss Jessel—a fully acceptable alternative. See "Britten's Bad Boys: Male Relations in *The Turn of the Screw*," chapter 6 above.

19. The criminologist D. J. West distinguishes between the pedophile and "ephebophile," a category into whose broad outline Britten fits remarkably well; see 211–15.

20. For the process of transformation in this opera, see my "Fiery Visions."

21. Boone, 102. Marjorie Garber proposes for "Boone's salutary substitution" of the homosexual male dancer that Said overlooks or represses, the further substitution of an irreducible transvestic spectacle, suggesting that "transvestism . . . *that* is the taboo against which Occidental eyes are veiled" (341–42).

22. For a full account, including Plomer's note and Britten's letter, see Alexander, 299–306. I am indebted to Mervyn Cooke for this reference.

CHAPTER NINE

Keeping the Straight Line Intact?

Britten's Relation to Folksong, Purcell, and His English Predecessors

The word "folksong" is likely to produce different and special reactions in musicians of all kinds. Many of us brought up in Britain are indelibly marked by early experiences of *The National Songbook*, edited by Sir Charles Villiers Stanford, or one of many subsequent schoolroom anthologies, such as the one edited by Cecil Sharpe. I remember pursuing the program, which in my day included initiation in "country dance," until the age when it seemed unbearably soppy. I was taught, in other words, along lines approved by Cecil ("it is Englishmen, English citizens we want") Sharp, Ralph Vaughan Williams, and other liberal or Fabian socialist authorities who wanted to construct a musico-nationality and

Originally published as "Toeing the Line: To What Extent Was Britten Part of the British Pastoral Establishment?" *Musical Times* 137 (September 1966), this essay reviews a selection of Britten's recordings that were released on CD in the 1990s. They include *The Folk Songs*—Felicity Lott, Philip Langridge, Thomas Allen, Carlos Bonell, Osian Ellis, Graham Johnson, Northern Sinfonia, Wenhaston Boys Choir, BBC Singers, Steuart Bedford—Collins Classics 70392 (3 CDs); *Complete Folk Song Arrangements*—Lorna Anderson, Regina Nathan, Jamie McDougall, Malcolm Martineau, Bryn Lewis, Craig Ogden—Hyperion CDA 66941–2; *Purcell Realizations*—Felicity Lott, Susan Gritton, Sarah Walker, James Bowman, John Mark Ainsley, Ian Bostridge, Anthony Rolfe Johnson, Richard Jackson, Simon Keenlyside, Graham Johnson—Hyperion CDA 67061–2; and *The Red Cockatoo; the Holy Sonnets of John Donne; and Other Songs*—Ian Bostridge, Graham Johnson—Hyperion CDA 66823.

certain standards in me and every other English child by means of a putatively classless music that would aim us in the direction of art music before we were perverted by decadent popular music or, worse still, seduced
by the lure of jazz.

It is ironic, then, that at my first school, deep in North Midlands countryside, the village children were unself-consciously engaged in traditional round games which they sang as they encircled the lofty oak on the
village green—a suggestive ritual that came to an abrupt end when the
Air Ministry felled the tree to clear the path to a temporary wartime air-
field and thereby killed the spirit of the village in a scene indelibly etched
on my memory. If authentic tradition were the criterion, we had no need
of the universalized, essence-distilled tunes of Sharp and Company; we
had the "real thing."

It is also ironic that for me (and I think many others) indoctrination
into folksong and its accoutrements at an early age produced the opposite of Cecil Sharp's stated intention to "arouse that love of country and
pride of race the absence of which we now deplore" (*English Folk Song*,
136). I suffered a reaction against it (and many other forms of cultural patronization) as I grew older. My sole moment of unalloyed patriotism occurred listening to Olivier deliver Shakespeare's speeches accompanied
by cosmopolitan Walton's music in the postwar film of *Henry V.* My bol-
shie attitude on the one hand put a barrier between me and the music of
the "pastoral" composers, and on the other made me unreceptive to the
movement in the United States that connected folksong to political concerns with which I identified in the 1960s.

Vaughan Williams's music still alas triggers resistance. On the other
hand I have recently begun to experience the eloquence of the Woody
Guthrie tradition—and recognize the historical and artistic importance
of Bob Dylan and his legacy, evident in the impassioned delivery of Bruce
Springsteen as well as the elegant lyricism of Sting, to mention two dis-
similar as well as remarkable contemporary musicians among the many
who might acknowledge that influence. I suspect that Sting was rather
more susceptible than me to those British schoolroom influences: his lat-

est album, *Mercury Falling* (A&M Records, 1996), contains two folksong episodes (in "I Was Brought to My Senses" and "Valparaiso"), one of them unaccompanied, the other harmonized in "traditional" fashion; and the back cover of the accompanying booklet is an iconic representation of frozen-looking-singer-with-dog-and-stick-in-country-lane in the best pastoral manner. I realize that Sting might more likely have been influenced by the British 1950s folksong revival, which Niall MacKinnon writes about interestingly in *The British Folk Scene*. This likewise utterly passed me by—or, in its Morris-dancing manifestation, brought on the same faintly hysterical response as early-music-in-tights. (A Folger Consort appearance in San Francisco prompted an inspired correction of this attitude problem from another gay man: "Why would *anyone* want to deny *these* girls their drag?")

It is important to ponder as wide a context as possible before taking a look at any single composer's attachment to or use of folk material in order to counter a modern tendency to view the entire phenomenon as noxious. In a book bent on "deconstructing" the so-called English Musical Renaissance but ultimately reinscribing it with a different cast(e) of hero-composers, Robert Stradling and Meirion Hughes write as though the use of folksong is always already tainted by "folklore's undercurrents of fascism" and on that basis affix such labels as "this 'national front'" to their composer-villains (146, 163). But from the Anglo-American context briefly sketched out here, and without even invoking the decidedly anti-Nazi if not completely invulnerable figure of Bartók, the musical material can support several, possibly opposing, ideologies; and the motives of the English "pastoral school" are not so very different from those of other twentieth-century composers, like Bartók, who accepted the task of constructing national identity through music at a time of increased ethnocentricity. Moreover, in a significant gesture just before he died, Vaughan Williams showed his willingness to abandon the purely conservative and prescriptive ideals of earlier days, throwing his support behind the 1950s revival by editing *The Penguin Book of English Folk Songs* (1959) together with one of its leaders, A. L. Lloyd: their preface "acknowledges . . . a curious but welcome phenomenon, this revival of folk music as a city music," and in a further gesture the composer limits himself to a couple of modest specimen accompaniments, presenting the majority of the songs without any adornment at all.

Benjamin Britten's being content to follow the pastoral composers in arranging folksongs while disapproving of their whole aesthetic is also disruptive of any single view of an ideology of folksong in British art-music circles. It is instructive to see how Britten critics have dealt with this phenomenon. Donald Mitchell, celebrating Britten's "Englishry" in the canonizing collection *Benjamin Britten: A Commentary on His Work from a Group of Specialists*, consigns the folksong arrangements to the "very many purely *external* signs of Britten's immersion in the English musical scene," and goes on to put as many miles as possible between Britten and the pastoral school by pointing out that, since the second volume is devoted to French songs, "even in this sphere Britten has to remind us of his European outlook." Furthermore, "it would . . . be a mistake to imply that Britten has been much influenced by folk song . . . since he is far too complex a figure for so simple a musical constituent to be a determinant of his style" (47–48). Later critics are not so generous with their attention to the issue. Peter Evans's magisterial *The Music of Benjamin Britten* dismisses both folksong and Purcell arrangements ("this book examines only the composer's original compositions," 558); and in *The Britten Companion* Graham Johnson gives only a paragraph (admittedly a very good one) to the folksongs, whereas the Purcell arrangements get their own chapter (304).[1] Arnold Whittall, in his essays "The Signs of Genre: Britten and the Pastoral" and "Along the Knife-Edge: The Topic of Transcendence in Britten's Musical Aesthetic," has begun recently to explore the issues involved through the lens of genre, and this is among the most interesting work on Britten at present.

Britten had a good deal to say himself on the topic in "England and the Folk-Art Problem," written for *Modern Music* during the American period. In this article, Parry and Elgar are projected as the binary opposition haunting English composition, the one having "stressed the amateur idea and . . . encouraged folk-art," the other emphasizing "the importance of technical efficiency and [welcoming] any foreign influences that can be profitably assimilated." Studiously avoiding any mention of Holst and Vaughan Williams, Britten names Walton, Lambert, Maconchy, Berkeley, Darnton, Lutyens, Rawsthorne and (with reservations) Ferguson and Rubbra as indicating that "since 1930 the influence of Parry has largely disappeared" (71). This is presumably a direct riposte to Vaughan Williams's famous statement about composers "who thought that their own country was not good enough for them and went off in the early stages to become little Germans or little Frenchmen" and whose names (as a result) "are unknown even to their fellow countrymen" (19).

Later in the article Britten reveals his current fascination with "the nearest approach to folk-music today" which he deems to be swing and the spiritual, the former coming from "jazz, rag-time, Victorian popular song back to the lighter Italian operas . . . and Johann Strauss, to be colored by the luscious harmonies of Debussy, Franck and Delius," the latter having "some of its roots obviously in Methodist hymns." The point of this is to throw the authenticity of folksong of any kind into question, so that "what we call folk-music is no product of a primitive society" and that the "whole conception of folk-song as a germ from which organized music grew may prove to be a false one" (73). The dependence on folksong as raw material is either unsatisfactory (as in *Sacre du Printemps*—Stravinsky gets better marks for its handling in *Les Noces*, and Bartók goes unmentioned), or the sign of a need for discipline which second-rate composers cannot find in themselves. Lurking behind much of the thought is W. H. Auden, a passage from whose momentous "New Year Letter" (1940)[2] is quoted on the last page as an indication to composers to "accept their loneliness and refuse all refuges, whether of tribal nationalism or airtight intellectual systems" (75).

Britten's few words about actual English folk tunes in this article are significant:

The chief attractions of English folksongs are the sweetness of the melodies, the close connection between words and music, and the quiet, uneventful charm of the atmosphere. This uneventfulness however is part of the weakness of the tunes, which seldom have any striking rhythms or memorable melodic features. Like much of the English countryside, they creep into the affections rather than take them by storm. (72)

In this account of "quiet, uneventful charm" juxtaposed with "weakness" we can identify the same ambivalent attitude to Englishness that Whittall locates in a Britten letter to Elisabeth Mayer (4 May 1942), in which "the country is *unbelievably* beautiful," but "the accent is horrible, and there is a provincialism & lack of vitality that makes one yearn for the other side" ("Signs," 364). It is an ambivalence that was about to be writ large in the person of Peter Grimes (progress on the libretto of which is enthusiastically reported in the same letter), and one that allowed (or possibly compelled) Britten to set and publish a really remarkable number of folk or traditional songs from the British Isles, as well as France, to which (thanks to Philip Reed and others at the Britten-Pears Library) can now be added many more left in manuscript.

Ultimately, then, Britten benefited as much as any composer from the Sharp syndrome and made sure that he had a stake in folksong while emphasizing his independence of the "pastoral school" by what means were available, largely the very different accompaniments he devised. There was, however, nothing very radical in principle about his approach, as the intelligent Graham Johnson points out:

The pathos and intensity of the greatest of the old unaccompanied folksingers is not easy for singers of our own age to recapture, cut off as they inevitably have been from hearing this music in its original context. . . . At least Britten removed these songs from the schoolroom where they have long been turgidly accompanied . . . and where folksong has sadly become associated with compulsory music-making. The fact is that Britten's folksong arrangements are not folksongs at all and have to be appreciated (or not, as the case may be) on their own terms. (304)

The performance problem so cogently discerned by Johnson affects the entire history of folksong-as-art-song. The composers of European art music, trained to think of music as text and technique as something demonstrable on paper, are often incapable of realizing the lack of any distinction, in the rural forms of folksong Sharp and Company were looking to find, between "text" and "performance." I am not trying to reinscribe an essence or authenticity that folk-music scholars like Philip Bohlman have exploded; rather I am pointing to a certain lack of awareness on the part of Cecil Sharp of the issues at stake in translating artistic experience from one medium to another, and from one social sphere and performance space to another. This comes out in the fundamental disagreement between him and Percy Grainger, whose very different methods and principles were outlined in an article entitled "Collecting with the Phonograph." As Sharp wrote in a letter of response to Grainger about that time,

> in transcribing a song, our aim should be to record its artistic effect, not necessarily the means by which that effect was produced [. . .] it is not an exact, scientifically accurate memorandum that is wanted, so much as a faithful artistic record of what is actually heard by the ordinary auditor.[3]

David Josephson has trenchantly argued Grainger's case in this controversy, largely on grounds of his increased class consciousness. But even if we take Sharp's part and endorse the "ordinary auditor" over and above Grainger's Platonic machine-aided attempt to represent the actual enunciation of the singer (an attempt which though more scholarly must also be only a partial representation, as Grainger was well aware), there is a further level of prescriptive idealization waiting for us in the form in which Sharp presents his songs outside the relatively austere pages of the *Journal of the Folk-Song Society.* In the preface to a collection entitled *One Hundred English Folksongs*, Sharp writes:

> If we frankly decorate our folk-tunes with the fashionable harmonies of the day, we may make very beautiful and attractive music . . . but we shall effectually rob them of their most characteristic folk-qualities, and thereby convert them into art-songs indistinguishable from the "composed" songs of the day. (xv–xvi)

Once again the idealized, indefinable artistic quality of the folksong (of *all* folksongs, one is led to imagine), a topic which also recurs a good deal in Vaughan Williams's *National Music*, is what is worth preserving. Sharp, bent on "fostering the growth and development of those things, like good music, [that] exercise a purifying and regenerative effect" (*English Folk Song*, 140) never understood, it seems, that any removal of folksongs from their context in performance "converts" folksongs into something "indistinguishable" from whatever constitutes the new context. Folksongs in a piece like *The Lark Ascending* become simply the melodic material of a Western high-art genre known as the "tone poem." They may be different in style from the tone poems of, say, Mendelssohn or Smetana, and their rhetoric may point in new directions, or contain subversive elements, but folksong and modal harmony are not enough to change the genre.

Sharp's failure to grasp all this becomes clearer by comparing his prescription with his product. He writes:

> Surely, it would be wiser to limit ourselves in our accompaniments to those harmonies which are as independent of "period" as the tunes themselves . . . and further, seeing that the genuine folk-air never modulates, never wavers from its allegiance to one fixed tonal centre, to avoid modulation, or use it very sparingly. Personally, I have found that it is only by rigidly adhering to these two rules—if I may so call them—that I have been able to preserve the emotional impression which the songs made upon me when sung by the folksingers themselves. (preface, xvi)

"Little Sir Hugh," the song to which I turned at random (Scout's honor!) in the limited time I had to spend with a copy of this anthology, is Schubertian or Gounod-like but for a few diatonic dissonance's characteristic of academic English counterpoint of the kind familiar from Royal College of Organist paperwork examinations (*One Hundred English Folk Songs*, 22–23). It could only be thought of as "independent of 'period'" by someone to whom the central German tradition was completely naturalized. In response to the horrifyingly anti-Semitic story of the little English aristocrat ensnared and murdered by a Jewess (it is the Hugh of Lincoln referred to at the end of "The Prioress's Tale" in Chaucer's *Canterbury Tales*), Sharp apparently hears only "merry Lincoln" where "all the boys come out to play . . . and toss their ball": the sexual suggestiveness and ethnic bigotry are completely ignored by his accompaniment. One is left wondering exactly what "emotional impression" was made on him by the folksinger from whom he collected this song, and exactly how and why he thought it might have a "purifying and regenerative influence" on others.

This might seem an odd point at which to turn to Britten's folksong arrangements. But it happens that "Little Sir William," the second song of his first published collection, is a not-too-distant cousin of "Little Sir Hugh" (Bronson, 3:76, 85). The tune, with its fine melodic curve downward from an initial high note and an anacrustic rhythm leading to repeated notes in the second phrase, is rather better than Sharp's—or at least more effective as art song. There is no sexual suggestion, and the murderess is the Jew's wife, not his daughter; but complete ideas and verbal phrases are shared between the songs. Britten's accompaniment adopts a broad narrative march-like style for the first few stanzas and then proceeds, after an almost Waltonian chord built of thirds has disrupted the mood, to portray the dead child's voice by expressive chords, one to a bar, and by creating in the accompaniment a pathetic echo of the anacrustic repeated-note motive: the song, like many in these collections, is dramatized.

A recent letter to *Musical Times* from representatives of the Britten Estate and the Britten-Pears Library suggests that when Britten "came to realize that the text, historical or not, perpetuated an ugly racist myth, he had the text amended . . . ["School wife" was substituted for "Jew's wife"] and he instructed his publishers to correct the printed edition accordingly." This had not happened when I bought my copy in the late 1950s, but in a recording of 4 January 1944, Pears sings the amended text. Interestingly, the setting is dedicated to William Mayer, the Jewish refugee with whose family Britten and Pears stayed for so long on Long Island. Humphrey Carpenter might see this weird dedication as one of Britten's unconscious expressions of aggression against his own father transferred to the psychiatrist husband of his Long Island benefactress, and in this case I would be tempted to agree with him. Silent modern bowdlerization, too, can often cause as much pain as authentic historical bigotry: the incongruous "School wife" will quickly alert the sensitive reader. But his self-conscious and surely repentant gesture sets Britten apart from Sharp no less than the unrepentant decision to become involved in the text.

It was obviously necessary for Britten, if he were to use folksongs, to find ways of distinguishing himself from all others. Already in a much-quoted diary entry of 3 March 1933, he had referred to "two brilliant folksong arrangements of Percy Grainger [. . .] knocking all the V. Williams and R. O. Morris arrangements into a cocked-hat" (Mitchell and Reed, 347). Identifying with the outsider Grainger was less important, musically speaking, than resisting Vaughan Williams, of course, and compared with wonderful Percy's zippy "wogglings," a good selection of which can be heard on a recent, highly successful Phillips CD (446 657-2) featuring the Monteverdi Choir and Orchestra under John Eliot Gardiner, Britten's is typically spare, economical and "cool" (in the colloquial as well as dictionary sense). The comparison lends support to Whittall's emphasis on a "classical" orientation that isn't simply "neo" ("Signs," 372). This is not incompatible, after all, with the kind of psychological "tracking" of the text that occurs in famous and much-discussed exemplars like "The Ash-Grove." In any case such songs take their place beside purely strophic settings that either simply emphasize the mood (e.g., the lullaby "O can ye sew cushions") or, following Schubert, add to this one distinctive moment that focuses the attention—everyone who has heard "Down by the Salley Gardens" will remember the E-flat–D-flat appoggiatura over a dominant ninth outline in the accompaniment (significantly the only time the repeated right-hand thirds move down by step) that packs so much regret and nostalgia into the word "foolish" of this splendid *carpe diem* song. The arrangement dedicated to Bobby Rothman, "The Trees Grow So High," starting out monophonically and adding a single contrapuntal voice in each stanza until the fifth, where a chordal accompaniment symbolizes the poor boy's arrested development from marriage, fatherhood, to death, prefigures the treatment of the "Dirge" in the *Serenade*, Op. 31, where the melody, far from folk-like, nevertheless obeys strophic decorum and is similarly the constant element in a musical discourse that grows and then decays.

It is natural enough to dwell on the first volume, *British Isles* (published in 1943 and representing arrangements from the American period), which sets parameters for the subsequent settings. It could be argued that by vol. 5 (1961), representing additional settings from the 1950s, the formula is threatening to tire on the composer as well as the listener. But listening to the ten settings from Moore's *Irish Melodies* of 1957 and 1958 (vol. 4, published 1960), makes one wish these had been more frequently played and performed: they make perhaps the most coherent and consistent set of all. Britten is clearly at home in the classic world of French chanson as represented in vol. 2 (1946): "Voici le printemps" or "La belle est au jardin d'amour" could be *hommages* to Fauré and the spirited "Fileuse" with its spinning figures brings the idiom up to date. There is something of a revival of interest in the last two volumes, because of the change of accompanimental medium, guitar and harp respectively. On the one hand the idiom becomes more rarefied and intriguing (as in the positively desiccated setting of "I Will Give My Love an Apple"—further revenge on Vaughan Williams, who collected it?) or more "genuinely" folk-like, as in the "Bird Scarer's Song."

The fifty-one arrangements preserved in these published collections are augmented in the Collins CD set by a further thirteen settings from various sources and dates (culminating in the ambitious but incomplete cantata, *The Bitter Withy*, intended for the London Boy Singers for whom two other settings were completed). This 3-disc collection fills itself out with orchestral versions of several of the published songs made for various occasions. Unfortunately, even this attempt at a "complete" edition omits without explanation four simple arrangements (of "Love Henry," "What's Little Babies Made Of?" "The Maid Freed from the Gallows" and "The Frog and the Mouse") that prefaced a 1968 folksong publication (Karpeles, 11–14). Another slightly irritating feature of this Aldeburgh-sponsored recording is the ubiquitous copyright notices. Can words captured from the mouths of country folksingers and published by London toffs in the first decade of this century really only be "reproduced by permission of the Britten Estate Limited"? If so, the law is an ass, and the Britten Estate, philanthropic to a fault, does itself a disservice to flaunt it. Legal constraints of some kind must also have infected the usually forthright Philip Reed's explanation of "I Wonder as I Wander" in the CD booklet as an "uncollected folk song" that (unknown to Britten) had been "collected" by John Jacob Niles and is therefore the property of G. Schirmer Inc. The words "uncollected" and "collected" are here presumably euphemisms for "collected" and "composed" respectively. Popular tradition has it that Mr. Niles passed off his own tune as one of the Appalachian folksongs he had collected. And his estate is now getting the benefit of his deceit? Shame on all concerned.

Given a choice between two rival recordings, it would be nice to be able to report that the Hyperion set makes up in youthful enthusiasm and musical qualities what it lacks in completeness. Alas, the very fact that this music is, as argued above, art song means that the more experienced the singer, the more satisfying detail will (and does) appear. One can point to a few instances where the Hyperion set is superior—in the guitar songs, for instance, Jamie McDougall and Craig Ogden take "I Will Give My Love an Apple" at a better tempo than Philip Langridge and Carlos Bonell, and the latter completely misses the gunshot effect of the guitar chords in "The Shooting of his Dear" from which Craig Ogden and Hyperion's close-up recording gain maximum effect. But the younger singers on the Hyperion set, all keen to let us know they have real voices, and oversinging as a result, are no match for experienced lieder singers like Felicity Lott and Philip Langridge, who have the added advantage of Graham Johnson's piano accompaniment on the Collins set—though even their interpretations are restrained (and fast) compared with those of Sophie Wyss, Pears and Britten in recordings made in the 1940s.[4] It was a mistake of the Hyperion producers to entrust all ten songs of the Irish set to Regina Nathan, who can't sustain them: Lott and Langridge sensibly share them as they do most of the other sets.

The attraction of the "pastoral school" to the music of late Tudor composers can be explained partially by the mere existence of the indefatigable editor, Edmund H. Fellowes, and partially by the apparently naturalized state of folksong in the virginalists' work, as well as by the actual music. Projecting the present onto the past, Vaughan Williams could write of "the great School of Tudor music . . . inheriting its energy and vitality from the unwritten and unrecorded art of its own countryside" (*National Music*, 92). Musically, Vaughan Williams ought to have been closer to the rhapsodic Eton composers and Taverner than to the virginalists, but once again folksong (as well as low-church attitudes to such Catholic music) was decisive. For Britten, therefore, the entire Tudor period was effectively ruled out of his official English antecedents: only Dowland the proto-Purcellian songwriter, as represented by Peter Pears's remarkable artistry, merited more than cursory mention. The choice of Purcell was both rational and literally in tune with Britten's own aesthetic program as a dramatic composer. Purcell was also arguably the first English composer to be completely comfortable with enjambed or non-end-stopped verse. His settings tend to announce their adherence to two traditions: a syntax and sense-oriented declamatory style; or to the older strophic style in which each phrase matched a single verse, whatever the syntax. (In *Job's Curse*, a notable example of the former, the final repeated tuneful section actually begins halfway through an iambic pentameter, something earlier composers would not have been able to con-template.) Britten had already shown himself attracted to Purcell's declamatory style in "Let the Florid Music Praise," the first song of the Auden cycle, *On This Island*, Op. 11, of 1937; and it is no surprise that, with the real predicament of recitals with Pears prompting folksong settings, Purcell realizations should follow.

The art of "realization," prominent up to the 1950s, suffered an eclipse at the hands of early-music puritanism, but, with theoretical ob-jections to it foundering on the same rock as the exclusive claim of com-posers' intentions, everyone can now relax and understand, even appre-ciate, it as part of the historical, social and aesthetic record. Constrained for the most part by Purcell's harmonic style (interpolated motives some-times take him beyond it), Britten can only explore modern piano sonori-ties and contrapuntal play as means to impregnate the songs with his per-sonality. A little of this goes a long way for all but the most ardent Aldeburghian. Seventeenth-century song as a whole works on the prin-ciple of impassioned delivery or lyrical impulse, neither of which needs much more than a firm bass and a few chords to support it. For all Gra-ham Johnson's incredible tact and understatement, Britten's contribution constantly vies for attention with Purcell's melodies or declamatory ges-tures. The bifocal effect inevitably becomes distracting and, for me and possibly many involved in the early music movement, often unbearably pretentious and precious. Not content with adding a gratuitously Schu-mannesque introduction to "How Blest Are Shepherds," for instance, the composer drizzles notes all over the repetition of the strains as if to sug-gest that the tune has the same effect on him as a lamppost on a dog. Needless to say, Britten is at his best when Purcell's music is at its strangest. His "Mad Bess" is endlessly suggestive (but so is the singing of the wonderful Sarah Walker), and the tiny cantata, *Saul and the Witch at Endor*, is simply inspired in his rendering. The wit of "Sound the Trum-pet" also surpasses other piano versions, including that of Tippett and Bergman. The Hyperion producers sensibly collected a large cast of good singers, and the different vocal colors as well as fine idiomatic vocal projection certainly help to hold one's attention. This is a valuable contribution to a sense of Britten's total musical activity, and a reminder of the time when early music performance was not dominated by historically based methods and ideals. But where one could perhaps enjoy a group of three of the songs amid a full-length recital, a two-CD set, containing forty items, many of them quite long, overwhelms one to such an extent that the "realization" process begins to seem more an act of appropriation or competition than homage, another Oedipal episode in the composer's complicated trajectory.

Three more realizations, dating from the Pears–Osian Ellis partnership of the 1970s, are of songs not by Purcell but his contemporaries (including a setting of Donne's *Hymn to God the Father* by Pelham Humfrey). They open another Hyperion record, made in association with the Britten Estate, that presents yet more music Britten decided not to publish. In a sense, it is a companion to the Unicorn-Kanchana disc (DKP[CD]9138) devoted to the Auden cabaret songs and various other bits of incidental music, for it not only duplicates one of those songs ("When You're Feeling Like Expressing Your Affection"), but adds other Auden settings and the three songs from the incidental music to Ronald Duncan's *The Way to the Tomb* (1945), for which Britten's "Boogie-Woogie" appears on the other record. The Auden settings look (and sometimes sound) like rejects from *On This Island*, but are good to have. Much of the rest of the record is devoted to the miscellaneous settings (of Blake, the Auden telephone song mentioned above, Beddoes, Peter Burra, an Arthur Waley translation from the Chinese, Louis MacNeice, Ronald Duncan's birthday poem for Erwin Stein and Goethe's "Um Mitternacht") gathered together in the recently published collection, *The Red Cockatoo and Other Songs* (1994).

The disc climaxes in a performance of the taxing *Holy Sonnets of John Donne*, whose Purcellian rhetoric is integrated into as painful an idiom as Britten ever managed to produce. This is a tall order for the single singer, Ian Bostridge, who only made his debut a couple of years ago. His singing is intelligent and, once he curtails a tendency to sing too much, gets the voice further forward and corrects a few awkward vowel sounds (words like "and" and "hath" come out as though their vowel were the same as that of the British rather than U.S. pronunciation of "aunt") he will undoubtedly be a serious contender in the prolific British tenor field. The best compliment I can pay is to say that his and Graham Johnson's *Donne Sonnets* stands up to comparison with the Pears-Britten 1945 performance on EMI Classics (CDC 7 54605 2): what one misses in the sheer intensity and comprehension of Pears's reading of the faster numbers (if only Bostridge could make "blacke" as palpable as Pears does at the opening of "Oh my blacke Soule!"), is more than made up for in the really moving account of the slower, quieter movements, "O might those sighes and teares" and "Since she whom I lov'd." The much better sound quality, as well as the artistry, make this a suitable second recording for anyone's library. The young voice captures the emotional intensity packed into these terrifying songs which overshadow most of the other pieces considered here.

Some of this music is undoubtedly of more historic than artistic significance, but it does help to reveal certain things about Britten, or at least to prompt thought about his position in English music. If one adds to the sixty-eight folksong arrangements the many folksongs and singing games, traditional or composed, in the operas, and the final *Suite on English Folk-Tunes*, and if one adds to that the forty-three realizations and the references to historic English music (e.g., in *Young Person's Guide, Gloriana* and elsewhere), it becomes clear that Britten had as great an investment in these two linked phenomena as any bona fide member of the "pastoral school." Furthermore, Britten's being asked to write the four sample folksong piano accompaniments for the Faber anthology compiled by Maud Karpeles, Cecil Sharp's co-researcher and successor, was surely an acknowledgment of his position as the leading English composer of the folksong movement since the death of Vaughan Williams, and therefore in some way to be accounted the latter's successor as leading national composer.

I think this was very cleverly staged by the composer—there is no reason why his talents as an opera composer could not be applied to his own professional life, after all. Once having distanced himself from Vaughan Williams and Co., both by the *Modern Music* manifesto (discreetly published abroad and not much remarked on since) but also by the very nature of his musical response to traditional musical material, he was nevertheless concerned to infiltrate and dominate their chosen fields of activity on his own terms. The sponsorship of the alternative Grainger and the reclamation of Holst through the incorporation of his daughter into the working household at Aldeburgh were only later touches to a plan that, looked at one way, seemed from the moment of return in 1942 to be matching the ideology of the "pastoral school" item by item. The invocation of the powerful British sea myth, again on the composer's own terms, in *Peter Grimes* and *Billy Budd*, and the substitution of Aldeburgh, Suffolk and East Anglia for Hereford, Gloucestershire and the West country, all seem to fit the pattern. "Finding one's place in society as a composer is not a straightforward job," wrote Britten in a speech, which, like *National Music*, was originally delivered to Americans, and which sounded remarkably like the earlier document in tone (*Aspen Award*, 14). Perhaps, as part of returning home, he had even consciously understood and applied to himself Vaughan Williams's passionate if politically incorrect comment on the indebtedness of an earlier generation (Walton, Bliss, Lambert and Hadley) to the folksong movement: "they may deny their birthright; but having once drunk deep of the living water no amount of Negroid emetics or 'Baroque' purgatives will enable them to expel it from their system" (*National Music*, 85). As has often been remarked, Britten certainly moderated his eclecticism during the very same period that the onset of folksong and Purcell arrangements occurred. Perhaps, then, he ultimately understood that, returning to his native country and exorcising certain fears in the cathartic score of *Grimes*, he also needed to fulfill his role in ways that were laid out by Vaughan Williams in a gracious review of the first volume of the folksong arrangements. The older composer, casting himself in the role of an "old fogey" welcomes the "divagations," either to right or to left, of the younger generation "so that in the end the straight line is kept intact" (Mitchell and Reed, 347). The line was kept indeed, arguably to run on through Maxwell Davies. Intact, perhaps, but not exactly straight.

NOTES

1. See Eric Roseberry, 356–66.

2. Britten, quoting from the MS, calls it "A Letter to Elizabeth Mayer," the title which (as Edward Mendelson has kindly informed me) Auden decided on in early November 1940 for its publication in the *Atlantic* in January–February 1941.

3. Letter of 23 May 1908, quoted in Bird, 114.

4. Available on EMI Classics (CMS 7 64727 2) together with excerpts from *Peter Grimes* and an abridged version of *The Rape of Lucretia* recorded in the 1940s.

CHAPTER TEN

Pacifism, Political Action, and Artistic Endeavor

Imagine the scene: a dignified Oxford college interior, setting for the Royal Musical Association's annual conference, somewhat daringly entitled that year "Music and Eros." We listened in polite if forced attentiveness as British éminences grises listed examples of the erotic in Berlioz or Wagner, and almost sighed with relief when a cultural studies scholar with a Manchester accent broached the topic of Mae West. Halfway through a morning session in which two young American women scholars had begun to unveil the meaning of some naughty sixteenth-century madrigals, the Oxonian chair, in a stentorian voice, declared his hand: "I think that, in the words of Maurice Bowra, one should avoid forcing interpretation onto unwilling objects. And now it is time for coffee."

As we filed out, my blood began to simmer and later to boil. At the conclusion of the morning session, I plucked up the courage to say what most of the U.S. scholars in the audience were too polite to articulate: "Why cut off discussion like that; why avoid *any* interpretation; why privilege the work of art over the listening subject, and why (in a conference

This essay was given as a talk at SUNY Fredonia, 30 April 2001. Its thoughtful discussion of centrally important issues warrants its inclusion here.

entitled 'Music and Eros') metaphorically sit on your hands and declare, 'No sex, please, we're British!'?" My antagonist, an expert of musical aesthetics, lost all his American and much of his British audience by opening his reply with the three words "We in Oxford." But he ended with a very significant statement in which he declared his continuing loyalty to the basic thesis of Hanslick's *Vom musikalisch-Schönen*.

Eduard Hanslick wrote his short treatise *On the Musically Beautiful* in 1854: this Oxford conference occurred in the early 1990s. Nothing could better indicate how music, or rather a certain kind of music that aestheticians denote when they employ this synecdoche, has been dominated for almost a century and a half by a theory derived from Kant, Hegel and some other German philosophers by a clever and polemical music critic still in his twenties. The core of this theory of Hanslick's, encapsulated in a preface to the 8th edition of 1891, is "that the beauty of a piece of music is specifically musical, i.e., is inherent in the tonal relationships without reference to an extraneous, extramusical content." "Music," Hanslick wrote in the final chapter, "consists of tonal sequences, tonal forms: these have no other content than themselves. They remind us of architecture and dancing, which likewise bring us beautiful relationships without content" (xxiii, 78).

You might want to know how Hanslick could discount the figurative content of music in a century celebrated for its invention of the tone poem and its intensification of the dramatic and psychological abilities of opera. He does so by dismissing the Aristotelian thesis of the imitation of nature by art as having been "flogged to death." "Art should not slavishly imitate nature," he goes on, "it has to transform it" (73). Whereas the other arts find a prototype in nature that is the basis of this transformation, according to Hanslick even the two realms of sound offered by nature on the one hand and the musical art of mankind on the other are separate, almost irreconcilable. "For music, there is no such thing as the beautiful in nature" (73), he firmly concludes, thus asserting the superiority of music over the other arts for the Age of Progress.

Other powerful forces worked in favor of this assertion. The early Ro-

mantic writer and critic E. T. A. Hoffmann had judged Beethoven's abstract instrumental music superior to his song cycle *An die ferne Geliebte*
("To the Distant Beloved") because the spirit of yearning at the heart of
Romanticism was enhanced by the absence of specificity: a generalized
and essentialized yearning is so much more powerful than desire fixed on
an object. Hanslick's ideas also were convenient to a European culture
busy imposing its ideas, values and political domination on the rest of the
world through imperialism. Music without content could assume universal and transcendent qualities for all mankind: it would indeed become
"absolute." The other arts were most of them quick to catch on to the degree that, toward the end of the nineteenth century, all art aspired to the
condition of music, in the well-known phrase.

Coded as feminine, art and musical works were placed on a pedestal,
giving them almost religious significance to counterpoise the age's increasing industrialization and materialism. Although a modernist reaction occurred against many aspects of Romanticism at the opening of the
twentieth century, artists and composers were not willing to forfeit the
attention that the autonomous state of art thrust upon them. Style had
to change, of course. In place of the mercurial genius, coattails and hair
a-flying, like Liszt, or clothed in enigmatic and androgynous satin bro-
cade, like Wagner, appeared the magisterial bank teller as embodied in
T. S. Eliot or the wizard-like craftsman image promulgated by Stravinsky. But except in a few exceptional areas, such as theater, the artistic content of art continued to predominate in the minds of both artists and critics. Interpretation, shying away from disclosing any real or practical
meaning in an art-for-art's sake climate, continued to focus on aesthetic
effect in spite of, or perhaps in answer to, the evils of the twentieth century. How else could Wagner's blatant anti-Semitism have gone only
half-remarked, even after the Holocaust?

In this climate, how was the artist, schooled in the autonomy of art, to
experience and show the effects of any of the twentieth century's cataclysmic events without being dismissed as a charlatan or traitor to art?
Some maintained a lofty stance, projecting a "humanity" every bit as ab-

stract as their art. (One of my modernist colleagues at Berkeley, the American composer Andrew Imbrie, would often defend the abstruse, dissonant and complicated nature of his music by referring to the complicated times in which we live without ever specifying how the one kind of complication might relate to the other.) Others became "committed" artists, usually on the Left (e.g., Soviet artists and composers), and were identified and devalued as such, unless they happened to be in fields, like theater, less affected by the doctrine of the autonomy of art. Still others made subtle negotiations that acknowledged the power of artistic autonomy but managed nevertheless to suggest ideas and attitudes to those who could decipher their messages. This guerrilla warfare of artists of all kinds against the ideology of modernism and autonomy is among the most interesting phenomena of the century to study.

The theme of the present conference is "A Culture of Peace," and I propose here to focus on efforts within the realm of art to further the aim of universal peace, and to do so in a specific context, that of twentieth-century Britain. In order to offer you what I know best, I will be trying to reveal for you the context which nurtured and made possible Benjamin Britten's extraordinary attempt to condemn war, promote reconciliation and further the case of universal peace in his momentous *War Requiem*, first performed in May 1962.

An important initial work in Britten's negotiation with the ideology of music is *Our Hunting Fathers* of 1936, his first major collaboration with the poet W. H. Auden outside the film studio. It upset a number of people at its first performance at the Norwich Triennial Festival in September, including critics like H. C. Colles of *The Times*, who treated it as "just a stage to get through." Perhaps the voice of the domineering master (Auden) ventriloquizes a little too insistently through his brilliant new pupil, yet it is arguably the first of Britten's major works to encapsulate a social or political issue (in this case the evils of fascism juxtaposed against those of the "ordinary" country pleasures of animal hunting) in a way calculated to challenge received opinion because of the unusual combination of high drama and biting irony in an up-to-date eclectic score brilliantly orchestrated—"a twenty-two-year-old's revolt against the stuffy and the sloppy," as Pears later put it (Mitchell and Keller, 63), but also more than that in its conviction and incisiveness. If this way of thinking about music and art were all that Auden gave Britten, it was ultimately the gift that turned him into a composer of lasting impact. When the composer spoke about this aspect of his work, moreover, he maintained a canny ability to have the traditional cake of autonomy and at the same time to eat away at it: "I don't believe you can express social or political or economic theories in music, but by coupling new music with certain well known musical phrases, I think it's possible to get over certain ideas."

Just how well Britten could get over those ideas may be indicated by an excerpt from the slightly later *Sinfonia da Requiem* of 1939–40, which Britten described as "combining my ideas on war & a memorial for Mum & Pop." This piece is a culmination of much of Britten's earlier symphonically conceived music; but it is also characteristic of the later music in combining personal and social concerns on an ambitious scale: it can have been no surprise that the Japanese government, who paid for it, rejected its being performed at the festival celebrating the 2,600th anniversary of their empire, and it is a sign of Britten's naïveté that he accepted the commission. Auden rescued him from the predicament, but not from the damage to his reputation among left-wing acquaintances at home. Significantly, though, Britten declared that "I am making it just as anti-war as possible." How does this manifest itself? The following example begins at the climax of the second movement, the scherzo, which Donald Mitchell has described as one of a series of "Dances of Death" in Britten's music of this time—another occurs in *Our Hunting Fathers*. Rather than being sustained and progressing to a further heroic apotheosis, as it would likely have done in a symphony of the nineteenth century, the music self-destructs through overassertive gestures of a hysterical kind which, becoming self-conscious of their very extremity, seem limply to collapse on to each other, like so many hollow men, and to die off in impotence.

The gesture, as so much else in this work, owes a good deal to the musical irony of one of Britten's heroes, Gustav Mahler, a composer then hated and reviled in Britain. The young composer fortunately worked his way through this influence toward a unique and unmistakable idiom based on the synthesis of a wider palette including many English elements he had earlier avoided in his search for a European voice and reputation. After writing *A Ballad of Heroes*, a work in honor of those who had fallen in the Spanish civil war, and one that offers glimpses of what the *War Requiem* would sound like, the young composer had emigrated to the United States with his life companion, Peter Pears, in 1939, just prior to the composition of the *Sinfonia*. There were many reasons for this, among them to get away from the war, and to follow their friends W. H. Auden and Christopher Isherwood, who had created a national stir by leaving earlier that year. It was in the States that many issues came to be resolved for Britten. He saw in the work of his friend Aaron Copland, for instance, the attempt to create an American sound in classical music, and how successful that could be. And in an epiphanic moment in—of all places—Escondido, California, he understood how to go back to begin that process in England by reading an essay by the novelist E. M. Forster on the poetry of George Crabbe beginning with the words, "To talk about Crabbe is to talk about England." In Crabbe's poem, *The Borough*, Britten found the material for his first major opera, and his first international success, the opera *Peter Grimes*. It is the story of an individual at odds with the society around him, and the theme of persecution it embodies is directly linked to pacifism in Britten's own statement about it. "A central feeling for us was that of the individual against the crowd. As conscientious objectors we were out of it. We couldn't say we suffered physically, but naturally we experienced tremendous tension" (Schafer, 116–17). *Peter Grimes*, a work that contains not one but two manhunts, and ends with the suicide of the title character as a result of internalized oppression, relates as much to Britten's outlaw status as a homosexual as it does to that of his conscientious objection. As we shall see, the two were inextricably intertwined, not only in him as an individual, but also in British culture, and for many specific reasons.

On their return, Britten and Pears immediately befriended a slightly older composer, one who not only shared their beliefs and their sexuality, but who did suffer for his pacifism. Michael Tippett, enjoined, like Britten, by the tribunal to undertake noncombatant duties, refused, and was given a prison sentence in Wormwood Scrubs. Britten was instrumental in getting Tippett to resuscitate his 1938 oratorio, *A Child of Our Time*, that is itself "widely recognized as a significant musical and extra-musical statement" (Gloag, 1). Britten helped Tippett to secure the first performance of 1944, in which Peter Pears was the tenor soloist. Tippett's inspiration for this work was the 1938 shooting of a German diplomat in Paris by a seventeen-year-old Jewish boy, Herschel Grynspan, in protest against the treatment of his parents and other Jews deported without notice back to Poland by the Gestapo. This event gave Goebbels the excuse he needed to unleash the pogrom, the so-called *Kristallnacht*. A rumor got out that Grynspan shot vom Rath as the result of a love affair between them that had gone sour. Tippett never mentions this, but, if he knew, as seems likely, it fits into the double pattern that I am proposing, as also does the fact that the work was conceived shortly after the breakup of Tippett's relationship with the painter Wilfred Franks, who had a great formative influence on him. The work is a forerunner of the *War Requiem*, if only in the influence of Wilfred Owen's poetry on Tippett's libretto, which he wrote himself, drawing on Jungian ideas in which he was immersed. But it adopts very different musical models, the passions of J. S. Bach, Berlioz's *L'enfance du Christ* and the English settings of Henry Purcell. As an example of Tippett's different musical approach to politics I consider two items, the first an aria on a tango-like bass that "had to express the frustrations of the ordinary man temporarily at odds with life," as Tippett puts it. "The sense of our time," he continues, "lies musically in the tango, not in any Purcellian turn of phrase" (Gloag, 40). The second is Tippett's idea of a contemporary version of Bach's interjected chorales: "Go Down, Moses" is one of five spirituals which the composer incorporated on what may now seem dubious grounds of universal musical significance masking an undoubtedly "liberal" and possibly patronizing attitude that has gone quite out of fashion but that was advanced thinking in 1938–44.

To return to Britten, his success after *Peter Grimes* and two following operas, as well as several other successful works, put him in a position in which the Arts Council could hardly avoid commissioning a major opera from him for the 1951 Festival of Britain. For this he finally invited the collaboration of E. M. Forster, the novelist who had been so important to his decision to return to England. Forster, author of a posthumously printed homosexual novel named *Maurice*, was in fact an "anti-heroic hero," as Isherwood put it, for the entire Auden group. And his anti-authoritarianism and belief in personal relations fired their imaginations and actions. Though not a pacifist, Forster had, after giving up writing novels after *A Passage to India*, written the biography of Goldsworthy Lowes Dickinson, or "Goldie" as he was known to his friends. A gentle, queer don of King's, Dickinson had been an influential cultural figure, and chief among the proponents of the League of Nations, ill-fated predecessor to the United Nations. Like Goldie, Forster saw the paradox of "making the bridge between speculation and art and that side of life and practical politics. For practical politics involves fighting, and the object of such a book as mine [Dickinson's *Modern Symposium*], as it was Plato's object long ago, is to raise the mind above the fighting attitude" (introduction, 8–9). Forster had gone further still. In a famous remark written at the opening of the European conflict in 1939, he had stated firmly: "I hate the idea of causes, and if I had to choose between betraying my country and betraying my friend, I hope I should have the guts to betray my country" ("What I Believe," 78). It is out of this personal and, we might add, homosexual, attitude that Isherwood's rationale for pacifism was born. In *Christopher and His Kind*, Isherwood supposes himself in charge of a button that can blow up the entire Nazi army. He reminds himself of his boyfriend Heinz, who was about to become an unwilling part of Hitler's war machine. "Once I have refused to press the button because of Heinz," Isherwood writes, "I can never press it. Because every man in that Army could be somebody's Heinz and I have no right to play favorites" (335–36).

It turns out that Britten was himself to have personal problems with authority during the early 1950s. In this era of conformism, the cold war and other factors caused authority to overstep its bounds. A key event was the defection to the U.S.S.R. of the British spies, Guy Burgess and Donald Maclean. The gentleman's agreement between the police and the leisured classes was as a result abrogated, and as part of the drive in 1953–54 that resulted in the landmark arrest of the Lord Montagu and some of his circle, Britten himself was reported to have been interviewed by Scotland Yard. Sometime during the same decade, and probably on account of their outspoken pacifist statements in the 1940s, he and Pears were declared "prohibited immigrants" by the U.S. immigration authority.

It is against this background that I would invite you to contemplate the Britten-Forster collaboration in bringing Herman Melville's story, *Billy Budd*, to the operatic stage. Forster at some level wanted to "rescue Vere from Melville," that is, from the excessive respect for authority and discipline he found in Melville's account of Vere. He also wanted to "make Billy, rather than Vere, the hero," and to suggest a very Forsterian kind of redemption-through-love, or at least eternal hope, through the image of the "white sail" which he saw as mitigating and limiting Melville's belief in Fate. But the Prelude-Epilogue frame in which the aging Vere recalls the action places the dramatic emphasis firmly on his moral choice and predicament, which is precisely that of choosing between loyalty to a fellow man and the authority of the state. In the penultimate moments of the Epilogue, Britten appears to dissolve and dispel the forces of both good and evil (the melody of Billy's lullaby, and the ominous brass motive associated with the evil Claggart) in a final, radiant B-flat chord. But that very epiphanic moment is undermined by the hefty drumbeat motive that underpins the trial and ultimately derives from the sea chase in Act II. The implication that underneath it all, so to speak, Vere is hopelessly contaminated by his role in killing men—as the leader in battle as well as the naval disciplinarian—is powerful on the social as well as personal level. The advance of *Billy Budd* in both dramatic and musical terms is nowhere so telling as in the culminating moment, which leaves the sad, lonely and self-deceiving old man, a failure in Forsterian terms, to whittle out the ages in an indeterminate and significantly unaccompanied vocal conclusion (example 10.1).

Example 10.1. *Billy Budd*, Epilogue

My story ends with Britten's television opera, *Owen Wingrave*, based on a Henry James ghost story. Broadcast simultaneously in Europe and America in May 1971, it is, at one level, a final testament on peace and pacifism. The hero, scion of a military family, determines not to embark on an army career. Disinherited as a result, he is goaded by his fiancée's taunt of cowardice into being locked into the haunted room of the family mansion, Paramore. On unlocking the door in remorse, she finds him dead. The opera places great condemnatory weight on the family, the power of which is maintained in the absence of serious male authority (a doddery old general represents its remains) by three women portrayed

Example 10.2. *Owen Wingrave*, conclusion

with unmitigated hostility in both music and television image as shoring up the patriarchy. Owen's determination to be true to himself in the face of the enemy—tradition and the family—leads to a classic "coming out" scene that Britten, schooled in an age of discretion, could never have contemplated for himself. James cannot resist the irony of Owen's embracing peace only to die, as he puts it "all the young soldier on the gained field," a point that Britten and his librettist Myfanwy Piper underscore—Owen's reaction to past military heroes, including his ancestors, is to want to "hang the lot." Similarly, Britten and James send Owen literally back into the closet at the end of the opera, and kill him off as well. At least he has meanwhile found "peace" (example 10.2). Musically this occurs in one of Britten's most celebrated arias not only accompanied by diatonic triads, always a sign of truth and goodness in his music, but also given an overlay of Balinese gamelan music, the kind that in Britten's earlier ballet, *Prince of the Pagodas*, signifies at best utopianism or nescience, at worst polymorphous perversity, not the dangerous erotic love that gamelan sounds evoke in Britten's setting of *The Turn of the Screw*.

This least known of Britten's operas is one that repays further study. For all the optimistic Forsterian declaration of Peace as Love that occupies this aria, other musical signs, and the ending, indicate a pessimistic view. Self-determination is a chimera, the opera seems to say, for there is always some ghost to disturb the perfect denouement. Just as the pacifist can fight militarism only in its own terms (and lose in those terms), so the problem of the homosexual is to escape the history of sexuality into a new life without replicating the old "straight" order, something understandably inconceivable to the closeted Britten.

And yet, reviewing Britten's work as a whole, including these examples and the *War Requiem*, something has surely been achieved, even in the admittedly limited framework of a national and "classical" music. In a recent book, John Champagne discerns the two critical responses to what he calls the Other, or the marginal. One, the liberal humanist response, grants the Other greater subjectivity by trying to remake it in the image of the dominant or center: this process has been at work in white responses to African American music, or in the male canon's tentative acceptance of women composers, for instance. The second valorizes or privileges the marginality of the Other, not by extending greater subjectivity to it, but by making a resistant and transgressive use of the very lack at the center which first caused the construction of the margin. These two processes are of course not separate but contingent on each other. I would like in my final remarks to argue for the effectiveness of Britten's own version of marginal politics. "All a poet can do is to warn" is the conclusion of the Wilfred Owen epigraph on the cover of the score of the *War Requiem.* But in order to warn, or do anything else, the poet/composer has to be heard. What North America may have taught Britten and Pears, then, was that to work for centrality at home would ultimately be more artistically and therefore politically effective than marginality abroad—as a means of articulating a message to society from that margin where Britten, at least, always imagined he lived, as countless tales of his depressions and darknesses attest. His old left friends like Auden were irritated to see him waltzing up and down church aisles on the arm of the Queen Mother; gay men like myself often have to work through a certain resentment at his exercise of privilege without disclosure; younger radicals presumably have no time for his compromised politics at all. But granted the isolated space of art music and the difficulty of any effective opposition along the lines indicated by Champagne's second option, especially in the pre-1967 conditions under which Britten lived and under which his social imagination was formed, one still needs to grant to Britten consistency and integrity in pursuing, sometimes to his friends' acute discomfort, a fairly incisive and certainly passionate line on the linked issues of pacifism and homosexuality in relation to subjectivity, nationality and the institutions of the capitalistic democracy under which he lived. This line he maintained in his work rather than his life, where he acted out a role of charm and compliance laced with occasional brutality. The political stance of the music is all the more remarkable because it really did overcome Hanslick's embargo in a way that barely exists anywhere else in art music outside avant-garde circles already too self-marginalized to offer any hope of serious intervention in the status quo. And, as a starting point, it certainly wins hands down over the tired and tiring credo of the many composers today who are openly gay but vow that homosexuality has absolutely nothing whatsoever to do with their music; or those composers—composers who just happen to be gay—who ask for homosexuality to be accepted as ordinary rather than seeing it as a site from which to disrupt present notions of subjectivity and from which to imagine different organizations of power and pleasure, as I believe Britten did.

Britten's artistic effort was an attempt to disrupt the center that it occupied with the marginality that it expressed. In this it was comparable to Forster's achievement which, though it did not specifically alleviate the persecution of his own kind, nevertheless contributed, in the novel *A Passage to India*, to the eventual downfall of the British Empire. "We are after all queer & left & conshies which is enough to put us, or make us put ourselves, outside the pale, apart from being artists as well," wrote Pears in response to a letter from Britten about "all those other dreary HRH's, you know" (Carpenter, *Britten*, 419–20). It was the achievement of the Britten era, then—and this achievement was in no way contradicted by Britten's contemporary Michael Tippett—that British classical or art music became during those years indelibly queer and left and conshie. And instead of being instantly marginalized, Britten's music has traveled all over the world. There is no need to argue that in the process of its inevitable assimilation it may have had some transformative effect; it is enough to note that, for anyone inclined to explore beyond its deceptively "conservative" and desperately inviting surface, it offers not only a rigorous critique of the past but also the vision of a differently organized reality for the future. It certainly invites us to contemplate a culture of Peace.

CHAPTER ELEVEN

Auden's Britten

At a recent symposium at the Huntington Library, the novelist Edmund White posed a question about Christopher Isherwood. What had enabled him, he asked, to write a novel with a homosexual central character who was neither pathologized nor sentimentalized at least a dozen years before anyone else would begin writing with comparable assumptions and ease? How could *A Single Man* have been written as early as 1964? This prompted me to a similar question about Benjamin Britten's opera *Peter Grimes* (for which, incidentally, Isherwood had been Britten's first choice of librettist). How could a work whose plot hinges on the internalized oppression of an allegorical figure inescapably signifying "the homosexual" have come to be written in 1945, twenty years before the liberation movements articulated the issue of internalized oppression and a quarter of a century before gay liberation began "consciousness-raising" to help lift lesbian and gay people out of their most damaging predicament?

White provided a threefold answer for Isherwood: his belonging to

This paper was given as the Distinguished Humanist Achievement Lecture at the Center for Ideas and Society, University of California, Riverside, on 18 January 2001. It is printed here for the first time.

the group of upper-middle-class British artists and intellectuals whom Samuel Hynes dubbed "the Auden generation"; his formative period in Berlin in the late 1920s; and his life in one of the liminal beach societies of the United States. He went on to talk about Berlin, the bars, the boys and about Dr. Magnus Hirschfeld, whose Institute of Sexology educated the embarrassed Isherwood in the lore of his tribe. In Britten's case, there was no equivalent to Berlin. He had a plan to go to Vienna. But he knuckled under when his parents scotched his studying there with Alban Berg, whom the authorities at the Royal College of Music had suggested was "not a good influence"—whether morally or musically is not clear, though English paranoia about Viennese expressionism would in any case have confused the two. Britten did visit around his twenty-first birthday, but typically with mother as chaperone and without meeting Berg. As for an equivalent to Isherwood's California beach life, Britten, after an abortive attempt to live in the United States, chose to dwell for the rest of his life on the stony shores of the North Sea in the very place, Aldeburgh, in which the eighteenth-century poet George Crabbe had set his grim story of Peter Grimes. I am left then with a single proposition. The emotional and intellectual development that enabled a modern allegory to be crafted out of Crabbe's poem is attributable in general to Britten's being a member of the Auden generation, and in particular to his being very close to Auden himself.

They met in the spring of 1935, shortly after the twenty-one-year-old Britten got his first job working under Albert Cavalcanti in John Grierson's documentary film unit, which operated then under the auspices of the General Post Office. They worked together first on a film called *Coal Face*, then on one about the West Indian slave trade. After a lull came their most famous collaboration, and the unit's most successful film. This was *Night Mail*, a documentary about the Railway Post Office that traveled from Euston station up to Glasgow each night. Most of the train sounds were not recorded at trackside, but, in the spirit of the unit's experimentalism, reproduced by Britten using compressed air, sandpaper on slate, miniature rails, studio booms and other found objects after a rainy night out by the tracks in Harrow observing the exact sounds the trains made. The composer even wrote out the score for this outlandish orchestra, closer to the world of Brian Eno than to that of Bach and Beethoven. The four-minute clip with which I began [the lecture, in 2001] is a coda to the film that answered to a need felt by Grierson to expand its meaning. The solution was Auden's verse set (in notated rhythms) to Britten's music. What I want to emphasize here is the meeting of these two minds under the auspices of social commentary moviemaking, a new form which, though Auden himself quickly condemned it for its compromised and upper-middle-class version of social realism, seemed to many to offer a new arena for political commitment on the part of artists.

"Auden is the most amazing man, a very brilliant & attractive personality" confided Britten to his diary the day after their first meeting in July 1935 (Carpenter, *Britten*, 66–67). He remained throughout their relation in awe of Auden as a "brain," allowing himself to be dominated and pushed around in ways that led with other people to an abrupt cutting off that became one of Britten's trademarks. Auden on his part quickly recognized Britten's talent and gave him the vacant post of musician in his "gang." In addition, Britten's almost painful youth and even more painful virginity evidently presented themselves as a challenge to the self-assured poet who had little compunction about interfering in the lives of his friends, and readily enlisted Isherwood's aid in what became a project to Bring Out Benjy.

Britten presents himself in his diaries and his letters as ingenuous, but this was part camouflage. People noticed things. When he met the couple Rupert Doone and Robert Medley, who ran the left-wing Group Theatre that produced the Auden-Isherwood plays, for instance, Medley noted that "over dinner and a bottle of inexpensive white wine Ben lost his reserve, and something of the complexity that lay behind the deceptively conventional persona was revealed" (Carpenter, *Britten*, 70). Britten had until now carried off the asexual British schoolboy role rather well, and for a definite purpose. It concealed the obscure wounds revealed in the stories, possibly fictional, of early sexual abuse from a schoolmaster and, even more surprisingly, of his puritanical father's liking for boys, told much later to his librettists Eric Crozier and Myfanwy Piper (19–25). But when he met Auden his undoubted desire for "his own kind" was beginning to break through the facade. Many of his new friends, including Auden, were openly queer, at least among themselves. Britten must have realized that the left-wing, pacifist, agnostic and queer model they offered him—a role whose construction in Britain dates from the First World War and perhaps earlier—provided a suitable identity-niche in which to lodge his particular set of personal concerns, though few of his friends believed that he was ever entirely comfortable with it. (I must explain that I am using the term "queer" historically, not in its 1990s sense, but as the term Britten would and Peter Pears did use, as when the latter wrote "we are after all queer & left & conshies.")

Earlier commentators on Britten invested in the public/private binary, especially Donald Mitchell his executor, but even Humphrey Carpenter, doyen of the let-it-all-hang-out school of biographers, have not wanted to see the connection between the personal and political awakening of Britten, and how the two worked together. Even Paul Kildea, a much younger critic, feels he has to declare that "to locate the themes [of the individual and the masses that occupy Britten's postwar dramatic music] solely within the confines of his homosexuality is to rob each work of its vibrant intellectual origins" (Cooke and Horn, 37). It seems that even today the motto that E. M. Forster, the unheroic hero of the Auden generation, fixed to his novel *Howards End* needs endlessly repeating: "only connect."

At the start of Britten's development, as in the case of so many others, the political stood in for, and was inextricably intertwined with, the personal: it would be a long time before Isherwood could take young Ben to the Jermyn Street Baths. The first thing the composer needed to do was to jettison the safety of Lowestoft, the family home to which he returned at the lightest excuse—even in London he began boarding with his straight sister Beth around this time. How he must have enjoyed, and been pained by, arguing with his widowed Mum over communism, and refusing to go to Communion with her. The ideas he gained from his smart new friends also worried the "Brits," that is, his composition

teacher Frank Bridge, his wife, and Marjorie Fass, the third member of
the odd ménage à trois surrounding the older composer in Felixstowe.

Britten's collaboration with Auden, meanwhile, progressed outside
the studio to a major musical project, an orchestral song cycle. Planning
took place early in 1936, with Auden choosing three older poems (of the
sort he had collected for his famous anthology *A Poet's Tongue*), and surrounding them with a Prologue and Epilogue of his own. Meanwhile the
personal friendship became more intimate: around March Auden wrote
and gave Britten the poem "Underneath the abject willow, / Lover, sulk
no more" with its call to action:

> Geese in flocks above you flying
>   Their direction know;
> Brooks beneath the thin ice flowing
>   To their oceans go;
> Coldest love will warm to action,
>   Walk then, come,
>   No longer numb,
> Into your satisfaction.

Britten set the poem toward the end of the year for two voices and
piano—"very light and Victorian in mood," as he said, evidently not
wishing to identify or be identified (Carpenter, *Britten*, 77).

Meanwhile serious work proceeded on the songs. *Our Hunting Fathers*
was designed as a large orchestral cycle in the manner of one of Britten's
main musical heroes, Gustav Mahler, whose ironic and subtle musical
fingerprints abound in the score. The social theme is human relations to
animals presented in a way that would both attack the fox-hunting set at
home and act as a parable for the worsening political situation abroad. In
the fourth movement, one of the several "Dance of Death" pieces that
Britten continued to write even when Auden's influence waned, the huge
list of hawks' names from a sixteenth-century poem is slowly weeded out
in Britten's setting until all that remains are "German," "Jew" and the
hawker's cry "Whurret!" Just as striking is the opening of the second

song (example 11.1). The acerbic, disjointed orchestral gestures, the almost hysterical vocal cadenza on the word "Rats," and the uncomfortable musical motive that follows, with percussion exploding everywhere like gunfire, locates the piece quickly enough in anti-fascist discourse. This harsh musical modernism came easily enough to the eclectically minded Britten, and he continued to draw on it, later imbued with atonal, serialist procedures, as a way of critiquing old Europe and its savage customs. In this way, Britten turned European musical modernism against itself.

"[Mum] disapproves thoroughly of 'Rats'—but that is almost an incentive," reads a diary entry during composition. The public reaction was stronger. As Donald Mitchell points out, "nothing quite like this music had been heard before in the UK of 1936" (*Britten and Auden*, 36). Largely unperformed after its broadcast in 1937, it was treated even by Britten himself as something of an embarrassment. Perhaps the voice of the domineering master ventriloquizes too insistently through his brilliant new pupil, yet it is arguably the first of Britten's major works to encapsulate a social or political issue. If this way of thinking about music and art were all that Auden gave Britten, it was ultimately the gift that turned him into a composer of lasting impact. When the composer spoke about this aspect of his work, moreover, he maintained a canny ability to have the traditional cake of autonomy and at the same time to eat away at it: "I don't believe you can express social or political or economic theories in music, but by coupling new music with certain well known musical phrases, I think it's possible to get over certain ideas," he said in connection with *Sinfonia da Requiem*, a slightly later work in the same vein of which, he declared, "'I am making it just as anti-war as possible" (Mitchell and Reed, 705).

I am tempted to dwell on this harsh-sounding, "political" side of Britten's work. Humphrey Carpenter has opened up a narrative of sublimated sadism as the fount for this and much else in Britten's music. I read it differently. It seems to me to stem from a release of that burning anger that builds up in queer adolescents toward all those in authority, even their parents, who rob them of the right to their own feelings. Isherwood

Example 11.1. *Our Hunting Fathers*, opening of "Rats"

Example 11.1. (*continued*)

would certainly have provided a model in this regard. And though in *Letters from Iceland* Auden wrote "To my friend Benjamin Britten, composer, I beg / That fortune send him soon a passionate affair," he would have been inclined to see Britten's problems whole. Interested in healing from early on, he had been much influenced by his friendship in Berlin in the late twenties with Richard Layard. Out of sources as diverse as W. H. Rivers, the psychologist who treated Wilfred Owen and Siegfried Sassoon at Craiglockhart, Blake, Freud, Jung, Lawrence, Groddeck and especially his psychoanalyst, the American Homer Lane, Auden developed a full-blown theory of the evil effects of repression and self-control. This suited Auden well because it allowed, nay commanded, him to act out the desires his religion named sinful, and authorized unconventional behavior. Following the Layard-Lane theory of the psychosomatic origin of all illness, Auden was only too ready for a patient like Britten, for whom ill health was seemingly the only defense against the punishing puritan work ethic instilled by his father and maintained by the composer all his life, along with a bath in cold water every morning.

On the last day of January 1937, Britten's mother died unexpectedly of influenza. Her darling son was both devastated and, at a level just beginning to find expression in his diary, relieved to be free from her controlling influence. An immediate result was an exploration of what he coyly termed "Life (with a capital S)" (Carpenter, *Britten*, 90). A month later, after a BBC Singers' rehearsal, he met a tenor whose name he wrote down as "Peter Piers." It would be some time before he corrected the spelling (never his strongest suit), and longer still before the two men entered on full partnership. A year later, however, they were sharing a London flat. Yet for some years the two maintained a mentor-student relation which precluded sexual intimacy. It was a fortunate match for Britten on account of his real need for protection. As the relation of two equal individuals, each with commensurable and connected talents that led to their spurring one another on, it defied the stereotypical model of cross-class (or -race, or -generation) desire that neither Auden nor Isherwood's life partnerships managed to avoid, a model that linked the cultural form of queer male relations in Britain to its class system, its school system, or its imperial ambitions, or all three.

In 1937 and for some time after, Britten was still trying out potential liaisons of a slightly different kind, for instance with the composer Lennox Berkeley and more characteristically with Wulff, the eighteen-year-old son of the conductor Hermann Scherchen, who underwent inspection by both Auden and Pears. With the younger schoolboy, Piers Dunkerley, Britten continued a mentoring relation suffused with constantly sublimated desire; this was to be a pattern throughout his life.

At this time something slightly different emerged in his music. When Wulff spent his first weekend at the Old Mill at Snape, a house Britten bought with his inheritance, the composer was working on the piano concerto which he himself premiered as soloist at the Henry Wood Promenade Concerts in August 1938. Taking Poulenc rather than Shostakovich as a model, it shocked the critics with its ebullient, almost campy first movement and with what Peter Evans calls the "irritatingly smart vulgarity of the final march" (47). Auden merely asked, "And what about its effect on a certain person of importance?" (121).

A year later Britten was sailing with Peter Pears for the United States. There were many reasons for him to leave England and try his hand abroad: the growing cloud of fascism over Europe; the plight of pacifists in the war that seemed inevitable; the influential departure of Auden and Isherwood to New York in January 1939; the frantic pace of his career and the need to determine his own direction; discouragement owing to patronizing or hostile reviews (Britten was the thinnest of the thin-skinned); the opening up of opportunities through his new friendship with Aaron Copland; and the curtailing of the personal situations from which Britten already appears (from his letters) to be trying to escape—from Lennox Berkeley, especially, but also from Wulff Scherchen, and perhaps others. At any rate, the way was now clear for a commitment to Peter Pears, and the consummation took place early in the visit—in Grand Rapids, Michigan, according to Pears. After a trip to New York, the two visited Copland at Woodstock, where they stayed for part of the summer. From there they went to Amityville on Long Island to visit Pears's friend Elisabeth Mayer, a German refugee with literary and artistic interests, who ended up not only accommodating them for more or less the rest of their visit (until 1942) but also providing a surrogate mother for Ben and, as it happens, for Auden as well.

The music Britten wrote during the American years reflects the emotional turmoil that engulfed him, and contains several triumphs, like the magnificent *Sinfonia da Requiem*, in memory of his parents. But *the* key work of this period is *Les Illuminations*, Op. 18. Completed in the October after arrival, it is the first substantial work to explore a more complicated erotic vision. Rimbaud's poems, to which Auden had introduced Britten, focus upon the inevitably confused and divided subject who "alone holds the key to this savage parade"—and Britten matches this image by presenting a typically double focus on the major triads of B-flat and E which not only sustains ambiguity over long musical stretches but also (as in the opening fanfare, example 11.2) simultaneously suggests exhilaration as well as confusion. Whatever one makes of the dedication of "Antique" to Wulff and "Being Beauteous" to Peter or of the direct sexual imagery with which the latter ends, never mind the cruising depicted in "Parade," it is hard to avoid the conclusion that the piece as a whole encapsulates a certain hard-won victory—like many similar gay triumphs, cast in a foreign language or executed on a foreign journey (in this case both)—over the distancing effect from the purely corporeal (reflected in both the athletic glorification of and mundane alienation from the body) to which British middle-class education of the period was dedicated. It joyously and unashamedly reclaims music as an immediate, physical act. Who could have imagined that a decade of technical struggle away from English amateurism and toward eclectic professionalism would lead to the moment when, after the transfigured exclamation "et je danse" on a top B-flat that concludes the exquisite "Phrase," the string orchestra turns into a giant guitar to accompany a deliriously diatonic melody supported by root position major chords? Copland was shocked—he was surely the "older American composer" who said of "Antique" that "he did not know how Britten dared to write the melody"; and even Peter Pears labeled this incandescent work "a trifle too pat" (Mitchell and Keller, 65–66). For the truth is, no one quite trusts erotic joy when they hear it (at least, when it is unclouded by Wagnerian chromaticism), and musical solutions of personal problems are equally suspect. It is for reasons like this that one can see the Britten of this period castigated by his friends and enemies alike for being too "clever," why even Copland "picked certain things in Ben to pieces," as the Canadian composer Colin McPhee put it, adding that "he must search deeper for

Example 11.2. Conclusion of "Phrase" and beginning of "Antique" from *Les Illuminations*

a more personal, more *interesting* idiom . . . in the order of today good craftsmanship is not enough" (Mitchell and Reed, 907–8). How threatening a figure he had become, this intense musician who still looked and spoke like a schoolboy, earnest and mischievous by turns.

The central Auden collaboration of the American period, the operetta *Paul Bunyan*, is also one of the most problematic, a patronizing attempt to evoke the myth and spirit of a nation not his own by W. H. Auden in which Britten was a somewhat dazzled accomplice—he was quite vague about the exact nature of the title role's manifestation and staging only six months before it opened. It was meant to be a Broadway musical, and ended up more like a socio-political oratorio. Listen to the Western Union boy's song. It is all stop and start in a Copland manner, but with a jaunty melodic quality that also betrays Britten and Auden's lifelong devotion to Cole Porter. The addressee is Johnny Inkslinger, the surprised intellectual of Bunyan's logging operation, who (like Isherwood) is to be a Hollywood movie consultant.

With encouragement Britten might have joined Bernstein and Sondheim in transforming musical theater; but a really sneering review from "old stinker Virgil Thompson," as Britten called him, and poor notices from the other New York critics were enough to close that avenue. The work was withdrawn and only revised after Auden's death. From that time must stem the cooling of the Auden friendship, something Pears seems to have encouraged. Exchanging the orderly Mayer household for Auden's louche and alcoholic lifestyle in a Brooklyn Heights villa owned by George Davis (and occupied by people as various as Carson McCullers and Gypsy Rose Lee) did not help. From this bohemian atmosphere, "sordid beyond belief," as Pears put it, the two lovers fled as soon as they could after the production of *Bunyan* at Columbia University in May 1941. They took up an invitation to stay in Escondido, where they came across the radio talk by E. M. Forster that began with the words "To talk about Crabbe is to talk about England" ("George Crabbe"). Dissatisfaction with all manner of things about American life had already surfaced in Britten's letters, and he had succumbed to an illness that Auden had diagnosed as the result of his indecision whether to stay or go back home. Reading Forster was the catalyst for the decision not only to write an opera out of Crabbe's *The Borough*, but also to return home where he had roots.

The flight to North America, for all its apparent failure, had enabled Britten to find out more about himself in general, to mature as an artist and person, to establish a lifelong partnership, and to find a certain level of acceptance among others and more importantly in himself about his sexual orientation (though many people recall signs of his continuing shame about it). He returned with a much firmer sense of his potential to become the leading English composer of his time, not a post to be turned down lightly for the anonymity and nonassimilation that Auden, who had been too much lionized in 1930s Britain, sought abroad. After a lunch with William Walton, Britten had jokingly referred to the latter as the Head Prefect of English music, with Williams (as he called Ralph Vaughan Williams) the Headmaster and Elgar a member of the Board of Governors. During his American stay he wrote (or did Auden write for him?) an article entitled "England and the Folk-Art Problem" that makes abundantly clear his relation to the tradition, and his opposition to English folk-based pastoralism, which Auden must have encouraged. The article ends with a quotation from Auden's then unpublished New Year Letter of 1940. On returning to England, as I have argued elsewhere, Britten followed a program calculated step by step to provide an alternative to each of the genres and institutions with which Vaughan Williams was associated—setting Britten's relations to folk music, the English historic musical tradition, and to choral music on entirely different footings. To this he added two unassailable trump cards: an international success in grand opera, the very first by an English composer; and a brilliant audience-creating endeavor—what we call today "outreach"—in school and amateur music. In 1956, when the small North Midlands grammar school I attended celebrated its millecentenary, Ben and Peter themselves came to perform Britten's cantata *Saint Nicolas*, with our school strings and chorus stiffened with a few professionals. Like countless others all over Britain, I was hooked, in my case from the very second chord.

But Britten did not escape America and Auden without a farewell and bruising lesson about "the dangers that beset you as a man and an artist." The letter that came close to the departure in 1942 began with a standard Auden lecture on the balance between Bohemianism which leads to "a mad jumble of beautiful scraps" and Bourgeois Convention, "which alone ends in large unfeeling corpses." Britten's bias was toward Bourgeois Conventions and technical skill. "Your attraction to thin-as-a-board-juveniles, i.e. to the sexless and innocent, is a symptom of this. And . . . your denial and evasion of the demands of disorder is responsible for your attacks of ill-health—sickness is your substitution for Bohemianism." Then Auden went even closer to the bone: "You see, Benjy dear, you are always tempted . . . to build yourself a warm nest of love (of course when you get it, you find it a little stifling) by playing the lovable talented little boy." And finally: "If you are really to develop to your full stature, you will have, I think, to suffer, and make others suffer . . . you will have to be able to say what you never yet have had the right to say—God, I'm a shit. . . . All my love to you both, and God bless you. Wystan" (Mitchell and Reed, 1015–16).

This remarkable document has been exhausted of all significance by Britten critics since it surfaced in 1981. Humphrey Carpenter uses it to interpret all the operas, and many other things besides. At one level, Britten took it absolutely literally. He behaved like a shit not only to Auden, whom he increasingly avoided meeting, but also to countless others who gave him their lives and souls only to be dropped unceremoniously when used up. Very few escaped this treatment. But, quite apart from the fact that in 1942 Britten was escaping from the most smothering part of that "warm nest of love"—Auden's own domination—I would also argue that the Bohemian/Bourgeois opposition can be seen more usefully as a projection of Auden's own problems onto his friend rather than a meaningful diagnosis of Britten the artist.

"I am getting to such a condition that I am lost without some children (of either sex) near me," confided Britten to his diary as early as April 1936 (Carpenter, *Britten*, 403). So it was to prove throughout his life. How easily he could enter into children's worlds as well as some of the precipitous moments in his encounters with young boys are outlined in some detail by Carpenter (341–54, et passim). It seems that the composer

was captured at many levels by the notion of return to a perfect state sym-
bolized by childhood—Britten commentators always call it "innocence,"
but it is more usefully thought of either as the Lacanian imaginary, or as
"nescience" in the words of Thomas Hardy's poem "A Time There Was"
set as the climactic final song in Britten's Hardy cycle, *Winter Words*, Op.
52. The entry into language and the patriarchal order make this state impossible to recapture, and much of Britten's music is about the difficulty
and pain of separation from it, but it arguably remains the principal fount
of nonverbal inspiration. Lack produces desire (in the already lost adult),
and the sexual element that occasionally obtrudes (and can never satisfy
or be satisfied) is a symptom of that lack. What Britten discovered—possibly aided by his constant invocation of presymbolic elements such as
the mother's voice (many noted that Peter's voice resembled Edith Britten's very strongly)—was a way of accessing powerful messages from beyond the preverbal barrier, even perhaps occasionally of breaking that
barrier, at a time when musical modernism was setting up barbed wire
fences everywhere and driving "art" music increasingly into the cold unfeeling camps of masculine intellect and order. So Britten's case was
surely the opposite of Auden's point: that this nostalgia produced an excess of desire, and that the social difficulty of that desire, coupled with
the moral difficulty over the question of power, produced in Britten the
passionate conviction and sense of justice required to examine and undermine every aspect of the law of the father that forbade it. Technique,
then, would always be balanced by the imperative of directness, of sim-
plicity, of the succinct. That is how I see what Hans Keller ages ago called
"the enormous creative advantage of Britten's homosexuality" (introduction, xxvi). It worked to produce a classically poised music of passion
that is the best antidote in the twentieth century to expressionist excess
or self-conscious neoclassicism. "The tradition of romantic pastoralism
died, one might say, on the Western front," writes Samuel Hynes (24),
but its manifestations were still all-powerful in British music until Britten came along with his new and distinctive approach.

Example 11.3. *Hymn to Saint Cecilia,* end

The answer to my initial question was provided by Britten himself. According to the Australian painter Sidney Nolan, he once said, "Auden is in all my operas" (Carpenter, *Britten,* 248). And in much else beside. At the heart of the Spring Symphony of 1948 lies a setting of four stanzas of Auden's "Out on the lawn I lie in bed," the work that celebrates the poet's vision of Agape, an event that led to his reconversion to Christianity, a path Britten also followed, perhaps with less fanfare owing to the agnosticism of his partner. Furthermore Britten's choice of stanzas includes the political thought he would have associated with Auden: "what doubtful act allows / Our freedom in this English house, our picnics in the sun."

The great farewell to Auden, and a work that symbolizes the poised classicism I have described, is Britten's setting of Auden's *Hymn to Saint Cecilia*, a magnificent reinterpretation of Dryden that locates music itself outside the symbolic ("I shall never be / Different. Love me"), but offers to those who hear it the possibility of change and forgiveness.

In conclusion, here is the end of this radiant and poised work (example 11.3), written on board ship as Britten returned to England, while Peter Pears, in the next cabin, was drafting the scenario of *Peter Grimes*.

Britten did not set the oratorio *For the Time Being* that Auden finished for him in August 1942. The cold-shouldering that came later was perhaps to some degree owing to Britten's guilt about this, and perhaps there was some resentment, too, from Peter, who explained that Ben "was no longer prepared to be dominated—bullied—by Wystan" (Carpenter, *Auden*, 323). Auden, on his part, made it clear how pained he was by the estrangement, and eventually said bitchy things, perhaps to amuse Chester, who always referred to the Britten and Pears's establishment as Addleborough. When the news came in 1973 that Auden had died in Vienna, Donald Mitchell was with Britten, and it was the only time he ever saw him weep (Carpenter, *Britten*, 561). Three years later, as Britten faced his own end, he asked Rita Thompson, the professional nurse who, after his 1973 operation, joined the ranks of the imposing women guarding the Red House, what dying would be like. She told Humphrey Carpenter what she had replied. "I told him I felt dying was like going to sleep, and that there was no problem. I said, 'And after all, there's going to be lots of friends waiting there for you. Wystan will be at the top of the stairs, waiting for you!' And he just laughed" (583).

CHAPTER TWELVE

The Britten Era

I have deliberately chosen to talk today about a fiction, the Britten Era. To reduce British musical history from the mid-1940s to the mid-1970s to a single expression of this kind is misleading or plain wrong on a number of counts. It would for instance ignore the second wave of the folk-music movement that started in the 1950s. Even more notably it would omit the British contribution to what was arguably the most important musical development of the postwar years: if the roots of rock 'n roll are embedded in the much-looked-down-on southern part of the United States, the vitality of that new synthesis was quickly picked up and reinterpreted in the similarly looked-down-upon northern part of England; and rock music since has been much indebted to the inventiveness, vitality or sheer bravado of the British contingent within it.

In the world of art music with which I am concerned today, there has been a notable tendency in Britain since the late nineteenth century to

From Sue-Ellen Case, Philip Brett, and Susan Leigh Foster, eds., *Decomposition: Post-Disciplinary Performance* (Bloomington: Indiana University Press, 2000), this essay originated as the 1997 Proms Lecture; it was delivered in the main concert hall of the Royal College of Music and broadcast live nationwide as part of a central "Britten weekend" of the BBC's annual summer music festival in London, the Henry Wood Promenade Concerts. Bringing together many of the author's ideas about Britten, it repeats several sections from earlier essays.

focus upon a single figure representative of national musical pride. As my friend Elizabeth Wood reminds me, there has been a kind of relationship between the leading composer of the day and his British public that might be characterized as serial monogamy. The reputation of Sir Edward Elgar, she feels, queered the pitch for Ethel Smyth, whose biography she is completing. There have been grumblings of late that Ralph Vaughan Williams, generous to a fault in his dealings with other musicians of all kinds, nevertheless caused the occlusion of some notable contemporaries of his own. A feature of this singling out has been a complementary doubling which has either bolstered the prestige of the central figure or provided a safety valve for dissenting connoisseurs: Stanford and Parry, Elgar and Delius, Vaughan Williams and Holst, and finally Britten and Tippett, perhaps the last of these pairs before the onset of pluralism and postmodernism made further such constructions impossible. The challenge for the professional composer within reach of the post of head boy in this earlier situation, then, has been how to work the school rules in favor of his candidacy. This Britten set out to do.

It surely helped in Britten's case that he decided to become a composer of opera. Not only was it a genre in which for one reason or another British composers had not managed to make an impact on the standard repertory, but it also encouraged thought about self-presentation. Of course, operas have to be about something. Britten never wanted to hide behind a cloud of abstract modernism or avant-garde ideas, and would have agreed with one of his librettists, Montagu Slater, in excoriating "that monster, the work of pure art 'unmixed,' as Mr. Eliot has put it somewhere, 'with irrelevant considerations'" ("Purpose," 364). It is one thing to reject the autonomous modernist view of art, of course, another to find stories that connect to a group beyond one's immediate friends and associates. The library shelves of opera houses are thickly populated with operas once performed and then discarded not because of any necessarily crippling defect in either musical or dramatic technique—well-known operas, after all, abound in these—but because they have very little to say to anyone in the audience. *Paul Bunyan* (1941) was a classic false start, a patronizing attempt to evoke the spirit of a nation not his own by W. H. Auden in which Britten was a somewhat dazzled accomplice—he was quite vague about the exact nature of the title role's manifestation and staging only six months before it opened.

Finding in an imported copy of *The Listener* a radio talk by E. M. Forster on the poetry of George Crabbe barely two months after the staging of *Paul Bunyan* in 1941 was a turning point. In Crabbe's poem *The Borough*, and more precisely in its story of the ruffian Peter Grimes, Britten and his partner Peter Pears found that "something to say." It was an unlikely and unpromising tale of a rough fisherman who beat and lost his apprentices, and finally went mad and died. Christopher Isherwood, the friend they first turned to as librettist, later told Donald Mitchell he was "absolutely convinced it wouldn't work" (Brett, *Peter Grimes*, 36). But they saw the potential of turning Grimes into a more sympathetic figure of "difference," a misunderstood dreamer, and worked on their vision as they prepared to return to England in 1942. After the plot had been further transformed by the librettist they eventually chose, the Communist playwright and journalist, Montagu Slater, it worked not only stupendously well, as public response to the opening production of 1945 bears out, but also in a way that uncannily connected the private concerns of a couple of left-wing pacifist lovers to public concerns to which almost anyone could relate in the late twentieth century.

The author Colin MacInnes confided to his private diary in the late 1940s that "Grimes is the homosexual hero. The melancholy of the opera is the melancholy of homosexuality" (Gould, 82). Its theme of the individual who is persecuted by the community for no other reason than his difference cried out to be interpreted in this way, but could not be publicly articulated in those days. A more remarkable and far more penetrating aspect of the allegory, however, had to do with the actual social mechanism of oppression. It is the classic condition of those who do not have access to full status in society that they themselves start believing in the low opinion they perceive others to have of them. Grimes's fate is ultimately determined not simply by his isolation but by his capitulation in this way to the Borough at the climax of Act II, scene 1, a much delayed and extremely powerful cadence on to B-flat, the Borough's own key. Upon striking his friend Ellen in response to her "We've failed!" Grimes literally takes up the offstage church congregation's "Amen" in his "So be it," proceeding to the cadence with "and God have mercy upon on me," set to a musical motive (*y*) that dominates the rest of the opera. David Matthews points out that its "curt, emphatically cadential quality seems graphically to seal Peter's fate" (Brett, *Peter Grimes*, 134), and the four triadic chords that define its limits and the angry brass canon it prompts both indicate that there can be no escape once the die is cast. In this symbolic moment, therefore, Peter internalizes society's judgment of him and enters the self-destructive cycle that inevitably concludes with his suicide. In this moment, Britten may at one level have been addressing his own concerns, because in spite of a certain sang-froid about what he would have called his "queerness" there are many signs and several testimonies to point to his not being comfortable about it.

There were other private issues the opera addressed. One was inevitably the return from the irksome freedom of the America he had never fully liked to a native land about which he was also ambivalent. Since there was a war on, and he and his friends were commonly thought to have shirked their responsibilities by emigrating, he was not likely to receive a universally warm welcome. As a conscientious objector he could have faced an unpleasant term in prison. The opera contains not one but two manhunts, the second of which is one of the most terrifying episodes in modern opera. They surely owe their intensity to Britten's own sense of foreboding and victimization, and served as some sort of catharsis. Imagining the worst is a good way of dealing with a difficult situation, and if Britten's imagination was overheated in this instance, it only served the opera and his career all the better.

If I have stressed the interrelatedness of Britten and Pears's private concerns with the larger themes of Britten's music, it is not simply a matter of my own interest in exploring the stories of other gay English musicians who went to the U.S.A., but also to combat the pointed neglect of the topic. When I began writing about Britten more or less twenty years ago, the subject of his homosexuality had not been broached in relation to his music in any serious way. Here was a composer with sixteen operas, or opera-like works, to his credit, many of which, after *Grimes*, dealt at rather important levels with male relations, often with an obviously homoerotic text or subtext; yet the subject had been ignored as though it didn't exist. There were some good reasons for this. The Sexual Offences Act, which finally legalized homosexual acts between consenting adults in private, did not pass until 1967. All mention of homosexuality on the stage was specifically forbidden until 1958, and all stage material was subject to state license until 1968. Britten himself never mentioned the topic, and it was only in 1980, after Peter Pears had declared the nature of their relationship in a prime-time Easter Sunday television broadcast (of Tony Palmer's film *A Time There Was*), that others felt fully comfortable alluding to the fact.

There was a further and more significant barrier to any criticism that would include material elements, such as politics or sexuality. Art music, like poetry, had become in this century the repository of transcendent or universal values, which is almost tantamount to saying masculine and heterosexual values. This came about for a number of reasons, but one very strong cause in my estimation was the threat to its status by a widespread notion encapsulated by Havelock Ellis in a single sentence in his book on what he referred to as *Sexual Inversion:* "it has been extravagantly said that all musicians are inverts" (295). In the aftermath of the trials of Oscar Wilde English musicians, like other artists, cultivated images that were as distant as possible from the connection of effeminacy, aestheticism and vice that had been discerned in those traumatic events; and this cultivation of masculinity and detachment extended from their personalities to their art, and remained virtually unchallenged until quite recently.

Although the attempted separation of life and art produces protection and an honored place for the arts, as Alan Sinfield observes, "it is at the cost of limited influence, marginality, even irrelevance. Their protected status confines them to a reserve, like an endangered species insufficiently robust to cope with the modern world" (*Literature, Politics*, 28). A particularly crucial misunderstanding about any relation that might exist between sexuality and music is that it will be or should be concerned exclusively with sexual attraction or with sexual acts, or alternatively with complex psychological scenarios arising from frustrated sexual drives rather than with social mechanisms. It is clear that not only was *Peter Grimes* intended to "cope with the modern world" but also that any suggestive psychological or pathological elements that might detract from its primarily *social* theme of the individual's tragic internalization of community values were steadily eliminated as the work grew to fruition. All mention of a domineering father incorporated into earlier versions of the libretto, for instance, was erased. The result was a brilliant appeal, made more palpable and convincing through music, to the alienation of every member of the audience. "In each of us there is something of a Grimes," wrote Hans Keller, "though most of us have outgrown or at least outwitted him sufficiently not to recognize him too consciously. But we do identify him, and ourselves with him, unconsciously" (Brett, *Peter Grimes*, 105).

If it was something of a feat to get the audience to identify with an allegorical figure who could most easily be interpreted as "the homosexual," the basest member of society, and furthermore to identify the problem not as one of the "homosexual condition" but of society's vicious treatment of difference, the opera certainly offered members of its audience a plateful of related social concerns to ponder. It laid bare the paranoid nature of society's scapegoating someone who it feels to be threatening but is not; and asks the audience to consider how each of them might feel at being similarly and inexplicably scapegoated. It questioned the operation of violence, which, as Edmund Wilson saw clearly on his first journey to Britain after the war, including a visit to this opera, affects both sides: everyone is brutalized, not merely the aggressor and the victim. Coinciding with the birth of the welfare state in Britain, it also posed the (always unresolved) question of responsibility in the relation of individual and state in modern capitalistic democracies, and this is where the question of homosexuality becomes so central. The "more liberal view" espoused by the welfare state's authors sees deviance in particular and criminality in general as a symptom of society's failure, and tends to want to deal with it accordingly by trying either to understand and allow for it, or, in a more problematic strategy, to control it by "medicalizing" it. The opposing view, espoused by those who resist state control in most other spheres, insists on maintaining individual conformity and responsibility, and uses institutionalization as a means of controlling deviance.

Homosexuality is deeply embedded in modern society's idea of itself. Since the trials of Oscar Wilde, exactly a half century earlier than the opera, the male homosexual in particular, as a notionally uniform but actually incoherent identity, had been foregrounded or represented in Anglo-American society and ideology as an internal enemy causing the dislocation of an otherwise ordered society—the McCarthy era saw an extreme manifestation of this homosexual conspiracy theory. But society is in a permanent state of dislocation stemming directly from its own blockage, its own contradictions. So the dislocation, this internal negativity, was displaced and projected onto those seen ideologically as society's enemies, among whom this "homosexual" was particularly important because of the fragile nature and infinite difficulties surrounding the institutions of heterosexuality, marriage and the family, and also because of the importance that had accrued since its invention in modern times to sexuality itself, which had replaced religion as the ultimate window onto the soul. The immanent failure of the patriarchy is especially demonstrated by, and projected on, those who exercise its privilege as men but undermine the principles of sexual relation and patterns of domination on which patriarchal authority is founded in the modern world. I shall return to this point in my conclusion.

The other operas of the 1940s, *Albert Herring*, *Lucretia*, even *The Little Sweep*, maintain the emphasis on oppression and internalization in different contexts and with different parameters and results. Interestingly, all except *Lucretia* also focus on working-class environments and people—though mixed in *The Little Sweep* with middle-class children to whom those in the audience who are helping to make the opera can more easily identify. And the revelation of the hypocritical nature of authority figures is powerfully continued in the person of Lady Billows and her minions in *Albert Herring* as well as in the *Beggar's Opera* realization, where the point is forcibly made that there would be no lawyers, police-man, clergymen and politicians if there were no thieves, rogues and whores. Peachum enunciates the lawyer's credo: "We protect and en-courage cheats, 'cos we live by them."

Developments in Britten's own life and in British society made the continuing exploration of the oppression/liberation theme an unlikely way forward—the repressive atmosphere of the 1930s, like so much else in British life, was swept away in the aftermath of World War II. Yet, par-adoxically, Britain under a socialist government seems to have been less stimulating for left-wing idealism than those earlier days. Alan Sinfield (*Literature, Politics*, 43–58) has shown how artists and writers responded negatively to the threat the welfare state presented to the notion of indi-viduality they prized so highly as a condition of art. In Britten's case, there appears to have been an increasing conservatism and social assim-ilation in his public behavior, but I do not find in his works any amelio-ration of his relations to the state. His adoption of Lytton Strachey's out-rageous Freudian view of Queen Elizabeth I for his coronation opera, *Gloriana*, was surely an ambivalent act of homage and aggression. On the other hand, it is true that the later operas, beginning with *Billy Budd*, focus on what might be called microcosmic politics, exploring power within relations themselves. The backdrop of society does not of course vanish but is localized even further into a number of small and sometimes claustrophobic worlds—the ship, the schoolroom, the family or, in *Mid-summer Night's Dream*, the wood, both literal and psychological, in which the courtiers, rustics and warring factions of fairies encounter each other.

In all these works ambivalence tends to reign. Some of it must stem from Britten's own life. In his rueful and moving tribute to Britten, John Gill notes that the partnership of Britten and Pears did not coincide with any of the classic British models (12). These were notable for their incorporation of a discrepancy, such as the age difference emblematic of classical pederasty, or the class difference characteristic of the relations of intellectuals like Carpenter, Forster, Ackerley and others, or the race difference nostalgically celebrated by Alan Hollinghurst in *The Swimming Pool Library*, all of which are obscurely and interestingly connected in an imperial and class-based culture such as that of Britain. Britten and Pears were not only of the same generation, class and ethnicity, but also both active and celebrated in branches of the same field, doing their bit for the balance of payments—the model of Thatcherite citizenry but for their pacifism, politics and homosexuality. But Britten's imagination was also caught up with boys, mostly young adolescents. Whether or not he ever acted upon his desires in this regard—Humphrey Carpenter examined the evidence and came to the conclusion he did not—he was clearly preoccupied to a great extent with the question of power which is posed by such relations. The odd stories he told his librettists about a schoolmaster's having raped him and his own father's desire for boys are telltale indications (*Britten*, 20, 23). But stronger evidence is contained in his music. His imagination really was focused on the plight of the weaker partner, or "innocent," for which he found musical expression in work after work in terms that no one else in the twentieth century has matched. But only in *Owen Wingrave*, where the "innocent" is arrayed against the bleak and crushing might of the patriarchal family in which the women identify with the phallic power of the father, is there possibly a clear identification of composer and victim. In *Billy Budd* and *The Turn of the Screw*, most notably, an ambiguity surrounds the figures of power, Vere and Claggart, Quint and the Governess, that allows for the contemplation of real moral dilemmas, not easy slogans. Those increasingly powerful drumbeats that underpin and undermine Vere's final epiphany in the epilogue to the opera show (along with other musical clues) that he is so hopelessly contaminated by his role in killing other men—as the leader in battle as well as the naval disciplinarian—that his putative "salvation" must be wishful thinking.

This preoccupation with authority does not always take the same turn.

The moral and tone of *The Prodigal Son* appear, for instance, to reverse the carpe diem anti-establishment attitudes of *Albert Herring* in favor of reconciliation, finally, to the law of the father, personified as all-merciful and munificent in this work in a way that suggests wish fulfillment, not like the Abraham who, in Wilfred Owen's vision incorporated in the *War Requiem*, sends his sons to destruction one by one instead of sacrificing the ram of pride. But the preoccupation with patriarchal characters of many kinds is never far distant.

Needless to say, it is impossible here to encapsulate an overview of the operas, and indeed one of their strengths, arising from their ambivalence and moral questioning, is that no two people will agree about their exact program. Critical thought will remain in dialogue about them for as long as they hold their place in the repertory. But the questions that are debated in them still seem in most instances real ones at the end of the twentieth century: questions of identity, of the relation of the individual to society, of power within individual human relations as a reflection of societal values, the liberal view of sexuality, and the exploration of loss and desire, all presented in music of great clarity, one that balances feeling with restraint in a way that even the conservative opera audiences of our time have been able to comprehend and enjoy.

As I observed at the opening, opera was not a central genre for the British music audience, which Britten could not afford to ignore in any bid for a central position. About the time of the conception of *Peter Grimes*, Britten accordingly began to define his relation to the British musical tradition more clearly. An early manifestation was the release of his aggression toward it, which is the noteworthy feature of an article entitled "England and the Folk-Art Problem" that he contributed to an American music journal in 1941. In this essay, Parry and Elgar are projected as the binary opposition haunting English composition, the one having "stressed the amateur idea and . . . encouraged folk-art," the other emphasizing "the importance of technical efficiency and [welcoming] any foreign influences that can be profitably assimilated." Studiously avoiding any mention at all of Holst and Vaughan Williams, Britten names Walton, Lambert, Maconchy, Berkeley, Darnton, Lutyens, Rawsthorne and (with reservations) Ferguson and Rubbra as indicating that "since 1930 the influence of Parry has largely disappeared."

Later in the article Britten reveals his current fascination with "the nearest approach to folk-music today": this he deems to be swing and the spiritual, which as he points out are the result of utterly diverse ingredients. The point is to throw the authenticity of folksong of any kind into question, so that "what we call folk-music is no product of a primitive society" and that the "whole conception of folk-song as a germ from which organized music grew may prove to be a false one." The dependence on folksong as raw material is either unsatisfactory (as in *Sacre du Printemps*—Stravinsky gets better marks for its handling in *Les Noces*, and Bartók goes unmentioned), or the sign of a need for discipline which second-rate composers cannot find in themselves. Lurking behind much of the thought is the presence of W. H. Auden, a passage from whose momentous "New Year Letter" (1940) is quoted on the last page as an indication to composers to "accept their loneliness and refuse all refuges, whether of tribal nationalism or airtight intellectual systems."

Britten's few words about actual English folk tunes in this article are marked by the same ambivalence that he showed about England in a letter back to America on his return, where he celebrates the country as "*unbelievably* beautiful" and yet finds that "the accent is horrible and there is a provincialism & lack of vitality that makes one yearn for the other side" (Whittall, "Signs," 364). "The chief attractions of English folksongs," he writes, "are the sweetness of the melodies, the close connection between words and music, and the quiet, uneventful charm of the atmosphere. This uneventfulness however is part of the weakness of the tunes, which seldom have any striking rhythms or memorable melodic features." The ambivalence expressed here, reflected in so many aspects of Britten's life, did not prevent the composer from making considerable use of these melodies, either by arranging them for recital use or incorporating them in original works.

Ultimately, then, Britten made sure that he had a stake in folksong while emphasizing his independence of the "pastoral school" by what means were available, largely the very different accompaniments he devised. In the exercise of arrangement, for instance, Britten understood clearly certain things that eluded Cecil Sharp and even Vaughan Williams, who tended always to assign to folksong an idealized, essential artistic quality that was somehow in Sharp's program "to exercise a purifying and regenerative effect" and produce good Englishmen (*English Folk Song*, 140). Sharp apparently believed that his own anodyne arrangements preserved, as he said, "the emotional impression which the songs made upon me when sung by the folksingers themselves" (preface, xvi). Such blindness to the effects of changing every single parameter of performance except the notes of the tune (themselves idealized in Sharp's transcriptions of course) is truly breath-taking viewed from this end of the century. How much more honest was Britten's recognition that the venue changed the genre and turned these songs in effect into lieder or art song.

"Little Sir William," the second song of his first published collection, may be taken as a fair example of the process. Britten's accompaniment adopts a broad narrative march-like style for the first few stanzas and then proceeds, after an almost Waltonian chord built of thirds has disrupted the mood, to portray the dead child's voice by expressive chords, one to a bar, and by creating in the accompaniment a pathetic echo of a motive from the second phrase of the tune. The song, like many in these collections, is dramatized mildly in a manner familiar to admirers of Schubert, and since it carries no obviously modal connotations it is not identifiable as a folksong at all except for its words. There is a delightful recording of Peter Pears singing it in 1946 (EMI Classics CMS 7 64727 2).

Folksong, as manifest for instance in sets of keyboard variations by the Elizabethan and Jacobean virginalist composers, had been an important ingredient of the pastoralists' relation to English musical history. Projecting the present onto the past, Vaughan Williams wrote of "the great School of Tudor music . . . inheriting its energy and vitality from the unwritten and unrecorded art of its own countryside" (92). For Britten, therefore, the entire Tudor period was effectively ruled out of his official English antecedents: only Dowland the proto-Purcellian songwriter, as represented by Peter Pears's remarkable artistry, merited more than cursory mention. The choice of Purcell was both rational and literally in tune with Britten's own aesthetic program as a dramatic composer. Everyone tends to pinpoint a different piece to mark the beginning of Britten's involvement with Purcell. My own candidate at present is "Let the Florid Music Praise," the first song of the Auden cycle *On This Island,* Op. 11, of 1937, which exactly captures the quality of Purcell's rhetorical style. Whenever it began, it is no surprise that, folksong settings having paved the way, Purcell realizations should follow. The art of "realization," prominent up to the 1950s, suffered total eclipse at the hands of historically informed performance, and is now mercifully extinct. Seventeenth-century song as a whole works on the principle of vocally impassioned delivery or lyrical impulse, neither of which needs much more than a firm bass and a few chords to support it. Britten's contribution constantly vies for attention with Purcell's melodies or declamatory gestures and the bifocal effect inevitably becomes distracting. Needless to say, Britten is at his best when Purcell's music is at its strangest: the tiny cantata *Saul and the Witch at Endor,* for instance, is simply inspired in its use of piano sonorities to re-compose the work. The character and extent of these pieces—they number forty, far greater than the demand for recital fodder might seem to require—may start us wondering whether the "realization" process is more an act of appropriation or competition than of homage, another Oedipal episode in the composer's complicated trajectory.

With a strong relation to folksong and the past, and a special investment in the comparatively neglected genre of opera, all that remained to become the national composer of the period was a clearly defined relation to the nation's choral tradition and success within it. Britten started out early on this project with his Op. 3, *A Boy Was Born;* but the work seems conceived more for instruments then voices—it is difficult to perform in ways uncharacteristic of the rest the composer's choral music and may have been conceived, as Peter Evans puts it, "to break away from the rather woolly archaisms that had made such collections as the *Oxford Book of Carols* so appealing to his fellow countrymen" (86). Again, a considerable change came about with the American years, in fact precisely with the journey back to the homeland on which both *A Ceremony of Carols* and *Hymn to Saint Cecilia* were composed, as though to think of England was to think of choral music. How triumphant these pieces are, combining a secure technique and exquisite sound palette, a modernistic coolness in expression with a plentiful supply of emotional intensity, a musical language distinguished at once by its distinct character as well as its restraint—all the marks of what we think of as classicism, an attribute that cannot easily be discerned in earlier British music of the century. No less successful is the cantata *Rejoice in the Lamb,* written shortly after the return and containing at its center, framed by a Purcellian prelude and postlude and cheerful choruses and solos, a surprisingly fierce choral recitative rehearsing the theme of oppression that was about to boil over in *Peter Grimes.* A pattern was set, which could have lasted through the composer's life, of works of subsidiary importance directed not so much at the church which commissioned many of them and provided a performance venue for the others but toward a social function which appealed to the composer—he often advertised, after all, his belief in the figure of the composer as a servant of the community.

In the *War Requiem* of 1962, however, Britten suddenly seemed to become a victim of his own success simply as a result of inscribing himself into the English oratorio tradition with a major work for soloists, massed choral forces and orchestra. This work even evoked an ingenious medievalism in its device of troping the liturgical Latin text with a vernacular commentary. The historical resonance, combined with an evocation of the sublime in the form of a bombed cathedral in the heart of Britain's industrial midlands and the metaphysical in the notion of reconciliation beyond the grave, gave the piece a portentous and grandiose character which seems oddly more of the age of Elgar than that of post-World War II. Some listeners have wondered, too, whether the evocation of the end of Elgar's *Dream of Gerontius* in the A major conclusion ("*In paradisum* / Let us rest now") is sufficiently undermined by the two interruptions of boys and bells sounding the portentous augmented fourth, itself so evocative of that angst-ridden genre of the period that David Drew so wittily christened it the "Cheltenham Symphony." In terms of politics, too, questions have arisen about the unilateral and unmodified application of a First World War pacifist message in a post–Second World War context as though the Holocaust were not an additional factor to be reckoned with. The integrity of Britten's homosexual politics explains a great deal here, particularly the use of fellow pacifist and homosexual Wilfred Owen's poetry as the means by which to transmit his very real anger about the fate of young men sent to their deaths by an unfeeling patriarchal system as well as his critique of empty religious forms that are in collusion with that system. And it may not be too much to suggest that a metaphorical extension of those young male bodies can be made to all innocent victims of patriarchal systems, including those who perished in the Nazi concentration camps. But the choice of a major establishment genre in which to couch these messages gives pause and leads to the connecting of several threads that I have tried to explore.

To return for a moment to the questions of folksong and realization. If one adds to the sixty-eight folksong arrangements the many folksongs and singing games, traditional or composed, in the operas, and the final *Suite on English Folk-Tunes*, Op. 90, and if one adds to that the forty-three realizations and the references to historic English music (e.g., in *The Young Person's Guide to the Orchestra, Gloriana* and elsewhere), it becomes clear that Britten had as great an investment in these two linked phenomena as any bona fide member of the "pastoral school." Furthermore, Britten's being asked to write the four sample folksong piano accompaniments for an anthology published in 1968 by Maud Karpeles, Cecil Sharp's co-researcher and successor, was surely an acknowledgment of his position as the leading English composer of the folksong movement since the death of Vaughan Williams, and therefore in some way to be accounted the latter's successor as leading national composer.

Once having distanced himself from Vaughan Williams and others, both by his "England and the Folk-Art Problem" manifesto (discreetly published abroad and not much remarked on since) and also by the very nature of his musical response to traditional musical material, Britten was nevertheless concerned to infiltrate and dominate their chosen fields of activity on his own terms. His sponsorship of the alternative Percy Grainger and his reclamation of Holst through the incorporation of his daughter into the working household at Aldeburgh were only later touches to a plan that, looked at one way, seemed from the moment of return in 1942 to be matching the ideology of the "pastoral school" item by item. The invocation of the powerful British sea myth, again on the composer's own terms, in *Peter Grimes* and *Billy Budd*, and the substitution of Aldeburgh, Suffolk and East Anglia for Hereford, Gloucestershire and the West country, a substitution formalized by the founding of the Aldeburgh Festival as the polar opposite to the Three Choirs Festival, all seem to fit the pattern, as did the co-opting of the British choral tradition along the way. "Finding one's place in society as a composer is not a straightforward job," wrote Britten in a speech, like Vaughan Williams's *National Music*, originally delivered to Americans, and sounding remarkably like the earlier document in tone (*Aspen Award*, 14). Perhaps, as part of returning home, Britten had even consciously understood and applied to himself Vaughan Williams's impassioned belief that younger British composers (he mentions Walton, Bliss, Lambert and Hadley) could not expel traditional music from their systems, even though they might deny what he called "their birthright." As has often been remarked, Britten certainly moderated his eclecticism during the very same period that the onset of folksong and Purcell arrangements occurred. Perhaps, then, he ultimately understood that, returning to his native country and exorcising certain fears in the cathartic score of *Peter Grimes*, he also needed to fulfill his role in ways that were laid out by Vaughan Williams in a gracious review of Britten's first published volume of folksong arrangements. The older composer, casting himself in the role of an "old fogey" welcomes the "divagations," either to right or to left, of the younger generation "so that in the end the straight line is kept intact" (Mitchell and Reed, 347). The line was kept indeed, arguably to run on through Maxwell Davies.

Intact, perhaps, but not exactly straight. For what makes the crucial difference between Britten and his predecessor as a notionally "leading British composer" is the different way in which he pursued a social and political agenda itself far removed from the liberal socialism of Vaughan Williams. Along the lines of interwar homosexual pacifist ideals, it puts personal relations above allegiance to institutions; it puts the individual before society; it tends to show institutions such as the law, the military and the church as hypocritical, unjust or simply evil; it favors erotic relations and exposes marriage; the patriarchal family it portrays as shallow and oppressive; justice for the victim and the victimized are passionately argued; and the difficulty of homoerotic relations is presented as a legacy of this society. In much work that has been done on the politics of marginality in recent years, it has been observed that the center needs the margin to supplement, or in other terms, to act as a symptom of, what is lacking in the center. Thus a certain contained use of the marginal is necessary for the maintenance of the center. For instance, what if Britten had been forced out of his already transparent closet by some unthinkable event? It is hard to believe that any public exposure of his homosexuality would have harmed his career greatly. When Sir John Gielgud was convicted of importuning in a Chelsea mews in 1953, I remember my mother's phrase, "idols with feet of clay," as we drove off to Stratford for yet another dose of his Prospero's vocal elixir. Even Michael Jackson does not seem to have been placed beyond the pale by his fans, and since most humans live with a sense of the complexity of gender and sexuality, it is quite likely that not only pop stars but also artists of all sorts gain from projecting their sexuality as "simultaneously provocative and reassuring," to borrow a phrase from Dave Marsh (216) quoted by Martha Nell Smith in the context of a discussion of the "blatant homoeroticisms" evident in Bruce Springsteen videos (204). Britten surely understood this, if only intuitively, since the unspoken nonmystery of a sexuality marked by his constant appearance with Peter Pears in every context (a gesture hiding the deeper complication of his sublimated pederasty) was as much part of his image as the constant presentation of his own childhood, of his pacifism and of his regional affiliations.

In a recent book, John Champagne discerns the two critical responses to what he calls the Other, or the marginal. One, the liberal humanist response, grants the Other greater subjectivity by trying to remake it in the image of the dominant or center: this process has been at work in white responses to African American music, or in the male canon's tentative acceptance of women composers, for instance. The second valorizes or privileges the marginality of the Other, not by extending greater subjectivity to it, but by making a resistant and transgressive use of the very lack at the center which first caused the construction of the margin. These two processes are of course not separate but contingent on each other. I would like in my final remarks to argue for the effectiveness of Britten's own version of marginal politics—realizing full well as I try that my own effort to represent difference may already be irretrievably compromised by my appearing under the auspices of *the* Proms Lecture funded by *the* BBC. "All a poet can do is to warn," is the conclusion of the Wilfred Owen epigraph on the cover of the score of the *War Requiem*. But in order to warn, or do anything else, the poet/composer has to be heard. What North America may have taught Britten and Pears, then, was that to work for centrality at home would ultimately be more artistically and therefore politically effective than marginality abroad—as a means of articulating a message to society from that margin where Britten, at least, always imagined he lived, as countless tales of his depressions and darknesses attest. His old left friends like Slater and Auden were irritated to see him waltzing up and down church aisles on the arm of the Queen Mother; gay men like myself often have to work through a certain resentment at his exercise of privilege without disclosure; younger radicals presumably have no time for his compromised politics at all. But granted the isolated space of art music and the difficulty of any effective opposition along the lines indicated by Champagne's second option, especially in the pre-1967 conditions under which Britten lived and under which his social imagination was formed, one still needs to grant to Britten consistency and integrity in pursuing, sometimes to his friends' acute discomfort, a fairly incisive and certainly passionate line on the linked issues of pacifism and homosexuality in relation to subjectivity, nationality and the institutions of the capitalistic democracy under which he lived. This line he maintained in his work rather than his life, where he acted out a role of charm and compliance laced with occasional brutality. The political stance of the music is all the more remarkable because it barely exists anywhere else in art music outside avant-garde circles already too self-marginalized to offer any hope of serious intervention in the status quo. And, as a starting point, it certainly wins hands down over the tired and tiring credo of the many composers today who are openly gay but vow that homosexuality has absolutely nothing whatsoever to do with their music; or those composers—composers who just happen to be gay—who ask for homosexuality to be accepted as ordinary rather than seeing it as a site from which to disrupt present notions of subjectivity and from which to imagine different organizations of power and pleasure, as I believe Britten did.

Britten's artistic effort was an attempt to disrupt the center that it occupied with the marginality that it expressed. In this it was comparable to Forster's achievement which, though it did not specifically alleviate the persecution of his own kind, nevertheless contributed, in the novel *A Passage to India*, as much as any uprising of colonized peoples to the eventual downfall of the British Empire. "We are after all queer & left & conshies which is enough to put us, or make us put ourselves, outside the pale, apart from being artists as well," wrote Pears in response to a letter from Britten about "all those other dreary HRH's, you know" (Carpenter, *Britten*, 419–20). It was the achievement of the Britten era, then—and this achievement was in no way contradicted by Britten's contemporary Sir Michael Tippett—that British classical or art music became during those years indelibly queer and left and conshie. And instead of being instantly marginalized, Britten's music has traveled all over the world.

There is no need to argue that in the process of its inevitable assimilation it may have had some transformative effect; it is enough to note that, for anyone inclined to explore beyond its deceptively "conservative" and desperately inviting surface, it offers not only a rigorous critique of the past but also the vision of a differently organized reality for the future.

AFTERWORD

Jenny Doctor

> *Ultimately it is not the causes that are of greatest concern when one tries to come to grips with works of art, but the effects.*
>
> Brett, postscript to "Britten and Grimes," 27 above

An afterword for and after this volume—for and after Philip—is indeed about coming to grips with effects: the effects of Philip's lifetime of producing works of art about music, criticism and humanity. To survey these effects in full, I've turned to his legacy in print, reading and re-reading everything I could get my hands on: many writings on Britten, of course (some of the later ones sent to me electronically as he finished them—exciting moments indeed), but also articles on other musics and musicians, his thoughts concerning trends in musicology, his perceptive and unusually musical reviews of newly issued scores, recordings and books and the few personal e-mails to me that I managed to save.

Poring through these writings, I am reminded of much within that af-

Many warm thanks to Paul Kildea, Byron Adams and Sophie Fuller for their thoughtful and thought-provoking suggestions for this afterword. I feel extremely privileged to have been asked to contribute to this volume of Philip's essays, and most sincerely thank George for the opportunity. I would also like to thank Mary Francis of University of California Press for her kind encouragement and copious patience.

fected me the first time I read them, either in print or on my screen. I am struck yet again by the cogent arguments, by the elegance of style, by the acute descriptions of thoughts and thought-patterns, and most especially (so rare in musicological writings) by the *feelings* of performing and experiencing music, of reading about music, of responding to the field of musicology itself.[1] Always taking the *personal* as a starting point, these works have readability and unusual impact that does not fade with time, perhaps because in Philip's case, the underlying personality comes across as so interesting, knowledgeable and worth knowing; perhaps because his reasons for writing involved personal issues, such as genuineness and integrity, leading to deep questioning of the status quo—often dropping in as hard-hitting "asides" the fundamental, but largely unspoken, judicial, political or social realities that so profoundly affected the psyche of twentieth-century human experience, both in art and in fact. Two authors and colleagues whom Philip often mentioned in his writings were Christopher Isherwood and E. M. Forster, the latter a friend during Philip's Cambridge days. The qualities Philip most admired in them—their "honesty, gentleness and decency"[2]—are the qualities I value and was most moved by in Philip's own writings and approach to life.

For Philip, music—any piece of music he performed, heard or wrote about—seemed to be inseparably bound up with a kaleidoscope of aspects, aspects that others often considered to be external to music, but that he could not see separately. In his "view," his inner ear, in fact, performances, pieces, recordings and the discipline of musicology itself were about people and the way they experienced art and life.

> Western classical music presupposes that nothing exists beyond the notes. An inspired composer (who just happens always to be male) records his intentions on paper in a form of notation which at any point of history devoted performers then realise. The styles of realisation change, of course, but only for the better, which means closer to the composer's intentions. The listeners, a silent majority except when they clap, benefit from the universal significance of the sounds thus created, returning to earth only to buy the CD of what they have just

heard. If they had sex on their minds at any time during the process, they would be accused by critics of reductive thinking. ("Are You Musical," 370)

The things Philip wrote about—music, musicology, sexuality—and the people who interested him—Byrd, Britten, Dent, Forster—were interwoven into his patterns of thought, expressed within extraordinary sentences punctuated with colorfully evocative words. It all seems supremely logical, once he fit the different pieces of the social, political and legal spectrum together in his elegant, but direct prose.

*   *   *

When I began writing about Britten more or less twenty years ago, the subject of his homosexuality had not been broached in relation to his music in any serious way. Here was a composer with sixteen operas, or opera-like works, to his credit, many of which, after Grimes, dealt at rather important levels with male relations, often with an obviously homoerotic text or subtext; yet the subject had been ignored as though it didn't exist.   —"The Britten Era," 208 above

Of course, Philip was by no means the first to write significantly about Britten, the subject of myriad books, articles, radio programs and television documentaries, both during his lifetime and since.[3] But after the composer's death in 1976, a distinct polarity in Britten scholarship developed around a recognizable "stable" of authors; as Philip described them, "Donald Mitchell, Britten's musical executor, [headed] a team including Paul Banks, Mervyn Cooke, John Evans, Colin Matthews, Philip Reed, and others, [producing] an enormous amount of documentary and musical material as well as critical insight in a very short time."[4] For the first fifteen years or so, commentators outside the stable who were noted for contributing important work on Britten included in particular Michael Kennedy, Peter Evans, Arnold Whittall—and of course Philip. Significantly, it was only Philip in those years who challenged an image of Britten closely guarded by "the composer's Trustees."[5]

The unspoken non-mystery of his sexuality (which hid the real complication of apparently sublimated pederasty) was as much part of his image as the constant presentation of his own childhood (to remind us of Mozart as well as to provoke hints of that other complication?), of his pacifism, and of his regional affiliations.[6]

With his remarkable, ground-breaking article of 1977, "Britten and Grimes," first presented at a national conference a month *before* the composer's death, Philip began his long career of saying the unsayable about Britten and his world.

But then, in the early 1990s,

> into this world the arrival of the professional biographer, Humphrey Carpenter, came as a cold shower in April. His unfettered account of Britten's life, mercifully short on adulation but perhaps overlong on sadism, produced a recognizable human being with a psychological profile in which the role of anger, cruelty and evasion figured large (and in which Pears often figures as Svengalian); he also revealed details about Britten's love of adolescent boys which some had thought unmentionable. Possibly his concern to reveal Britten's pathology meant that he rarely looked beyond the psychological traits toward their grounding in social causes and conditioning. ("Benjamin Britten," 4:388)

In fact, three works changed the face of Britten scholarship in the early 1990s: Carpenter's biography of Britten, Headington's biography of Pears and the initial volumes of Britten's correspondence.[7] Since then the stream of contributions written from "without" the stable has gradually increased, both in number and interest; in addition to Philip's extensive and thought-provoking writings on Britten (a number reissued in this volume), works by Arnold Whittall, Clifford Hindley, Stephen McClatchie, Philip Rupprecht, Lloyd Whitesell and Paul Kildea are worth noting in particular.

Nevertheless the polarity continues, with contributions from "within" continuing to emerge, though with less frequency. The insiders still attempt to control the Britten image, as in the most recent volume of Britten's correspondence.[8] It is indeed noteworthy that the letters were selected and in large part annotated *before* the Carpenter biography was published, *before* the last decade of Britten scholarship, *before* the seismic shifts in musicological approaches of recent years. Donald Mitchell's extensive introduction is eloquent and thoughtful, as his writings always are, but at the same time apologetic for not having produced the long-expected "straight biography" he'd planned with Britten's approval.[9] His justification involves a fundamental disagreement with current biography, which has become "an unthinking pursuit of what is often represented to be the 'dark' side of the biographer's subject . . . that [which] is compulsive, socially unacceptable, and therefore concealed; and the main task of the biography is to strip away the wrappings and reveal the dark 'truth'; and the 'truth,' need one hardly add, has become inextricably associated with sex."[10] One of Philip's finer articles was his *JRMA* review of the initial volumes of Britten letters; I deeply regret that he won't be able to respond to the publication of this next volume—the progress of which he asked about frequently over the years.

*   *   *

[Donald Mitchell] has a great deal invested in Britten's stature, and on other occasions leaps to defend Britten from certain interpretative moves, including those, coming from gay-identified positions, that he sees as reductive because he tends to recognize only the sexual aspect of sexuality, not its broader cultural and societal implications.

—*JRMA* review, 151

"Outsiders" involved in Britten criticism often painfully challenged precepts of the Aldeburgh "court,"[11] those, including Donald Mitchell, who have been enormously determined to protect their view and definition of Britten's image. In doing so, of course, they invisibly reinforced their own personal identities, intrinsically fused with that of the famous composer many of them knew, but all felt had altered and somehow redefined their lives. Though some faces have changed, the Britten "establishment"[12] remains a powerful crowd, imposing a forceful illusion of boundaries: not only rhetorical, in what may be thought and written about "their" composer, but also physical, in providing access to Britten-related source ma-

terials, and financial, in decisions regarding grant awards for projects relating to British music and Britten's interests.

Dealing with "the composer's Trustees" was a recurrent theme from
the first in Philip's conversations with me, since obstacles he had encountered in the past with respect to accessing Britten materials were
substantial factors in his long hesitation before accepting the commission
for a new article on Britten to appear in the revised *New Grove Dictionary
of Music and Musicians.* Having turned his musicological focus onto
other spheres, Philip told me he was reluctant to return to what he perceived as a mine-filled, cloistered world: tempting in terms of fascination
with what was on offer—he'd always wished to write Britten's biography
as he felt it should be written—but dangerous. Relations between Donald and Philip were always perfectly cordial, and they respected and often
publicly admired each other's work.[13] But Philip was wary about how information relating to Britten was controlled, and he deplored the difficult atmosphere he had encountered at the Britten-Pears Library—
though he adored and had huge regard for Rosamund Strode, keeper of
the manuscripts in the years when he did most of his Britten research.
On several occasions he told me about the process of their getting to
know each other and winning each other's confidence. He made the pil-
grimage to Aldeburgh several times before he was finally allowed to view
one page of a manuscript score! He thought that was hilarious—and very
indicative.

*   *   *

> *I have done my own genuflections at the Britten shrine, of course, but
> it seems to me now important to cool the rhetoric, and to question the
> complacency behind it. New interpretations (whether "homoerotic" or
> not) arising from the sort of considered affection and curiosity to which
> I refer are what keep the music alive.*
>
> —"Authority of Difference," 634–35

Philip was not the first to write about Britten's homosexuality.[14] But he
addressed the personality of a creator in relation to his creations in a

uniquely integrated way, with sexuality vividly pivotal to understanding the works produced. As we can admit now—largely thanks to Philip's persuasive and illuminating campaigns—it wasn't ever as simple as "exposing" in print the obvious, open secret of Britten, or any other composer for that matter, as homosexual.

> We should avoid making the simplistic claim that here lies the single key to Britten's creative personality: no inner mystery in the music is revealed by the simple acknowledgment of his homosexuality and its consequences, but the way is at least cleared for us to approach the works a little closer and with more understanding. (Postscript to "Britten and Grimes," 28 above)

Indeed, further "acknowledgments" were needed relating sexuality to broader and equally significant issues of personality, background and social contexts.

> The phenomenon of "homosexuality" becomes less relevant than the psychological effects of the labeling and its social consequences. And Britten's preoccupation with a predominantly negative "homosexual vision" shows how crucial for him was the effect of this labeling and the concomitant oppression. (Postscript to "Britten and Grimes," 27 above)

> [Britten's] works are preoccupied with *the social experience* of homosexuality. ("Authority of Difference," 633 [emphasis added])

What is important is what these acknowledgments may *mean*, with respect to the music, with respect to the man, and ultimately with respect to both their places in relation to the society that shaped them.

Philip's quiet but remarkable powers enabled us to understand *why* hidden, covert meanings were of essential importance, not for the sake of superficial, sensational exposure, but as a means of permitting us to perceive music we'd known all our lives in completely different, often far-reaching lights. This collection of essays gathers Philip's various views of Britten through the operas, each glance of his rich, widely read gaze provoking powerful verbal images that penetrate deep below the surface, and often across and through it, too, weaving together the personal, the music, the characters, the dramas, the society and the politics, enunciating what often seems nearly apparent (in retrospect), but which had often never before been said.

*   *   *

You cannot get horny listening to classical music. It is a sublime form of
sublimation.   —"Are You Musical," 370

In terms of Britten and the themes he developed throughout the course of his life and within his music ("no one with his sense of stage-craft as well as professional know-how could be entirely innocent of staging his own life so well"),[15] the following few sentences summarize Philip's understanding of this composer's motivations—sentences that rather magnificently encapsulate Britten through his operatic subjects:

> Positioning himself so that his partnership with Pears, projected as "normal," masked his paedophilia, Britten pursued a political agenda far removed from the liberal socialism of his predecessor Vaughan Williams. It was similarly rooted in the past, and involved "a sense of disengagement from immediate politics" that increased as Britten grew older (Carpenter, 486). Along the lines of interwar homosexual pacifist ideals, it placed personal relations above allegiance to institutions; it put the individual before society; it tended to show institutions such as the law, the military and the church as hypocritical, unjust or simply evil; it favoured erotic relations over marriage; it portrayed the patriarchal family as shallow and oppressive; it passionately argued justice for the victim and the victimized; and it presented the difficulty of homoerotic relations as a legacy of this society. Britten's assimilation into the British establishment, and his silence on contemporary issues, effectively camouflaged the quite devastating extent of this social and political critique in his works. ("Benjamin Britten," 4:388–89)

This blending of biography with artistic output was the primary basis of disagreement for the courtside commentators: "what we experience, what we hear, is not an item of biography but its transformation, if you like, into a musical experience or communication of relevance and important to us all, irrespective of our sexual orientation."[16] This fundamental difference in approach—whether or not comprehending an artistic creation *can* be independent from comprehending its creator—was absolutely vital to Philip, and one that he brought home to me in a slightly different context: that of distinguishing artworks as public or private.

I have always perceived a significant divide in Britten's output between works that had a public guise and those that seemed more personal. The private works had a more intimate musical tone, and often included codes to express the unsayable, imagery that would be accepted in one guise, but to the knowing could mean something entirely different. For instance, Britten and Pears presented plentiful, popular and surprisingly public performances of the intimate *Seven Sonnets of Michelangelo*, Op. 22, beginning in wartime CEMA performances and continuing throughout their many years as a performing duo. To me, their performances of this song cycle embody an overt symbol, a public celebration of their private love for each other. The performances passed unquestionably as socially acceptable, due to long-held social pacts between performers and audiences: obscuring communication through the use of foreign language texts was one key factor (though Britten and Pears insisted that English translations of the Italian sonnets be included in every recital program); another excuses performers from any personal connection with the powerful emotions they express on stage.

However, Philip assigned a deeper, murkier association to the distinction between public and private, in which political and legal interventions blurred the lines:

> One can characterise this (as straight people tend to do for themselves) as "conflict between the public and private." But it is the total confusion over what belongs appropriately to these two spheres that is characteristic of a homosexual experience of society. ("Authority of Difference," 635)

Philip points out the obvious: the invisible source behind such public–private illusions was the illegality of homosexual relations in the U.K. during most of Britten's lifetime. But Philip refocuses the implications of this source so that essential consequences may be glimpsed. The perceived polarity may be interpreted solely in terms of Britten's compositional and performance choices, but Philip implores us to remember to ask: how much was the shaping of these decisions induced by his growing up and living within a society led by discriminatory laws that endorsed social prejudices? How much "stem[s] from a release of that burning anger that builds up in queer adolescents toward all those in authority, even their parents, who rob them of the right to their own feelings"?[17]

*   *   *

Of course there is no "lesbian and gay musicology": anything quite so serious as musicology is already self-defined as heterosexual beyond all hope of recall. —"Are You Musical," 373

Philip's infractions against the unsayable affected broader horizons and challenged many more people than the few concerned with the study of Benjamin Britten. As Susan McClary recounts so evocatively in her preface, Philip was a primary contributor to the changing visage of musicology in the 1990s, a leader particularly in the development of gay and lesbian scholarship as a fully fledged and recognized subdiscipline. As for Britten, his "artistic effort was an attempt to disrupt the centre that it occupied with the marginality that it expressed."[18] Acknowledging the relevance of the personal in musicology was not only a vital thread in his work, it became a guiding principle, both permeating and providing the essential motivations for his writings. This practice related subject to musical output, as in the cases of Britten and a musical contemporary of his, Edward Dent[19]—and, just as significantly, author to subject.

> Our scholarship always reflects our selves however hard we try to objectify it. The truths we discover and reveal are never so much about historical situation as they are about our own situations, tastes and per-

ceptions. . . . Critical judgments, however "right" they feel, are only further aspects of the training, personality, associations and predilections of each of us. (*JRMA* review, 145)

One of the things that attracted me to Philip's writings, even before I met him, was his willingness to challenge the status quo of musicology, looking honestly, personally and intuitively, rather than "objectively," at the way music and musicians work. This not only made sense to me, it was a hugely refreshing and releasing reminder of why I turned to musicology in the first place: why shouldn't my work in musicology relate to what music means to me personally? what is the liminality of music in all its guises? To find a way to understand and express *personal* responses to music, in terms of its construction in conjunction with its context—what a delightful mixture! Philip pioneered a means of approach and expression that, in my view, did it all.

*   *   *

> *In real life Britten was himself an excellent role model for that 10% of the youth of Kent and East Sus[s]ex who are gay or lesbian (and who need no Teach-Yourself-Guide to recognise this in the quietness of their desperation).*[20]

In fact, how much do these issues and approaches still apply to the world today? To what extent does the political still shape personalities and artistic decisions in the U.K. since the legal ban against sexual relations between consenting male adults was lifted in 1967?

When current events provoked Philip into issuing public responses, he wrote directly, sharply and forcefully, seeming to remove those elegant gloves that in some respects cushion his scholarly writings; his reaction to the banning of performances of Britten's *Death in Venice* in Kent and East Sussex schools in 1989 is a case in point.

> The way to combat the present bigotry (the only one that can be officially indulged in Western societies which have banned racism and sexism, and that has recently intensified because of AIDS) is surely not to

reinterpret homosexually oriented works like Brit[t]en's operas as "actually" about something else altogether, but to insist on their relevance to questions of sexuality and politics. [21]

In fact, social issues pertaining both to the U.K. and to the U.S.A. often evoked eruptions in Philip's later writings, the injustice of current events reinforcing the relevance of Britten—and musicology, for that matter—to life today.

> At a time when many still scapegoat the homosexual minority, when wealthy governments turn a blind eye to the poor and sick, and fail to agree to relinquish their nuclear weapons, when toxic waste poisons the environment and business successfully portrays itself as victimized by government controls, when the effects of ethnic strife can barely be contained in Europe, *Peter Grimes* speaks out clearly from the anger of the past. It is an opera for today, as unsafe and as disturbing a choice for English National Opera now as it was for Sadler's Wells in 1945. ("'Grimes' Today")

I wonder how Philip would have responded to the recent folding of *The Pink Paper*, the U.K.'s only lesbian and gay weekly newspaper. Financial reasons were blamed of course (it was apparently never profitable), but in a radio program exploring the issues, some interviewees distinguished between "the battles of the 80s and 90s" and the "modern age," when "there are more people willing to talk about lesbian and gay issues and act on lesbian and gay issues";[22] some felt that greater equalities in the current social climate left little for a campaigning paper to write about. Peter Tatchell disagreed:

> We've made significant gains . . . but there are still many lesbian and gay people in this country who are not part of the great gay nirvana. I would suggest that more than half of all lesbian and gay and bi-sexual people are still in the closet. They fear coming out. The scale of queer-bashing violence has rocketed. And without a specific gay press, I don't think our community can defend its gains and make more in the future.[23]

A few weeks after its demise, this campaigning, cultural icon was resurrected as a glossy magazine—an ironic evolution, illustrating the more relaxed attitudes of the "modern age." But like Tatchell, Philip too felt uneasy in latter years with complacency, with the triumphs of hard-won successes masking the persistence of deeper, darker issues. In a late article, he expressed his concern that even in musicology, hard work was required to save the new, "other" disciplines from glossy complacency, "from dullness and conformity."[24]

* * *

Owen's declaration is very much to the point of modern gay identity: "I was surrounded with love, nursed in hope, spoiled with admiration, but all for the image they made of me, for the man they planned to make of me. . . . [aria:] In peace I have found my image, I have found myself."[25]

So why Britten? Why was Philip Brett so drawn to thinking of, writing about and seeking to explain Britten? The answer to this is certainly no secret. Just as Philip's role in the development of lesbian and gay musicology rose from his inner being, so did his long association with Britten and his music. And since Philip applied the philosophy of drawing on the personal to exemplify professional thought patterns, reading through many of his works not surprisingly uncovers autobiographical information about the author and his motivations.

In his *New Grove* article on Britten, Philip clarified:

The account presented here, although mindful of the views of others, is written by one who (a generation later and a social rung or two lower) grew up contending with surprisingly similar British social attitudes (especially to sexuality)—he recognises and understands a good deal about the composer's story and interprets it accordingly.[26]

Philip alluded to childhood influences, musical, social and political impressions that mingled to form the conditioning atmosphere and "attitudes" he remembered.

I was taught . . . along lines approved by Cecil ("it is Englishmen, English citizens we want") Sharp, Ralph Vaughan Williams, and other liberal or Fabian socialist authorities who wanted to construct a musico-nationality and certain standards in me and every other English child by means of a putatively classless music that would aim us in the direction of art music before we were perverted by decadent popular music or, worse still, seduced by the lure of jazz.

. . . I suffered a reaction against it (and many other forms of cultural patronization) as I grew older. My sole moment of unalloyed patriotism occurred listening to Olivier deliver Shakespeare's speeches accompanied by cosmopolitan Walton's music in the postwar film of *Henry V.* ("Toeing the Line," 154–55 above)

It was of course not only folksongs and patriotic conditioning that defined background elements that Philip recognized he shared with Britten. Repressed homosexual identities, emotions and drives were fundamental, and the expectations of professional life, both as performing musicians and music commentators, also contributed. Philip had begun his work as a teacher of musicology when all these elements featured in a personal epiphany, one that led Philip to determine that his professional aspirations must change course.

One day, an undergraduate who came to me from another [Cambridge] College read an essay on Schubert that focused entirely on the male circle in which the composer lived and for which he composed. I knew what I was being told but, firmly locked in the closet and maintaining a painful asexual exterior, I was unable to respond in any but the most ridiculous and trivial way—like a real musicologist, I have since supposed. A week later, I learned from the Dean of the other College that my student had attempted suicide by sealing his room and turning on the gas fire. Unwilling to hear about Schubert then, I have found myself strangely reluctant to deal with him even now, after Solomon's pioneering and imaginative work has opened a hermeneutic window. But this event in which I failed, like a fuse smoldering inside me, has been the motive behind many of the subsequent public moves of my career. It is ultimately to a homosexual Schubert that I owe my coming out professionally and making an issue of sexuality in music. ("Piano Four-Hands," 168)

*　*　*

Another fundamental impulse must also have been at work: namely that desire, so common in young gay men, to seek anonymity and free-dom by going to the big city, the far-off country—any place, that is, away from the home where they feel at best half-accepted.
　　　　　　　　　　　　　　　　—"Britten and Grimes," 21 above

Perhaps it was similarities in social background that led not only Philip and Britten, but also Philip's literary mentors, Isherwood and Forster, to a common, vital decision they all faced in their twenties: whether or not to remain "in a country where homosexuality is tolerated as an eccentricity but not accepted as a way of life."[27] All left the U.K. to seek adventures abroad—Isherwood and Britten (and Auden and Pears, of course) to the U.S.A. in 1939, Forster to India and Egypt during the 1910s and back to India in the early 1920s, and Philip to California, briefly in 1962 and then permanently from 1966. Each at some point faced crucial questions: where did they belong? where could they best flourish artistically and professionally? . . . and personally?

Philip returns to these questions several times when addressing his subjects' psyches and formative motivations, and in fact compares decisions in his early essay "Britten and Grimes." The oldest author, Forster, felt compelled to return to England—to King's College, Cambridge, in fact, the very place at which Philip earned his degrees and began his professional life (and where he became friends with Forster).

> The tension between society's conventions and demands on the one hand and [Forster's] own wishes as a creative artist on the other finally led to the painful and difficult decision to abandon the writing of fiction for publication, as several entries in his personal diary indicate. . . . Given Forster's love of England, then, his acceptance of himself as a homosexual had an effect amounting almost to suicide as a novelist. (22 above)

For Britten, likewise, Suffolk's pull (sparked by Forster's published radio talk on Aldeburgh poet George Crabbe)[28] was too great, and he and Pears returned to a war-torn Britain in 1942, to face not only the social environment they had fled three years before, but the consequences of their beliefs as conscientious objectors.

> I believe it was *Peter Grimes*, representing the ultimate fantasy of persecution and suicide, that played a crucial role in [Britten's] coming to terms with himself and the society which he both distrusted and yet wished to serve as a musician. Unlike Isherwood, Britten needed to live and work where he had roots; unlike Forster he was not prepared to damp down the creative fires. (23–24 above)

Philip further assessed Britten's assimilation, analyzing how he developed his own character on society's stage and the resultant effects on creative choice.

> In writing [*Grimes*] Britten was somehow coming to terms with—by artistically experiencing the dark side of his feelings toward—the embattled society to which he was returning when he left the United States. While it is dangerous to connect an artist's personal life with his work too closely, it might even be suggested that there is some connection between the happiness and warmth of *Albert Herring* and the success of that particular decision in terms of the acceptance Britten found among English society. This "acceptance" grew over the years, and as Britten became more established so his mistrust of—even his connection to—society seems to have diminished, and his own private and deeply spiritual preoccupations came closer and closer to the surface: the corruption of innocence, the poignancy of age and decay, the theme of human reconciliation, compassion for the weak, lonely and helpless, and the Christian notion of salvation. ("Salvation at Sea," 73–74 above)

Britten's decision to return to England and the Suffolk landscape, his decision to forge a creative life despite repressive social conditions—in effect, the ways in which Britten took on and recomposed British society to serve and admire his creations, his performances, his organizations and his court—all this fascinated Philip. In my opinion, the consequences of Britten's decision to return to the homeland proved even more compelling than shared backgrounds as a force demanding Philip's attention. He examined the psychological and social consequences in particular, absorbed not only by the results of Britten's coping and creating, but also by British society's encumbered responses, the converted always admiring, yet in some ways, perhaps secretly, identifying with the disconcerted, disapproving, denying reactions of so many. Moreover, it is now rather amusing to remember that primary issues marginalizing Britten from professional circles during the 1960s and 1970s were not social or sexual, but tonal, in nature. As Philip remarked in 1981, "it will take some time for the dust of such irrelevant questions as his 'conservatism' to settle before we can see what the really critical issues are."[29] He later remembered, "by the modernist tenets that are still quite powerfully held in many quarters he was woefully conservative—I could barely mention his name to my composing colleagues in California when I first arrived there in the sixties."[30] Nevertheless, for Philip, the fundamental thing about Britten was, to redirect Forster's words of 1941, "he never escaped from Aldeburgh in the spirit, and it was the making of him as a poet."[31]

If Britten represented what might be achieved if you returned home—despite the turmoil and angst of contending with what British society offered a young, intelligent, talented gay man, both before 1967 and after—Philip was quite explicit in celebrating Isherwood's opposite decision:

> Christopher Isherwood, who settled in the Los Angeles area where he has remained to this day, has not become any the less a British novelist for the remove. His perception of America is brilliant, but it is the view of an outsider, like the hero of his novel, *A Single Man*, who is a British homosexual man teaching at a Southern Californian State College. Yet as an exile Isherwood has been able to write freely on sexual matters. He was the only writer of his time to explore the English phenomenon of male homosexuality. . . . Maintaining a reputation as one of the most distinguished living writers of English prose, he has also taken a prominent part in the activities of the gay movement in the U.S.A.[32]

The parallels with Philip's own decisions, career choices, professional focuses and contributions are obvious.[33]

*   *   *

"All a poet can do is to warn," reads the War Requiem *epigraph: but to warn, or do anything else, the poet has to be heard.*
—"Benjamin Britten," 4:389

Developing a way to be heard was a common aim for Forster, Britten, Isherwood and Brett, and their tactics in relation to their environments and life choices determined not just the audibility of the poetry, but its very nature. Philip explained his music-related strategies:

> My own tactics for dealing with any music with which I identify is to insist on the possibility of its difference, to hear its separateness rather than its indebtedness to models, to emphasize the value of distinct critical hearings of it, and to try gently to disrupt any totalizing vision as being characteristic of a dominant ideology that has for much of my life contested my right to a valid sentient experience. ("Piano Four-Hands," 168)

Extending such techniques may perhaps let us glimpse Philip's life tactics. Like Isherwood, he deliberately chose to live in a foreign country, thus guaranteeing that he would always be cast as a distinctive outsider (that's what happens to foreigners, no matter how thorough assimilation may seem—even in the easier, freer-thinking climate of California). Perhaps, having grown up experiencing an "other" world, he felt, again like Isherwood, that it was important to find ways to express, exploit and fight to expunge the loneliness, inner turmoil and pain of social marginalization. He needed to be a "foreigner" in its complete sense to attain a vantage point from which he could feel comfortable and feel *heard* when addressing issues that particularly mattered to him. As a social "other"— one whose accent gave him away instantly—he would be politely tolerated, even welcomed, as an elegant, beautifully spoken and mannered, well-dressed, Anglo-attractive commentator; this kind of otherness gave him special license to comment on and condemn quite impolite, discriminatory and damaging practices in society as he encountered it, even in his professional arena. In California, he could live a more comfortable life, he could both warn and be heard—and perhaps achieve significant "differences" (I believe we can agree he most certainly did, in any number of spheres).

Thus Philip's fascination with Britten may have arisen in part from wondering about "the road not taken." In Britten he saw someone from a similar background who, when faced with a similar decision, chose to "come home." Britten achieved an extraordinarily creative and powerfully effective life inspired by the sea, reeds, winds and open skies of rural Suffolk, but at great psychological and emotional cost, as his operas signify.

> It was Britten's achievement . . . to turn British art music during his years of ascendancy into something indelibly queer and left and conshie. And instead of being instantly marginalised, it has travelled all over the world. ("Benjamin Britten," 4:389)

Isn't it rather remarkable that Philip did the same thing for musicology?

∗　　∗　　∗

> *In* Death in Venice, *the composer's last opera, beauty enchants and then destroys: it leads as far as self-knowledge but does not reach the full distance to salvation.*   —"Salvation at Sea," 79 above

While preparing these after-thoughts, I repeatedly asked George if he was able to find any notes or essays that Philip may have written about *Death in Venice*, since I was particularly keen to know Philip's thinking on this work. Setting Mann's novella completed Britten's operatic epic, which began with Auden in early 1940s America and progressed through sixteen operas and three decades to this deeply moving piece, "[viewing] the great themes of his music, from a fundamentally different and freshly revealing viewpoint."[34] It interests me that George was unable to unearth an essay on this final opera. But perhaps that is fitting, perhaps Philip's words about it, and about Britten, in his seminal article in *The New Grove* should provide the most persuasive treatment possible at this time in relation to this enigmatic composer.[35] The words in this volume, along with those in that article, draw together Philip's interpretations and carefully constructed conclusions, resulting from a lifetime of thinking about music, about Britten, about sexuality, about society—about his life, his social experiences and what it meant to be true to them.

> *I have always kept a close watch over my development as a writer, over my behaviour as a man. Should I now, without thought, break my habit, my summer of work in the mountains, to holiday in the warm and lovely south? . . . Yes, it can be justified—but the truth is that it has been precipitated by a sudden desire for the unknown. So be it! I will pursue this freedom and offer up my days to the sun and the south. My ordered soul shall be refreshed at last.*
>
> —*Death in Venice*, Act I, scene 1

NOTES

1. One of Philip's most poignant articles about feeling the performance of music and musicology is "Piano Four-Hands: Schubert and the Performance of Gay Male Desire."

2. "Britten and Grimes," 22 above.

3. As early as 1952, a venerating volume was issued by Hans Keller and Donald Mitchell (then editors of the progressive journal *Music Survey*), *Benjamin Britten: A Commentary on his Works from a Group of Specialists* (London: Rockliff, 1952).

4. "Benjamin Britten," manuscript of submitted version (7 January 2000), article for *The New Grove Dictionary of Music and Musicians*, 2nd ed.

5. Mitchell, introduction to *Letters from a Life: Selected Letters of Benjamin Britten*, 3:5.

6. Review of Mitchell and Reed, *Journal of the Royal Musical Association* 119, no. 1 (1994): 148.

7. See Carpenter, *Britten* (1992); Headington, *Peter Pears: A Biography* (1992); and Mitchell and Reed (1991; corrected paperback ed. 1998).

8. Mitchell, Reed, and Cooke.

9. Mitchell, introduction, 3:3.

10. Mitchell, introduction, 3:6.

11. As Philip noted in his *New Grove* article on Britten (4:385), the term was first applied in an *Observer* article entitled "At the Court of Benjamin Britten" (7 June 1970). It has recently featured as a chapter heading, "Aldeburgh's Court Composer," in *Selling Britten Music and the Marketplace*, by Paul Kildea (Oxford: Oxford University Press, 2002), 148–93.

12. Personal e-mail from Philip, 18 September 1998.

13. Donald Mitchell expresses this mutual respect admirably in his introduction, 3:5.

14. Philip credits this to the highly individual musicologist Hans Keller, "the first writer in England to my knowledge to deal openly and seriously with Britten's homosexuality as an element ('enormous creative advantage,' he calls it) in his operatic character" (review of Evans and of Herbert, *Notes*, 2nd ser., 37, no. 3 [March 1981]: 579). As early as 1963, Robin Holloway related sexuality to output in an "Oedipally" blasting student essay ("Britten—the Sentimental Sublime," *Cambridge Review*, 30 May 1964); in a recent collection, Holloway reminisced: "the late Philip Brett was still around at the time and certainly picked up the vibes when the piece was printed in the *Cambridge Review* to coincide with Britten's visit to conduct the *War Requiem* with university forces; perhaps he even contributed to the subsequent correspondence, predictably if fatuously headed 'Battle of Britten'" (*On Music: Essays and Diversions, 1963–2003* [Brinkworth, Wilts.: Claridge Press, 2003], 204–8, esp. 204). Michael Kennedy wrote about Britten's sexuality as a matter of fact in *Britten, Master Musicians* (1981), and later in the 1980s, "the different views of Clifford Hindley are also written from the declared position of a gay man" ("Benjamin Britten," submitted version).

15. *JRMA* review, 148.

16. Mitchell, introduction, 3:9.

17. "Auden's Britten," 191 above.

18. "Benjamin Britten," 4:389.

19. "Musicology and Sexuality."

20. "Letters to the Editor: *Death in Venice*," *Musical Times* 131 (January 1990): 10.

21. "Letters to the Editor," 11.

22. David Bridle and Lisa Power, interviewed by Nigel Wrench, in "Open and Shut" story, *PM* [news program], BBC Radio 4, 30 Dec 2004, 5:25 P.M.

23. Peter Tatchell, in "Open and Shut."

24. "Musicology and Sexuality," 186.

25. "Benjamin Britten," submitted version.

26. "Benjamin Britten," submitted version.

27. "Britten and Grimes," 23 above.

28. E. M. Forster, "George Crabbe: the Poet and the Man," *The Listener* (29 May 1941).

29. *Notes* review, 577–78.

30. *JRMA* review, 151.

31. Forster describing Crabbe, in "George Crabbe."

32. "Britten and Grimes," original version; cf. 21–22 above.

33. Philip spoke to Isherwood about his decision, and Isherwood explained very simply: "I live here." Philip began citizenship proceedings immediately after that visit to Isherwood in 1976.

34. "Benjamin Britten," 4:385.

35. Shortly before his death, Philip was awarded a Guggenheim Fellowship to convert his *New Grove* article on Britten into a book-length biography.

PHILIP BRETT'S
BRITTEN SCHOLARSHIP

PUBLICATIONS
Books and Collections of Essays

Benjamin Britten: Peter Grimes. Edited by Philip Brett. Cambridge Opera Hand-
book Series. Cambridge: Cambridge University Press, 1983.
Queering the Pitch: The New Gay and Lesbian Musicology. Edited by Philip Brett,
Elizabeth Wood, and Gary C. Thomas. New York: Routledge, 1994.
*Cruising the Performative: Interventions into the Representation of Ethnicity, Nation-
ality, and Sexuality.* Edited by Sue-Ellen Case, Philip Brett, and Susan Leigh
Foster. Bloomington: Indiana University Press, 1995.
Decomposition: Post-Disciplinary Performance. Edited by Sue-Ellen Case, Philip
Brett, and Susan Leigh Foster. Bloomington: Indiana University Press,
2000.

Articles

"Britten and Grimes." *Musical Times* 117 (December 1977): 995–1000. Re-
printed, with postscript, in Brett, *Peter Grimes*, 180–96.
"Salvation at Sea: Britten's *Billy Budd.*" *San Francisco Opera Magazine* (1978), 61 ff.
Revised as "Salvation at Sea: *Billy Budd.*" In *The Britten Companion,* edited by
Christopher Palmer, 133–43. London: Faber and Faber, 1984.
"'The more vicious the society, the more vicious the individual': The Message of

Peter Grimes." Notes with the compact disc re-release of the Decca (London) recording of Britten's opera *Peter Grimes* (1985).

"Character and Caricature in 'Albert Herring.'" *Musical Times* 127 (October 1986): 545–47.

"Grimes and Lucretia." In *Music and Theatre: Essays in Honour of Winton Dean*, edited by Nigel Fortune, 353–65. Cambridge: Cambridge University Press, 1987.

"Homosexuality and Music: A Conversation with Philip Brett." Interview by Lawrence Mass, *Christopher Street* 115 (October 1987): 12–26. Reprinted in vol. 2 of *Homosexuality as Behavior and Identity: Dialogues of the Sexual Revolution*, by Lawrence Mass, 36–54. New York: Haworth Press, 1990.

"Britten's *Dream.*" *Performing Arts Magazine* (Los Angeles Music Center Opera edition) 22, no. 2 (1988).

"'Peter Grimes': Dal poema al libretto." In *Programma* (official publication of the 51st Maggio musicale fiorentino), 29 April–4 July 1988, 65–79.

"'Grimes' Today." In program book for the English National Opera's new production of Benjamin Britten's *Peter Grimes*, March 1991.

"Britten's *The Turn of the Screw.*" *Performing Arts Magazine* 25, no. 6 (June 1991): 14–24. Revised and extended as "Britten's Bad Boys: Male Relations in *The Turn of the Screw*," *repercussions* (a graduate student journal) 1, no. 2 (Fall 1992): 5–25.

"Albert Herring and the Celebration of Liberation." *Performing Arts Magazine* 25, no. 6 (April 1992).

"The Authority of Difference: Philip Brett reviews recent Britten offerings." *Musical Times* 134 (November 1993): 633–36.

"Britten's *Dream.*" In *Musicology and Difference: Gender and Sexuality in Music Scholarship*, edited by Ruth A. Solie, 259–80. Berkeley and Los Angeles: University of California Press, 1993 (a much revised and expanded version of the 1988 opera program note).

"Musicality, Essentialism, and the Closet." In Brett, Wood, and Thomas, *Queering the Pitch*, 1–23.

"Eros and Orientalism in Britten's Operas." In Brett, Wood, and Thomas, *Queering the Pitch*, 235–56.

"Are You Musical?" ("Musicology Today II"). *Musical Times* 135 (150th anniversary issue) (June 1994): 370–76.

"*Peter Grimes:* The Growth of the Libretto." In *The Making of "Peter Grimes"* (a facsimile of Benjamin Britten's composition draft issued by the Britten Estate to celebrate the fiftieth anniversary of the opera), vol. 2, *Notes and Commen-*

taries," edited by Paul Banks, 53–78. Woodbridge, Suffolk: Boydell Press, 1996. Reprinted in paperback as *The Making of Peter Grimes: Essays and Studies*, edited by Paul Banks, 53–78. Aldeburgh Studies in Music no. 6, edited by Jenny Doctor. Woodbridge, Suffolk: Boydell Press, 2000.

"Toeing the Line: To What Extent Was Britten Part of the British Pastoral Establishment?" *Musical Times* 137 (September 1996): 7–13.

"Cultural Politics" (position paper for Round Table VIII at the 16th Congress of the International Musicological Society, London, 14–20 August 1997). *Acta Musicologica* 59 (1997): 45–52.

"The Britten Era" [1997 Proms Lecture]. In Case, Brett, and Foster, *Decomposition*, 95–110.

"'Grimes Is at His Exercise': Sex, Politics, and Violence in the Librettos of Peter Grimes." In *Siren Songs: Representations of Gender and Sexuality in Opera*, edited by Mary Ann Smart, 237–49. Princeton: Princeton University Press, 2000.

"Britten, (Edward) Benjamin." *The New Grove Dictionary of Music and Musicians.* Edited by Stanley Sadie and John Tyrrell. 2nd ed. London: Macmillan, 2001.

"Musicology and Sexuality: The Example of Edward J. Dent." In *Queer Episodes in Music and Modern Identity*, edited by Sophie Fuller and Lloyd Whitesell, 177–88. Urbana: University of Illinois Press, 2002.

Reviews

The Music of Benjamin Britten, by Peter Evans (Minneapolis: University of Minnesota Press, 1979); and *The Operas of Benjamin Britten*, edited by David Herbert (New York: Columbia University Press, 1979). *Notes*, 2nd ser., 37 (March 1981): 577–80.

Albert Herring (recording, conducted by Britten), London OSA 1278. *Opera Quarterly* 4, no. 3 (Autumn 1986): 161–63.

Letters from a Life: The Selected Letters and Diaries of Benjamin Britten, 1913–1976, edited by Donald Mitchell and Philip Reed (London: Faber and Faber, 1991). *Journal of the Royal Musical Association* 119, no. 1 (1994): 144–51.

The Beggar's Opera, Op. 43, full score, edited by David Matthews (London: Boosey & Hawkes, 1997); *Who Are These Children?* Op. 84, new ed. (London: Faber and Faber, 1997); and *King Arthur: Suite for Orchestra* (1937), arr. Paul Hindmarsh (Oxford: Oxford University Press, 1996). MLA *Notes* 55 (March 1999): 735–39.

Liner Notes and Program Notes

Notes for the CD reissue of the original recording of Britten's *Owen Wingrave* (London/Decca), 1993.

Program note for production of Britten's *Peter Grimes*, Danish Opera production, Royal Theater, Copenhagen, 1993, and for the Vancouver Opera, 1994.

Notes for new London/Decca recording of *Peter Grimes*, 1995.

Notes on Britten's *Peter Grimes* for BundesTheater, Vienna, 1996; Teatro Real, Madrid, 1997.

Notes to accompany DGG recording of Britten's Spring Symphony, 1996.

"To Be Played with Love Later On." Article on Britten for BBC Proms Booklet, 1997.

Program note for a production of Britten's *The Rape of Lucretia*, the Canadian National Opera, Fall 1999.

Program note for a production of Britten's *Billy Budd*, the Canadian National Opera, Fall 2000.

Program note for a production of Britten's *Peter Grimes*, Teatro La Scala, Milan, 2000.

LECTURES AND INVITED PAPERS

"Britten in America: a composer in search of himself." Paper presented at the national meeting of the American Musicological Society, Washington DC, November 1976.

"'Fiery Visions' (and Revisions): The Making of *Peter Grimes*. Paper presented at the American Musicological Society chapter meeting, UCLA, February 1982.

"Britten's *Saint Nicolas*." Invited lecture at Pomona College, 3 December 1982.

"Grimes and Lucretia: Innocent or Guilty?" Paper presented at the Brown Symposium, "Benjamin Britten and the Ceremony of Innocence," Southwestern University, Georgetown, TX, 20–22 February 1985.

"Britten's *Grimes* and *Lucretia*." Invited lecture at Eastman School of Music, Rochester, NY, 17 March 1986.

"Britten's Music." Paper presented at a day-long symposium on Britten at UCLA, 13 December 1986.

"The Choral Music of Benjamin Britten." Invited lecture at "Podium '90," the fifth national biennial conference of the Association of Canadian Choral Conductors, University of Calgary, 9–12 May 1990.

"Musicality: Innate Gift or Social Contract?" Paper presented at the national meeting of the American Musicological Society, Society for Ethnomusicology and Society for Music Theory, Oakland, 11 November 1990.

"Britten's *Turn of the Screw*." Paper presented at the conference "Towards a Feminist Theory of Music," Minneapolis, 26–30 June 1991.

"Musicality, Essentialism and the Closet." Paper presented at a conference on music and gender, King's College, London, 6–7 July 1991.

"Eros and Orientalism in Britten's Operas." Paper presented at the Royal Musical Association's 27th annual conference, "Music and Eroticism," Exeter College, Oxford, 27–29 March 1992; also at the first meeting of the Music Department Colloquium, UC Riverside, 28 April 1992; University of East Anglia, Norwich, England, 26 October 1992; University of Virginia, Symposium on "Opera, Voice, Gender, and Sexuality," 2 February 1993; UC Berkeley, 15 March 1993.

"Displacing Homosexuality: An Aspect of Pacifism in Britten's Music." Paper presented during a weekend symposium on Britten and Pacifism at the Britten-Pears School, 2–4 October 1992.

"Overcoming Orientalism: Benjamin Britten's *Curlew River*." Convocation address, Carleton College, Northfield, MN, 30 April 1993.

"Britten's Queens." One of two keynote addresses in the symposium "Music, Sexuality, and Performance: Anything Goes," Music & Sexuality Study Group and the Doreen B. Townsend Center for the Humanities, UC Berkeley, 8–10 October 1993; Gay and Lesbian Workshop, University of Chicago, 28 February 1994.

"Queerister." Keynote address at the graduate studies conference "Can You Feel It?: Sound/Vision/Body," Humanities Institute & Ethnomusicology Workshop, University of Chicago, 25–27 February 1994; also UC San Diego, 5 May 1994; University of Denver, Boulder, 24 October 1994.

"'Grimes Is at His Exercise': Violence, Sex and Politics in the Librettos of Britten's *Peter Grimes*." Invited lecture at the NEH-funded conference "Representations of Gender and Sexuality in Opera" at University of Alberta, Edmonton, 12 September 1995; and at SUNY Stony Brook, 14 September 1995. Also given on 2 March 1996, at the Symposium on Music and Gender at Columbia College, Chicago as part of the celebration of the twentieth anniversary of the interdisciplinary Program in the Arts.

"Britten's Operas." Presentation to the interdisciplinary seminar in opera studies, Humanities Center, Stanford University, 6 May 1996.

"The Englishness of English Music and the Question of 'Renaissance.'" Invited lecture at Amherst Early Music Festival, 5 August 1996.

Paper on Benjamin Britten's *Turn of the Screw* and panelist on a symposium on the opera at the Music Department of Washington University, St. Louis, 15 March 1996, in connection with a production of the opera there.

"The Britten Era." The 1997 BBC Proms Lecture, Royal College of Music, London, 17 August 1997 (broadcast live over BBC Radio 3); UC Riverside, Music @ One, 29 October 1997; musicology seminar at University of Southern California, 5 March 1998.

"Musicology and Cultural Politics: The Case of Edward J. Dent (1876–1957)." Invited lecture at Round Table VIII, 16th Congress of the International Musicological Society, London, 20 August 1997; meeting of the Pacific Southwest Chapter of the American Musicological Society, UC Riverside, 21 February 1998.

"Queer Orientalism." Invited paper for the Society for Ethnomusicology forum "Queering Ethnomusicology" at its 42nd annual meeting, Pittsburgh, 22–26 October 1997.

"Musical Ambiguities and Dramatic Consequences in Britten's *The Turn of the Screw*." Invited lecture at Interdisciplinary Humanities Center, UC Santa Barbara, 27 February 1998.

"Benjamin Britten: The Politics of a Musical Life" (a revised version of "The Britten Era" above). Invited lecture in the new series "Music, Culture, Critique," University of Texas, Austin, 27 March 1998; University of Wisconsin at Madison, 4 December 1998; University of Michigan (eighth Ethel V. Curry Distinguished Lecture in Musicology), 19 February 1999.

"Queer Musical Orientalism." Invited paper at the Conference on Aesthetics and Difference, UC Riverside, 23 October 1998; Cornell University, 22 February 1999; Oxford University, Faculty of Music, Graduate Students' Colloquium, 12 October 1999; Indiana University Music School, 25 February 2000; UCLA Musicology Colloquium, 11 April 2000.

"Williams the Headmaster and Britten the Promising New Boy in the National School of Composition." Invited paper at the conference "Vaughan Williams in a New Century," sponsored by the Royal Musical Association, the British Library, and the Royal College of Music at the British Library, 19–20 November 1999.

"'Queer & left & conshies': British Composers at Mid-Century." Invited paper at the Los Angeles Philharmonic symposium "Music and Conscience in the 20th Century," 22 January 2000.

"Auden's Britten." Distinguished Humanist Achievement Lecture, UC Riverside, 18 January 2001.

"Pacifism, Political Action, and Artistic Endeavor." Invited talk at SUNY Fredonia, 30 April 2001.

PERFORMANCES

1977   Conducted the UC Berkeley Repertory Chorus program "Benjamin Britten 1913–1976: a memorial concert," with performances in Hertz Hall on 14, 15 May; and at the First Congregational Church, Palo Alto, on 21 May.

1985   Conducted the UC Berkeley Collegium Musicum in a Christmas program in the Art Museum, works by Tallis, Byrd, and Britten, on 8 December.

1986   Prepared the UC Berkeley Chorus for a concert of works including Britten's *Saint Nicolas*, 1 and 2 November at Hertz Hall (unable to conduct because of illness).

1989   Conducted the UC Berkeley Chorus (with John Butt, organ) in works by Britten at Hertz Hall, on 1 April.

WORKS CITED

Abbate, Carolyn. *Unsung Voices: Opera and Musical Narrative in the Nineteenth Century.* Princeton: Princeton University Press, 1991.

Alexander, Peter F. *William Plomer: A Biography.* Oxford: Oxford University Press, 1989.

Altman, Dennis. *Homosexual Oppression and Liberation.* 2nd ed. New York: Discus Books, 1973.

Attali, Jacques. *Noise: The Political Economy of Music.* Trans. Brian Massumi. Minneapolis: University of Minnesota Press, 1985.

Auden, W. H. *New Year Letter.* London: Faber and Faber, 1940.

———. *A Poet's Tongue.* London: G. Bell and Sons, 1935.

Auden, W. H., and Louis MacNeice. *Letters from Iceland.* London: Faber and Faber, 1937.

Banks, Paul, ed. *The Making of "Peter Grimes."* Woodbridge, Suffolk: Boydell Press, 1996.

Barber, C. L. *Shakespeare's Festive Comedy.* Princeton: Princeton University Press 1959.

Bird, John. *Percy Grainger.* London: P. Elek, 1976.

Blyth, Alan, ed. *Remembering Britten.* London: Hutchinson, 1981.

Bohlman, Philip. *The Study of Folk Music in the Modern World.* Bloomington: Indiana University Press, 1988.

Boone, Joseph A. "Mappings of Male Desire in Durrell's *Alexandria Quartet.*" *South Atlantic Quarterly* 88 (1989): 73–106.

Brett, Philip. "Are You Musical?" ("Musicology Today II"). *Musical Times* 135 (150th anniversary issue) (June 1994): 370–76.

———. "The Authority of Difference: Philip Brett Reviews recent Britten offerings." *Musical Times* 134 (November 1993): 633–36.

———. *Benjamin Britten: Peter Grimes*. Edited by Philip Brett. Cambridge Opera Handbook Series. Cambridge: Cambridge University Press, 1983. (Cited as *Peter Grimes*.)

———. "Britten, (Edward) Benjamin." *The New Grove Dictionary of Music and Musicians*. Edited by Stanley Sadie and John Tyrrell. 2nd ed. London: Macmillan, 2001. (Cited as Benjamin Britten.")

———. "'Fiery Visions' (and Revisions): *Peter Grimes* in Progress." In Brett, *Peter Grimes*, 47–87.

———. "'Grimes' Today." In program book for the English National Opera's new production of Benjamin Britten's *Peter Grimes*, March 1991.

———. "*Peter Grimes*: The Growth of the Libretto." In Banks, *Making of "Peter Grimes*," 53–78.

———. "Piano Four-Hands: Schubert and the Performance of Gay Male Desire." *19th-Century Music* 21 (1997): 149–76.

———. Review of Mitchell and Reed, *Letters form a Life* (1991). *Journal of the Royal Musical Association* 119, no. 1 (1994): 144–51.

Brett, Philip, Elizabeth Wood, and Gary C. Thomas, eds. *Queering the Pitch: The New Gay and Lesbian Musicology*. New York: Routledge, 1994.

Britten, Benjamin. "England and the Folk-Art Problem." *Modern Music* 18 (1941): 71–75.

———. Introduction to Crozier, *Peter Grimes*. Reprinted in Brett, *Peter Grimes*, 148–49.

———. *On Receiving the First Aspen Award; a Speech by Benjamin Britten*. London: Faber and Faber, 1965.

———. "Some Notes on Forster and Music." In *Aspects of E. M. Forster*, edited by Oliver Stallybrass, 81–86. London: Edward Arnold, 1969.

Britten, Benjamin, Ronald Duncan, John Piper, Henry Boys, Eric Crozier, and Angus McBean. *The Rape of Lucretia: A Symposium*. London: Bodley Head, 1948.

Bronson, Bertrand H. *The Traditional Tunes of the Child Ballads with Their Texts*. Princeton: Princeton University Press, 1966.

Buckland, Sidney, ed. and trans. *Francis Poulenc: "Echo and Source," Selected Correspondence 1915–1963*. London: Victor Gollancz, 1991.

Carpenter, Humphrey. *Benjamin Britten: A Biography*. London: Faber and Faber, 1992.

————. *W. H. Auden: A Biography*. London: Allen and Unwin, 1981.

Case, Sue-Ellen, Philip Brett, and Susan Leigh Foster, eds. *Decomposition: Post-Disciplinary Performance (Unnatural Acts)*. Bloomington: Indiana University Press, 2000.

Castle, Terry. *Masquerade and Civilization: The Carnivalesque in Eighteenth-Century English Culture and Fiction*. Stanford: Stanford University Press, 1986.

Champagne, John. *The Ethics of Marginality*. Minneapolis: University of Minnesota Press, 1995.

Clark, Don. *Loving Someone Gay*. Millbrae, CA: Celestial Arts, 1977.

Conrad, Peter. "The Top Line and the Sub-Text." *Times Literary Supplement*, 10 July 1981, 781–82.

Cooke, Mervyn. "Britten and Bali." *Journal of Musicological Research* 7, no. 4 (1988): 307–39.

————. *Britten and the Far East: Asian Influences in the Music of Benjamin Britten*. Rochester: Boydell Press, 1998.

————. "Britten and the Gamelan: Balinese Influences in *Death in Venice*." In Mitchell, *Death in Venice*, 115–28.

Cooke, Mervyn, and David Horn, eds. *The Cambridge Companion to Jazz*. New York: Cambridge University Press, 2002.

Crozier, Eric. "'Peter Grimes': An Unpublished Article of 1946." *Opera* 16 (1965): 412–16.

————. "Staging First Productions I." In Herbert, *Operas of Benjamin Britten*, 24–33.

————, ed. *Benjamin Britten: Peter Grimes*. Sadler's Wells Opera Handbooks. London, 1954.

Davison, Archibald T., and Willi Apel, eds. *Historical Anthology of Music*. Cambridge, MA: Harvard University Press, 1949.

Dean, Winton. Review of *Albert Herring*." *Musical Times* 127 (August 1986): 454–55.

Donaldson, Ian. *The Rapes of Lucretia: A Myth and Its Transformations*. Oxford: Oxford University Press, 1982.

Duncan, Ronald. *How to Make Enemies*. London: R. Hart-Davis, 1968.

————. Libretto for Britten et al., *The Rape of Lucretia*.

————. *The Way to the Tomb*. 1945.

————. *Working with Britten*. Welcombe, Devon: Rebel Press, 1981.

Eagleton, Terry. *The Rape of Clarissa*. Minneapolis: University of Minnesota Press, 1982.

Ellis, Havelock. *Sexual Inversion.* Vol. 2, pt. 2, of *Studies in the Psychology of Sex.* 3rd ed. 1915. Reprint. New York: Random House, 1936.

Evans, Peter. *The Music of Benjamin Britten.* Minneapolis: University of Minnesota Press, 1979.

Forster, E. M. *Aspects of the Novel.* 1927. London: Edward Arnold, 1974.

———. "George Crabbe: The Poet and the Man." *The Listener,* 29 May 1941. Reprinted [as part of "Two Essays on Crabbe,"] in Brett, *Peter Grimes,* 1–6.

———. "George Crabbe and Peter Grimes." In *Two Cheers for Democracy,* 178–92. Reprinted [as part of "Two Essays on Crabbe"] in Brett, *Peter Grimes,* 7–21.

———. *Howards End.* London: E. Arnold, 1910.

———. Introduction to *A Modern Symposium,* by Goldsworthy Lowes Dickinson. London: George Allen and Unwin, 1962.

———. "Letter from EM Forster." *Griffin* 1 (1951): 4–6.

———. *The Life to Come and Other Stories.* London: Edward Arnold, 1972.

———. *Maurice.* London: Edward Arnold, 1971.

———. *Two Cheers for Democracy.* London: Edward Arnold. 1951.

———. "What I Believe." In *Two Cheers for Democracy,* 77–85.

Fortune, Nigel, ed. *Music and Theatre: Essays in Honour of Winton Dean.* Cambridge: Cambridge University Press, 1987.

Foucault, Michel. *The History of Sexuality: An Introduction.* Trans. Robert Hurley. New York: Vintage, 1978.

Furbank. P. N. *E. M. Forster: A Life.* 2 vols. London: Secker and Warburg, 1977–78.

Garber, Marjorie. *Vested Interests.* New York: Routledge, 1991.

Garbutt, J. W. "Music and Motive in *Peter Grimes.*" In Brett, *Peter Grimes,* 163–71.

Gill, John. *Queer Noises: Male and Female Homosexuality in Twentieth-Century Music.* London: Cassell, 1995.

Gloag, Kenneth. *Michael Tippett: A Child of Our Time.* Cambridge: Cambridge University Press, 1999.

Gould, Tony. *Inside Outsider: The Life and Times of Colin MacInnes.* London: Chatto and Windus, 1983.

Grainger, Percy. "Collecting with the Phonograph." *Journal of the Folk-Song Society* 3 (1908–9): 147–242.

Greenfield, Edward. "Gramophone Records: Britten, *Albert Herring.*" *Musical Times* 105 (1964): 908.

Hanslick, Eduard. *On the Musically Beautiful.* Trans. Geoffrey Payzant. 1854. Indianapolis, IN: Hackett Publishing, 1986.

Hatch, Ronald B. *Crabbe's Arabesque: Social Poetry in the Poetry of George Crabbe.* Montreal: McGill-Queen's University Press, 1976.

Headington, Christopher. *Britten.* The Composer as Contemporary Series. London: Holmes and Meier, 1981–82.

Heilbrun, Carolyn G. *Christopher Isherwood.* New York: Columbia University Press, 1970.

Henze, Hans Werner. *Music and Politics: Collected Writings 1953–81.* Trans. Peter Labanyi. London: Faber and Faber, 1982.

Herbert, David, ed. *The Operas of Benjamin Britten.* New York: Columbia University Press, 1979.

Hindley, Clifford. "Why Does Miles Die? A Study of Britten's *The Turn of the Screw.*" *Musical Quarterly* 74 (1990): 1–17.

Hodges, Andrew. *Alan Turing: The Enigma.* London: Burnett Books, 1983.

Hollinghurst, Alan. *The Swimming Pool Library.* London: Chatto and Windus, 1988.

Holloway, Robin. "The Church Parables (II): Limits and Renewals." In Palmer, *Britten Companion,* 215–26.

Howard, Patricia. *The Operas of Benjamin Britten.* London: Barrie and Rockliff, 1969.

———. "Myfanwy Piper's *The Turn of the Screw:* Libretto and Synopsis." In Howard, *Turn of the Screw,* 23–62.

———. "Structures: An Overall View." In Howard, *Turn of the Screw,* 71–89.

———, ed. *Benjamin Britten: The Turn of the Screw.* New York: Cambridge University Press, 1985.

Hynes, Samuel. *The Auden Generation: Literature and Politics in England in the 1930s.* Oxford: Bodley Head, 1976.

Isherwood, Christopher. *Christopher and His Kind.* New York: Farrar, Straus and Giroux, 1976.

———. *A Single Man.* New York: Simon and Schuster, 1964.

James, Henry. *The Art of the Novel: Critical Prefaces by Henry James.* Edited by Richard P. Blackmur. New York: Scribner's, 1934.

———. "The Turn of the Screw." In Vol. 10 of *The Complete Tales of Henry James,* edited by Leon Edel, 15–138. London: R. Hart-Davis, 1964.

Johnson, Graham. "Voice and Piano." In Palmer, *Britten Companion,* 286–307.

Johnson, Paul. Review of *E. M. Forster: A Life,* by P. N. Furbank. *The New Statesman,* 22 July 1976.

Jones, Vivien. "Henry James's *The Turn of the Screw.*" In Howard, *Turn of the Screw,* 1–22.

Josephson, David. "The Case for Percy Grainger, Edwardian Musician, on His Centenary." In *Music and Civilization: Essays in Honor of Paul Henry Lang*, edited by Edmond Strainchamps, Maria Rika Maniates, and Christopher Hatch, 350–62. New York: Norton, 1985.

Karpeles, Maud, ed. *Eighty English Folk Songs from the Southern Appalachians*. London: Faber and Faber, 1968.

Keller, Hans. Introduction to Herbert, *Operas of Benjamin Britten*.

———. "*Peter Grimes:* The Story; the Music not Excluded." In Brett, *Peter Grimes*, 105–20.

———. *Three Psychoanalytic Notes on "Peter Grimes."* Edited by Christopher Wintle. London: King's College Institute of Advanced Musical Studies, 1995.

Kennedy, Michael. *Britten*. Master Musicians Series. London: J. M. Dent, 1981.

Kerman, Joseph. "*Grimes* and *Lucretia*." *The Hudson Review* 2 (1949): 277–84.

———. *Opera as Drama*. 1952. Rev. ed. Berkeley and Los Angeles: University of California Press, 1988.

Kobbé, Gustav. *Kobbé's Complete Opera Book*. Edited and revised by the Earl of Harewood. 9th ed. London: Putnam, 1976.

Koestenbaum, Wayne. "The Queen's Throat: (Homo)sexuality and the Art of Singing." In *Inside/Out: Lesbian Theories, Gay Theories*, edited by Diana Fuss, 205–34. New York: Routledge, 1991.

Lambert, Constant. *Music Ho! A Study of Music in Decline*. London: Faber and Faber, 1934.

Locke, Ralph P. "Constructing the Oriental 'Other': Saint-Saëns's *Samson et Dalila*." *Cambridge Opera Journal* 3 (1991): 261–302.

MacKinnon, Niall. *The British Folk Scene*. Buckingham: Open University Press, 1994.

Marsh, Dave. *Glory Days: Bruce Springsteen in the 1980s*. New York: Pantheon, 1987.

Matthews, David. "Act II scene 1: An Examination of the Music." In Brett, *Peter Grimes*, 121–47.

McClary, Susan. *Georges Bizet: Carmen*. Cambridge Opera Handbook Series. Cambridge: Cambridge University Press, 1992.

McDonald, Ellen. "Women in Benjamin Britten's Operas." *Opera Quarterly* 4, no. 3, (1986): 83–101.

McIntosh, Mary. "The Homosexual Role." *Social Problems* 16, no. 2 (Fall 1968). Reprinted in Plummer, *The Making of the Modern Homosexual*, 30–44.

McPhee, John. *A House in Bali*. 1946. Reprint. New York: Oxford University Press, 1987.

———. *Music in Bali.* 1966. Reprint. New York: Da Capo Press, 1976.

———. *A Club of Small Men.* New York: John Day, 1948.

———. "Scores and Records." *Modern Music* 21 (1943): 48–50.

Mellers, Wilfrid. "The Truth of the *Dream.*" In Palmer, *Britten Companion,* 181–91.

———. "Turning the Screw." In Palmer, *Britten Companion,* 97–103.

Melville, Herman. *Billy Budd.* Edited by Milton R. Stern. Indianapolis: Bobbs-Merrill, 1975.

Miller, D. A. *The Novel and the Police.* Berkeley and Los Angeles: University of California Press, 1988.

Mitchell, Donald. *Britten and Auden in the Thirties: The Year 1936.* London: Faber and Faber, 1981.

———. "Catching On to the Technique in Pagoda-land." In Palmer, *Britten Companion,* 192–210.

———. Introduction to Mitchell, Reed, and Cooke, *Letters from a Life,* vol. 3.

———. "Montagu Slater (1902–1956): Who Was He?" In Brett, *Peter Grimes,* 22–46.

———. "What Do We Know About Britten Now?" In Palmer, *Britten Companion,* 39–45.

———, comp. *Benjamin Britten, 1913–1976: Pictures from a Life.* With the assistance of John Evans. New York: Charles Scribner's Sons, 1978.

———, ed. *Benjamin Britten: Death in Venice.* Cambridge: Cambridge University Press, 1987.

Mitchell, Donald, and Hans Keller, eds. *Benjamin Britten: A Commentary on His Works from a Group of Specialists.* London: Rockliff, 1952.

Mitchell, Donald, and Philip Reed, eds. *Letters from a Life: Selected Letters and Diaries of Benjamin Britten from 1923–1945,* vols. 1–2. Vol. 3, *Letters from a Life: Selected Letters of Benjamin Britten, 1946–51,* edited by Donald Mitchell, Philip Reed, and Mervyn Cooke. London: Faber and Faber, 1991–2004.

Montgomery-Hyde, Hartford. *The Love that Dared not Speak Its Name: A Candid History of Homosexuality in Britain.* Boston: Little, Brown, 1970.

———. *The Other Love.* London: Heinemann, 1970.

Montrose, Louis. "'Shaping Fantasies': Figurations of Gender and Power in Elizabethan Culture." *Representations* 1 (1983): 61–94.

Moon, Michael. "Disseminating Whitman." *South Atlantic Quarterly* 88 (1989): 256.

Morris, Mitchell. "Reading as an Opera Queen." In Solie, *Musicology and Difference,* 184–200.

Newman, Ernest. Review of *The Rape of Lucretia*. *Sunday Times*, 28 July 1946.

Obey, André. *Le Viol de Lucrèce*. Paris: Nouvelles Éditions latines, 1931.

Oja, Carol J. *Colin McPhee: Composer in Two Worlds*. Washington DC: Smithsonian Institution Press, 1990.

Oliver, Michael. Interview with Jon Vickers. *Opera* 33 (1982): 362–67.

Orgel, Stephen. "Nobody's Perfect: Or Why Did the English Stage Take Boys for Women?" *South Atlantic Quarterly* 88 (1989): 7–29.

Palmer, Christopher. "The Colour of the Music." In Howard, *Turn of the Screw*, 101–25.

———, ed. *The Britten Companion*. London: Faber and Faber, 1984.

Palmer, Tony. *A Time There Was*. 1980. ITV Film.

Pears, Peter. "Neither a Hero nor a Villain." *Radio Times*, 8 March 1946. Reprinted in Brett, *Peter Grimes*, 150–52.

Piper, Myfanwy. "Writing for Britten." In Herbert, *Operas of Benjamin Britten*, 8–21.

Plummer, Richard, ed. *The Making of the Modern Homosexual*. Totowa, NJ: Barnes and Noble Books, 1981.

Poizat, Michel. *L'Opéra, ou le cri de l'ange*. Paris: A. M. Métailié, 1986. Translated by Arthur Denner as "'The Blue Note' and 'The Objectified Voice and the Vocal Object,'" *Cambridge Opera Journal* 3, no. 3 (1991): 195–211.

Porter, Andrew. "Britten's *Billy Budd*." *Music & Letters* 33 (1952): 11–18.

———. "What Harbour Shelters Peace." *New Yorker*, 3 August 1978. Reprinted in *Music of Three More Seasons, 1977–1980*, 206–12. New York: Knopf, 1981.

Reed, Philip. "Finding the Right Notes." In Banks, *Making of "Peter Grimes,"* 79–114.

———. "A 'Peter Grimes' Chronology, 1941–1945." In Banks, *Making of "Peter Grimes,"* 21–52.

Rich, Adrienne. *Of Woman Born*. New York: Norton, 1976.

Roseberry, Eric. "The Purcell Realizations." In Palmer, *Britten Companion*, 356–66.

Sackville-West, Edward. "The Musical and Dramatic Structure." In Crozier, *Peter Grimes*, 27–55.

Sadie, Stanley. "ESSAY." *Musical Times* 126 (1985): 548.

Said, Edward. *Orientalism*. New York: Random House, 1979.

Schafer, Murray. *British Composers in Interview*. London: Faber and Faber, 1963.

Sedgwick, Eve Kosofsky. *The Epistemology of the Closet*. Berkeley and Los Angeles: University of California Press, 1990.

Sharp, Cecil J. *English Folk Song: Some Conclusions.* 3rd ed., rev. Maud Karpeles. London: Methuen, 1954.

———. Preface to *One Hundred English Folksongs.*

———, ed. *A Book of British Song for Home and School.* London: John Murray, 1904.

———. *One Hundred English Folksongs.* Boston: Oliver Ditson, 1916.

Shawe-Taylor, Desmond. Review of *Peter Grimes. Sunday Times*, 20 July 1975.

———. "*Peter Grimes:* A Review of the First Performance." In Brett, *Peter Grimes*, 153–58.

Sinfield, Alan. *Literature, Politics, and Culture in Postwar Britain.* Berkeley and Los Angeles: University of California Press, 1989.

———. "Private Lives/Public Theater: Noel Coward and the Politics of Homosexual Representation." *Representations* 36 (Fall 1991): 43–63.

Slater, Montagu. *Peter Grimes and Other Poems.* London: John Lane, 1946.

———. "The Purpose of a Left Review." *Left Review* 1, no. 9 (June 1935): 362–67.

Slights, William W. E. "The Changeling in *A Dream.*" *Studies in English Literature* 28 (1988): 259–72.

Smart, Mary Ann, ed. *Siren Songs: Representations of Gender and Sexuality in Opera.* Princeton: Princeton University Press, 2000.

Smith, Martha Nell. "Sexual Mobilities in Bruce Springsteen: Performance as Commentary." In *Present Tense: Rock & Roll and Culture*, edited by Anthony DeCurtis, 197–218. Durham, NC: Duke University Press, 1992.

Smith-Rosenberg, Carroll. "Sex as Symbol in Victorian Purity." *American Journal of Sociology* 84 Supplement (1978): 212–47.

Solie, Ruth, ed. *Musicology and Difference: Gender and Sexuality in Music Scholarship.* Berkeley and Los Angeles: University of California Press, 1993.

Spender, Stephen. *Love-Hate Relations: English and American Sensibilities.* New York: Random House, 1974.

Stallybrass, Oliver. Introduction to *The Life to Come and Other Stories*, by E. M. Forster. London: Penguin, 1972.

Stanford, Sir Charles Villiers, ed. *The National Song Book: A Complete Collection of the Folk-Songs, Carols, and Rounds Suggested by the Board of Education. Edited and Arranged for the Use of Schools.* London: Boosey, 1905.

Stimpson, Mansell. "Drama and Meaning in *The Turn of the Screw.*" *Opera Quarterly* 4, no. 3 (1986): 75–82.

Stradling, Robert, and Meirion Hughes. *The English Musical Renaissance 1860–1940: Construction and Deconstruction.* Manchester: Manchester University Press, 1993.

Strode, Rosamund. "Reverberations." In *Peter Pears: A Tribute on His 75th Birthday*, edited by Marion Thorpe, 89–90. London: Faber Music/The Britten Estate, 1985.

Suleri, Sara. *The Rhetoric of English India*. Chicago: University of Chicago Press, 1992.

Tippet, Michael. Obituary. *The Listener*, 16 December 1976. Reprinted in Blyth, *Remembering Britten*, 71.

Treitler, Leo. "The Politics of Reception: Tailoring the Present as Fulfilment of a Desired Past." *Journal of the Royal Musical Association* 116 (1991): 280–98.

Weeks, Jeffrey. *Coming Out: Homosexual Politics in Britain, from the Nineteenth Century to the Present*. London: Quartet Books, 1977.

———. "Discourse, Desire, and Sexual Deviance: Some Problems in a History of Homosexuality." In *The Making of the Modern Homosexual*, edited by Kenneth Plumber, 76–111. Totowa, NJ: Barnes and Noble Books, 1981.

———. *Sex, Politics, and Society: The Regulation of Sexuality since 1800*. New York: Longman, 1989.

West, D. J. *Homosexuality Re-examined*. London: Duckworth, 1977.

White, Eric Walter. *Benjamin Britten: His Life and Operas*. Edited by John Evans. 1970. 2nd ed. Berkeley and Los Angeles: University of California Press, 1983.

Whittall, Arnold. "Along the Knife-Edge: The Topic of Transcendence in Britten's Musical Aesthetic." In *On Mahler and Britten: Essays in Honour of Donald Mitchell on His Seventieth Birthday*, edited by Philip Reed, 290–98. Woodbridge, Suffolk: Red House Press, 1995.

———. "Benjamin Britten." *Music Review* 23 (1962): 314–16.

———. *The Music of Britten and Tippett*. Cambridge: Cambridge University Press, 1982.

———. "'Twisted Relations': Method and Meaning in Britten's *Billy Budd*." *Cambridge Opera Journal* 2 (1990): 145–71.

———. "The Signs of Genre: Britten's Version of the Pastoral." In *Sundry Sorts of Music Books: Essays on the British Library Music Collections, Presented to O. W. Neighbour on His 70th Birthday*, edited by Chris Banks, Arthur Searle, and Malcolm Turner, 363–74. London: British Library, 1993.

Wildeblood, Peter. *Against the Law*. London: Weidenfeld and Nicolson, 1955.

Williams, Ralph Vaughan. *National Music*. London: AMS Press, 1934.

———. "Essay." *Journal of the English Folk Dance and Song Society* 4, no. 4 (December 1943): 164.

———. *The Penguin Book of English Folk Songs*. Harmondsworth: Penguin, 1959.

Wilson, Edmund. *Europe Without Baedeker*. New York: Farrar, Straus and Giroux, 1947. Reprinted in Brett, *Peter Grimes*, 159–62.

Woodforde-Finden, Amy. *Four Indian Love Lyrics*. Edited by Arthur Lamb. 1903. Reprint. London: Boosey and Hawkes, 1990.

Žižek, Slavoj. *The Sublime Object of Ideology*. London: Verso, 1989.

INDEX

Wilde, Oscar, 49–50; trials, 89, 208,
210. PUBLICATIONS: *The Importance of
Being Earnest*, 119; *The Picture of Do-
rian Gray*, 89; *Salome*, 50
Wildeblood, Peter, 148
Williams, Wayne B., 29
Wilson, Angus, 23, 122
Wilson, Edmund, 46, 48, 111, 209
Wolfenden Report, 50, 122

Wood, Elizabeth, 2, 6, 205
Woodforde-Finden, Amy, 129–130, 148
Woodward, S. B., 104n1
Wrench, Nigel, 246n21
Wyss, Sophie, 166

Yeats, William Butler, 139

Žižek, Slavoj, 49

Compositor:	Binghamton Valley Composition
Music engraver:	Louis Niebur
Indexer:	George E. Haggerty
Text:	10/15 Janson
Display:	Janson
Printer/Binder:	Maple-Vail Manufacturing Group

DATE DUE

			Printed in USA

HIGHSMITH #45230